MATAWHERO
RIVERPOINT RD
GISBORNE   N.Z.

Y0-CAR-261

$34.95
35 4.

The Wines and Vineyards of New Zealand

PHOTOGRAPHIC ACKNOWLEDGEMENTS

Auckland Institute and Museum 12,
From Frank Thorpy's *Wine in New Zealand* 15,
From Dick Scott's *A Stake in the Country* 20,
Khaleel Corban 20
Corbans Wines 10, 11, 187
D. Sawyer 60, 72, 106, 107, 112, 125, 149, 193, inside back cover
Pamla Toler 8, 85, 131, 162, 172, 173, 178, 182, 183

CARTOGRAPHY

Maps reproduced by permission of the Dept of Lands and Survey.

Copyright © 1984 Michael Cooper
First published 1984
ISBN 0 340 358289

All rights reserved. No part of this publication may be
reproduced or transmitted in any form or by any means,
electronic or mechanical including photocopy, recording, or
any information storage and retrieval system, without
permission in writing from the publisher.

Book design by Suellen Allen
Cartography by Sue Gerrard
Typesetting by Glenfield Graphics, Auckland
Printed and bound in Hong Kong for Hodder &
Stoughton Ltd., 46 View Road, Glenfield, Auckland,
New Zealand

The Wines and Vineyards of New Zealand

Michael Cooper

PHOTOGRAPHY BY ROBIN MORRISON

HODDER AND STOUGHTON
AUCKLAND LONDON SYDNEY TORONTO

Foreword

New Zealand has been quietly establishing a tradition of wine making for more than a century and a half. In Victorian times the wines of 'the land of the Long White Cloud' won praise from visiting foreigners — even Frenchmen! Around the turn of the century they were winning international competitions and attracting the notice of respected authorities, who saw the possibilities for developing quality as well as quantity.

In recent years, New Zealand producers have dedicated themselves to the task of bringing their wines into the contemporary scene so that, as well as providing for domestic palates, they can enter the international wine world without hesitation. Aiming for individuality and quality, all of those involved, ranging from small family producers to scientifically up-to-the-minute large concerns, are making steady and impressive progress. New Zealand enjoys many advantages of climate and soil and, certainly, working in some of the most beautiful wine country in the world must be a constant inspiration. I have been fortunate enough to watch some of these 'Kiwi wines' growing up and it is a joy to see them attracting increasing attention in export markets at all price levels. They promise to be among the respected classic wines of tomorrow — and those of us who look forward to their success welcome them abroad with a sincere 'Haere Mai!'

Pamela Vandyke Price
London, 1984

Contents

Preface 7
Introduction 9

Chapter One: THE HISTORY OF NEW ZEALAND WINE 11
The nineteenth century 12
Wine growing from 1900 to 1960 18
Wine growing from 1960 to 1983 26

Chapter Two: VITICULTURE 33
Climate and soils 34
Climate; Soils; Climate and wine styles.
The grapes 38
Vitis vinifera; Vitis labrusca; The hybrids; Vineyard surveys; Baco 22A; Chardonnay; Chasselas; Chenin
Blanc; Gewürztraminer; Grey Riesling; Muscat; Müller-Thurgau; Palomino; Pinot Gris; Rhine Riesling;
Sauvignon Blanc; Sémillon; Sylvaner; Albany Surprise; Cabernet Sauvignon; Gamay Beaujolais; Merlot;
Pinotage; Pinot Meunier; Pinot Noir; Seibels; Shiraz.
The seasonal cycle in the vineyards 50
Research 56
Te Kauwhata; Grapes and Regions; New Grape Varieties; Virus Diseases; Clonal Selection; Phylloxera;
Rootstocks.

Chapter Three: WINE MAKING IN NEW ZEALAND 61
White wines 64
Crushing; Sulphur; Juice Separation; Clarifying the Juice; Sugar; Acidity; Water in Wine; Yeasts;
Fermentation; Clarification; Aging; Sweetening; Bottling.
Red Wines 70
Fermentation; Wood Maturation.
Rosés 72
Sparkling Wines 72
Sherries 74
Port 75

Chapter Four: THE PRINCIPAL WINE REGIONS 77
Northland 80
Continental; Whatitiri.
Kumeu/Huapai/Waimauku 82
Abel and Co.; Coopers Creek; Glenburn; Markovina; Matua Valley; Nobilo; San Marino; Selaks.
Henderson 94
Babich; Balic; Collard Bros; Corbans; Delegat's; Fino Valley; Lincoln; Mayfair; Mazuran; Pacific; Panorama;
Pechar's; Penfolds; Pleasant Valley; Soljans; Windy Hill.
South Auckland 122
Villa Maria.
Waikato/Bay of Plenty 124
Aspen Ridge; Cooks; de Redcliffe; Morton Estate; Totara SYC.
Poverty Bay/East Cape 136
Matawhero; Montana; Ormond.
Hawkes Bay 148
Brookfields; Eskdale; Glenvale; Lombardi; McWilliam's; Mission; Ngatarawa; Te Mata; Vidal.
Nelson 168
Korepo; Neudorf; Victory; Weingut Seifried.
Marlborough 176
Hunters; Montana.
Canterbury 182
St Helena.

Chapter Five: BUYING, CELLARING AND DRINKING WINE 185
Buying New Zealand Wine 186
Vineyards; Wholesalers; Hotels; Wine Resellers; Restaurants; Labelling; Reading a New Zealand Wine Label;
Vintages (1976-1984); Wine Competitions; 1983 Gold Medals.
Cellaring 193
Tasting and Drinking Wine 194
Wine Glasses; A Vocabulary of Wine Tasting.

BIBLIOGRAPHY 197
INDEX 201

Preface

This book has sprung from a love of wine, and particularly from a fascination with New Zealand wine, which began many years ago.

Back in student days, my friends and I would return to Auckland from tours of the Henderson Valley, laden down with flagons of Medium Dry Red, which for us at the time represented the pinnacle of the drinking experience. Then one day I opened a bottle of McWilliam's 1970 Cabernet Sauvignon, and a new world opened up. I had now become aware of the standard that top New Zealand wines could reach, and during a subsequent search for every New Zealand label, my apprenticeship in wine tasting began.

Eventually my tasting notes, plus the research for a Master's thesis on the wine lobby, paved the way for this book. There followed work in vineyards and wineries, where I have since found my chosen career, and then an extended tour of New Zealand vineyards, in the company of Robin Morrison, who took most of the photographs in this book.

Other pens than mine have already written of this unique, controversial industry: there has been Dick Scott's elegant treatise, *Winemakers of New Zealand*, for instance, which examines wine making here up to the early 1960s — in acknowledging his contribution I would like to feel the historical section of this book helps to complete the picture up to the present day. Another heavyweight which pulls no punches is Frank Thorpy's *Wine in New Zealand*, and there have been briefer but most valuable guides by John Buck, Peter Saunders and J.C. Graham. In choosing to add this large, comprehensive volume to the list, I have aimed at giving both depth and scope to a fascinating and complex subject.

I would like to thank many people for their help during the preparation of this book. Robin Morrison has brought a sensitive understanding to the wine makers and their vineyards: all the photographs are his unless otherwise stated. Pamla Toler's photographs are also a fine contribution to the text, and I am grateful to David Sawyer for photographs I needed at the eleventh hour.

Peter and Joe Babich, and Ross Spence of Matua Valley, were kind enough to read parts of the manuscript. Alan Clarke of the DSIR, and Joe Corban, assisted in the positive identification of grapevines and bunches. Sue Gerrard prepared the maps; Anna and Maureen Radford and Noeline Sadgrove typed the manuscript. My editor, Cheryl Hingley and Suellen Allen, who designed the layout, both made crucial contributions to the finished book.

Lastly, and most importantly, I must acknowledge the willing assistance of the wine makers themselves, who so generously shared their wines and thoughts with me.

Sapich vineyard, Henderson.

NA TE RA NGA MAMAHI

Introduction

The pleasures of wine have been known to man for over seven thousand years, ever since the people of Asia Minor first converted grape juice, by inadvertence or a happy miracle, into the true monarch of beverages. Cultivated in ancient times throughout the Mediterranean Basin, wine came to fulfil a multitude of purposes, restorative, medicinal, religious and domestic, and became inseparable both from the humble pleasures of daily life and the exhilarating pomp of great occasions. Hundreds of years before the birth of Christ, grapes were being grown in France, to spread throughout Europe into what are now known as some of the great wine-producing regions of the world. Names like Bordeaux, Burgundy and the Rhine have a special redolence for the wine lover, evoking visions of luscious purple grapes ripening under clear skies, soft green vines spilling down steep hillsides, or pale grape flowers blooming over the dark red soil of the Rheinhessen.

Explorers, pioneers, missionaries and colonists spreading into new worlds over the centuries, brought with them the techniques of wine making, and above all the desire to perpetuate in their new lifestyle a most enjoyable element of the old — the benefits and joys of consuming wine.

Different soils and climates, viticultural histories marked by constant trial and error, have led to the successful establishment of many New World wine industries, the most familiar to New Zealanders being those of California, South Africa, and Australia.

This book begins with the history of our own wine growing. It is the tale of small isolated efforts, early failures, and tiny but significant successes, which eventually contributed to the growth of one of New Zealand's most promising industries. It not only traces the introduction of grape varieties to early New Zealand, and the vagaries of their cultivation, but looks at perhaps the most important side of New Zealand viticulture, the people who pioneered wine growing in the nineteenth century, those who learned the value of research in the early twentieth century, those who lent their talents to the burgeoning of the industry in the 1960s, and finally the ones who remain the inspiration for wine production in New Zealand today.

The second and third chapters deal with the realities which New Zealand wine makers are involved with all year round — those of the vineyard and those of the winery.

Chapter Two takes a close look at our climate and soils in relation to vine cultivation, and then at all the major grape varieties. Then follow sections on vineyard practice and the national development of wine research, both essential to an understanding of wine production in New Zealand.

Chapter Three explores in detail the transformation of the black and green grape varieties into the different wines: white, red, rosé, sparkling, sherry and port.

The heart of the book follows: the fourth chapter is a region-by-region commentary on every wine company of importance. I have visited almost all at least once, and returned to some of course many times; there is nothing to compare with the satisfaction not only of knowing the soils, terrain and vines of different regions and vineyards, but of understanding the goals and dreams of the wine makers themselves. This chapter explores the perfumes, tastes and myriad delights which New Zealand wines offer, linking them to their origins, and presenting what I hope is a fair, intelligible and nonetheless personal account of their character. Photographs, maps and labels fill out the picture of what is, in my opinion, one of New Zealand's most complex and endlessly fascinating industries.

The final chapter is concerned with two things of great importance to all wine lovers — the pocket and the palate. A section on the buying of New Zealand wine maps out the tempting range of choices offered to the consumer, and touches on both the last decade's vintages and the wine competitions, in the belief that if such knowledge is within the reach of everyone, it can only serve to enhance the appreciation of wine drinking. For those who want to take advantage of the excellent aging qualities of many New Zealand wines, there are notes on cellaring.

Finally, there is the section on tasting and drinking wine. This offers simple guidelines only, as there are no special mysteries here — the real miracles have occurred already, with the tender cultivation of the grapevine, the careful fermentation of the juice, and the subtle ministrations of the wine maker as he or she has coaxed a wine into clarity, balance and fragrance.

Hugh Johnson, a perceptive author of formidable knowledge and impeccable accuracy, writes in *Hugh Johnson's Wine Companion*, published in London in 1983: 'New Zealand's natural gift is what the wine makers of Australia and California are constantly striving for: the growing conditions that give slowly ripened, highly aromatic rather than super-ripe grapes. It is too soon to judge yet just how good her eventual best wines will be, but the signs so far suggest that they will have the strength, structure and delicacy of wines from (for example) the Loire, possibly the Médoc, possibly Champagne.'

Johnson is the world's most authoritative and widely read writer about wine. Thus the wine makers of New Zealand, with all their natural advantages and with superb wines already in the bottle, begin to stir up excitement in the leading wine centres of the world.

CHAPTER ONE
The History of New Zealand Wine

THE NINETEENTH CENTURY

Vitis vinifera, the great species of vine for wine making, originated in the northern hemisphere and stayed there, until carried south in the ships of the early colonists. Thus the grapevine sank its roots into New Zealand soil during the first years of European settlement. Such eminent enthusiasts as Samuel Marsden, who made the first known planting of grapevines in New Zealand and James Busby, our first recorded wine maker, ensured that grapes were among the early pioneering fruits.

Without the benefit of the grapevine as a native plant, the pre-European Maori sometimes made a non-intoxicating drink from the juice of poisonous tutu berries. The colonists attempted to make 'wine' from the same plant — with startling results. Exploring the area north of Wakatipu in March 1864, A.J. Barrington noted in his 'Diary of a West Coast Prospecting Party' that: 'Simonin [a Frenchman in the group] gathered a handkerchief full of the tutu berries, beat them up, squeezed them, and got a pint of wine, which was first-rate drink. The refuse, or seed, he threw on the beach, which the dog ate. In an hour afterwards he showed every symptom of being poisoned, foamed at the mouth, and lay down in fits; I believe he would have died but for a good supply of salt and water we managed to pour down his throat.'[1]

Fortunately the fruit of the tutu plant never won favour as the basis for a potentially unique antipodean wine industry.

When Charles Darwin called at the Bay of Islands in 1835 during the global voyage of the *Beagle*, he saw well-established grapevines. Samuel Marsden, on his second trip to New Zealand as Anglican missionary and chief Chaplain to the Government of New South Wales, had decided to make a settlement at Kerikeri. In his journal for Saturday 25 September 1819 he wrote: We had a small spot of land cleared and broken up in which I planted about a hundred grape-vines of different kinds brought from Port Jackson. New Zealand promises to be very favourable to the vine as far as I can judge at present of the nature of the soil and climate.'[2]

Other early colonists followed Marsden's example and planted vines in the North. Lieutenant Thomas McDonnell R.N., who had settled at Hokianga ('I think in the year 1830') and later at Kaipara, told a House of Commons Select Committee on New Zealand in a report printed in July 1844 that he had 'cultivated the vine to a great extent at Hokianga: I have nearly four hundred varieties of the grape-vine.'[3] Further north at Whangaroa Harbour, William Powditch was also growing grapes and he gave vine cuttings and viti-cultural advice to his neighbours.

These early vine growers are not known to have attempted wine making. The honour of being the first to produce wine in New Zealand therefore belongs to James Busby. A Scot, Busby emigrated to Australia in 1824, published a series of pamphlets fervently advocating the pursuit of wine making in Australia and New Zealand, and established a forty-acre (16.2ha) vineyard in the Hunter River Valley of New South Wales. He is widely regarded as the father of Australian viticulture.

James Busby was born in Edinburgh in 1801. While British Resident at the Bay of Islands between 1833 and 1840, he made the earliest recorded New Zealand wine.

After Busby was appointed in 1832 to the position of first British Resident in New Zealand, a small vineyard appeared between the house and the flagstaff at Waitangi. Writing to his brother in 1836 Busby told how 'the vines were planted out under the most favourable circumstances, just after a soaking rain. I think the majority of them are likely to survive.'[4]

The vines flourished, and the wine Busby made and sold to Imperial troops also found favour in 1840 with the French explorer Dumont d'Urville. Touring Busby's estate, d'Urville saw 'a trellis on which several flourishing vines were growing ... with great pleasure I agreed to taste the product of the vineyard that I had just seen. I was given a light white wine, very sparkling, and delicious to taste, which I enjoyed very much.'[5]

Within a decade of their establishment, Busby wrote that his vines were under attack, prey 'to the ravages of horses, sheep, cattle and pigs. The leaves are ripped off as soon as they come out.'[6] The vineyard was completely destroyed in 1845 by soldiers camped at Waitangi during the clashes with Hone Heke. Although Busby thereafter channelled into land speculation the energies he once devoted to viticulture, he deserves to be remembered as the pioneer whose enthusiasm for the spread of vine growing yielded the first New Zealand wine.

Other early outposts of viticulture included Port Nicholson and Auckland. A propagandist for the New Zealand Company, the Honourable Henry William Petrie, spent a year with the first settlers at Port Nicholson before returning to England in 1841. Petrie later wrote that: 'When I quitted the Colony, several vines had been planted, but had not then produced grapes. I myself took about one hundred cuttings of different sorts from Sydney, many of which were flourishing...'[7]

At Auckland, vines were planted from the very beginning of European settlement. The first colonists arrived in September 1840; in 1843 the Agricultural and Horticultural Society of Auckland reported that 'the vine plants brought from Sydney in October, 1840, have already produced grapes, and others procured from different sources, and planted subsequently in gardens, have thriven surprisingly ... the experiments carried on in the gardens will show what success may be reasonably anticipated, and ultimately lead to the formation of extensive vineyards.'[8]

At the Agricultural and Horticultural Society's exhibition held in March 1849, the wine on display was from Northland, rather than Auckland. *The New Zealander* reported that 'the attendance was both numerous and select, His Excellency the Governor and Lady Grey, and almost all the elite of Auckland being present ... There were half a dozen bottles of a claret from Wangaroa [sic] manufactured without any of the necessary means of wine making. It was much too new to form even an idea of its quality, but its colour was clear and good.'[9]

The 'claret' was probably made by French Marist missionaries. The first Catholic Bishop of the South Pacific, Bishop Pompallier of Lyons, had arrived at Hokianga in 1838 with French vine cuttings on board. To supply the missionaries' need for table grapes and for sacramental and table wines, vines were planted wherever mission outposts were established.

Brother Elie-Regis at Whangaroa wrote to Lyons in May 1842: 'We cultivate the vines, they do very well here, the first which we planted three years ago already commence to bear fruit.'[10] In 1851 Catholic priests established the first vineyard in Hawkes Bay and the oldest wine making enterprise in New Zealand, the Mission Vineyards, is descended from these early ventures.

Failure was common. Petrie had observed in the 1840s that a major drawback to the spread of the grape-vine was that the English knew little about viticulture. 'To cultivate them [vines] to any extent,

we shall require French and German cultivators, to whom the most liberal encouragement should be given.'[11] French peasants did plant vines at Akaroa in 1840 and three years later, German wine makers arrived at Nelson, but by the late nineteenth century little trace remained of either venture. Two shiploads of German vintners who had been promised perfect opportunities for viticulture by the New Zealand Company, arrived on our shores, contemplated the steep bush-clad hills surrounding Nelson, and left for South Australia.

At Akaroa grapevines sprouted in clearings around the small clay cottages and wine was made, but heavy forest cover and the spread of British influence on Banks Peninsula combined to defeat hopes for a flourishing wine-growing industry. A Government report near the end of the century pointed to the temporary nature of most early attempts to make wine in New Zealand: 'The wine industry [at Akaroa] prospered so long as those by whom it was started remained at the helm, but immediately they began to die off, the vineyards became neglected, and in consequence the vines died out.'[12]

An Englishman was the first to prove the commercial possibilities for wine growing in the colony. Charles Levet, a Cambridge coppersmith, and his son planted seven acres (2.8ha) of mainly Isabella grapes on an arm of the Kaipara Harbour and from 1863 to 1907 earned a living from making and selling wine. The Levets regularly shipped wine to Auckland customers including, in the 1890s, the Earl of Glasgow in Government House. After more than forty years of wine making, father and son died within two years of each other and the trickle of wine from the Kaipara ran dry.

The most successful non-British wine maker was a Spaniard, Joseph Soler, who made his first wine at Wanganui in 1869 and until his death in 1906 sold wine all over New Zealand. From grapes grown on his two and a half acre (1ha) property in Wanganui and other grapes purchased by the canoe-load from Wanganui River Maoris, each year Soler produced around 20,000 bottles of wine.

Soler's entries at first won three of five gold medals awarded at the Christchurch International Exhibition in 1906. Then Cabinet intervened at the urging of rival Australian entrants and ordered a re-tasting. This time, Soler emerged totally triumphant by capturing all five golds.

Later that year, however, Soler died and his sons abandoned the effort to grow grapes in a region climatically ill-suited to viticulture. They went sheep-farming.

There were numerous other small vineyards scattered around the country in the second half of the nineteenth century. Five settlers with eight acres (3.2 ha) of grapes between them were 'principally engaged in vine-growing' on the Mangawhai River south of Whangarei. The largest vineyard, according to *The Daily Southern Cross* in March 1875 was the 'well-known and old-established one of Mr Wendolin Albertz, who has three acres in a high state of cultivation ... There are about 1,000 gallons of wine on hand in the cellars ... Mr and Mrs Albertz were most hospitable, and produced a wine at once pleasant, wholesome and invigorating; a wine entirely free from adulteration, of a good bright colour, light in strength and having a fine bouquet.' The newspaper's 'rambling reporter' enthused: 'The wine made throughout the district is of fine colour and flavour, and only wants to age to make it equal to foreign wines usually imported, and better than some Australian.'[13]

By 1884 a German settler, Heinrich Breidecker, had a small two-acre (0.8 ha) plot of Isabella vines trained along low manuka poles at Kohukohu in the Hokianga. With additional grapes bought from local Maoris, Breidecker in most seasons to the end of the century produced and sold 1200 gallons (5400 litres) of wine at 10/- a gallon.

Generally, however, there was little wine being made in New Zealand in the latter part of the century. Partly to blame was the onslaught of a powdery mildew (oidium) from America which had invaded European vineyards at mid-century. Oidium first appeared as small whitish patches on young leaves and shoots, and eventually attacked all the green parts of the vine. The grapes became covered with a felt-like mould and split open, exposed to the ravages of fungi and insects.

When in 1876 oidium invaded the vineyards of Wendolin Albertz and his fellow vine growers on the Mangawhai River, the 'rambling reporter' observed on 27 March that 'nothing but leaves and wood are to be seen where last year tons of grapes were gathered'. The devastation was widespread. Evidence submitted to a Government committee in 1890 told how 'the chief difficulties with vine cultivation in New Zealand now arise from the presence of minute fungi, which in some seasons reduce the plants to such a condition that no fruit can be perfected'.[14]

The fledgling wine industry soon came under attack from another quarter. The rigours of pioneering life made for hard drinking and public drunkenness was common, much more so than today. The grog shops of the early settlements had set a pattern of squalid drinking conditions that prevailed through the century. Perhaps inevitably, there was a strong reaction.

The 1860s witnessed the foundation of a large number of temperance societies which increasingly called for the total prohibition of liquor. The Licensing Act of 1881, which severely restricted the conditions under which new liquor licences could be granted, was the prohibition movement's first major success, and from 1881 to 1918 there were more and more restrictions.

These laws severely inhibited the development of the wine industry. Representing the New Zealand Viticultural Association before the Industries Committee in 1919, Dawson Smith told how the viticultural pioneers 'had a very uphill fight ... owing undoubtedly to the prejudice which you would naturally expect in respect of an article of that description made in the Colony.'[15] The annual consumption of local and imported wines dropped from two bottles per capita

in 1882 to less than one bottle by 1894. Later *The New Zealand Graphic* disapprovingly noted the 'difficulty in the way of obtaining wine licenses for the retail sale of our native wines.'[16]

Wine growers succeeded in extracting a few concessions from Government before the power of the prohibition movement peaked in the early twentieth century. In 1881 special licences were introduced to govern the sale of New Zealand wine. Previously vineyard sales had been banned and hotels had been the sole legal outlet. Vineyard sales were now authorised but restricted to a minimum quantity of two gallons (9.1L) for consumption off the premises.

A new wine-shop licence was created which allowed consumption on or off the premises – mercifully without the two-gallon (9.1L) requirement. Only four of these licences were ever issued. Then in 1891 Parliament awarded wine makers the right to operate their own stills to produce spirits for wine fortification, thereby releasing them from the financial burden of having to purchase heavily-taxed imported spirits.

At the end of the century, the future of the wine industry hung in the balance. On the one hand, pressure mounted for the prohibition of alcohol; on the other, there were many attempts to find new industries that could boost the country's economy. Increasingly through the 1890s the wine industry came to be viewed as a new and potentially major avenue for economic development. According to Wairarapa wine maker William Beetham the feeling of the times was that 'anything that adds to the value of land, and to the prosperity of the country and the people, might well be taken in hand by the Government.'[17] In this context, development of the wine industry 'would add value to a large area of land in New Zealand that is not of very great value at the present time.'[18] A Government viticultural expert received in 1895 'letters from several agriculturalists, asking for information regarding the viticultural industry' who, 'one and all express their willingness to plant vines on a large scale...'[19]

New vineyards appeared as several Hawkes Bay landowning families explored the economics of wine making. Their interest was aroused by Beetham, who as a young man had spent several years in France and returned, as he later put it 'sure that a very large area of New Zealand could be profitably planted with the vine, and that excellent wine could be made.'[20] Beetham planted his first vines in 1883 and by 1897 he was producing about 1850 gallons (8410L) of wine from Pinot and Hermitage grapes.

Beetham's brother-in-law J.N. Williams planted an acre of Pinot grapes at Hastings in 1893 and later expanded the vineyard to seven acres (2.8 ha) producing 4000 gallons (18,184L) of claret and hock per year. At the Te Mata Station, Bernard Chambers planted his first vines in 1892, and by 1909 he was making 12,000 gallons (54,552L) of claret, hock and madeira.

A speaker at a conference of Australasian fruit-growers held in Wellington in 1896 asserted that 'more pioneer work has been done at the Green Meadows

Diary of S.F. Anderson, Manager of Greenmeadows Vineyard in 1902. Note the classic vinifera *grape varieties recorded on the right-hand page.*

Vineyard, Taradale, than elsewhere. Here we find the premier vineyard of New Zealand.'[21] The owner, Henry Tiffen, had arrived in New Zealand in 1842 as a surveyor with the New Zealand Company. Tiffen visited Masterton in 1890 and was deeply impressed with Beetham's wine. Six years later he had 25 acres (10.1ha) under vines and a mechanised presshouse on which no expense had been spared.

Tiffen died in 1896, whereupon control of Greenmeadows passed to his daughter Mrs A.M. Randall. She initially expanded the vineyard, but was subsequently influenced by a prohibitionist to uproot many of the vines, and by 1914 more than half of the vineyard had vanished.

The expansion of wine making activities had earlier come under renewed threat when in 1893 it seemed for the first time that a total prohibition of liquor might be imposed in New Zealand. The prohibitionists succeeded, by Act of Parliament, in having the issues of 'continuance', 'reduction' and 'no-licence' put to a three-yearly popular vote. When the Clutha electorate voted no-licence in 1895 and was soon followed by others, the wine industry, regardless of its recent growth, faced a real threat of extermination. It took an outsider to resolve the dilemma.

Romeo Bragato, a Dalmatian-born graduate of the Royal School of Viticulture and Oenology in Italy, came to New Zealand in 1895 on loan from the Victorian Government to investigate the possibilities for viticulture and wine making in the Colony. Bragato travelled widely through the country and furnished

Romeo Bragato was New Zealand's first Government Viticulturist. A graduate of the Royal School of Viticulture and Oenology at Corregliano, Italy, Bragato was born in the village of Mali Losinj in Dalmatia. In New Zealand, conscious of anti-'Austrian' feeling, he appears to have preferred an Italian identity.

15

Prime Minister Richard Seddon with a very favourable report.

Bragato wrote that 'there are few of the places visited by me which are unsuitable to the cultivation of the vine.' Hawkes Bay and Wairarapa were 'pre-eminently suited' to viticulture. The potential for wine making was enormous: 'the land in your Colony, if properly worked, should yield a very large quantity of grapes per acre from which wine of the finest quality, both red and white and champagne could be produced … I look hopefully forward to the development in the near future of an industry that will by far eclipse any other that has hitherto been prosecuted here.'[22] Bragato's enthusiasm tipped the balance in favour of the industry's expansion, vine growers' associations sprang up in North Auckland and Central Otago, and a surge in vineyard plantings followed.

Bragato's other major contribution to New Zealand wine makers in 1895 was the identification of phylloxera, a parasitic disease of the vine that rampaged like a prohibitionist zealot through French vineyards in the 1870s. In New Zealand it had wiped out entire vineyards; Government viticulturist S.F. Anderson recalled in 1914 that 'from the invasion of many of the vineyards by the phylloxera many promising starts fell through.'[23]

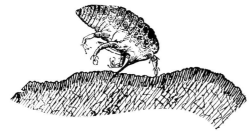

Phylloxera sucking tube in a vine root.

The Government was thus early in receipt of sound advice, but it failed to act decisively. Following Bragato's positive identification of phylloxera, infected vines were destroyed, prompting the *Auckland Star* to declare in December 1898 that 'phylloxera is gone'.[24] The *Star* was wrong. The Department of Agriculture chose to ignore Bragato's advice to distribute phylloxera-resistant vines grafted on American rootstocks. The replacement vines supplied by the department proved equally susceptible to phylloxera, which recurred massively in 1901.

Perhaps the most important of all nineteenth-century developments in the wine industry was also one of the very last. In the 1890s, Dalmatians in the kauri gumfields of the Far North began to make wine.

The promise of quickly acquired wealth attracted the first wave of Dalmatians to New Zealand. Gumdigging required little investment other than hard work and offered a solid financial return. There were over five hundred Dalmatians on the northern gumfields by the 1890s and their presence quickly attracted widespread criticism. The Dalmatians were seen as transitory, and indeed before 1920 most had no intention of settling here. This was directly at odds with the official view of 'settling the North', which held

that gumdiggers should be prepared to invest the fruits of their toil in the development of self-sufficient northern farms. New Zealanders at the time tended to mistrust persons of non-British origin, so racial prejudice was also brought to bear on the Dalmatians. Gumfields poet Ante Kosovich conveys a bitter impression of gumfields life in this excerpt from his 1908 poem 'Longing for Home' (translation by Amelia Batistich)[25]:

Ah! Dalmatia, if I could but give you
    news of your dear sons,
how this wild, hard country beats them down,
in what plight they find themselves
in the lonely hell of gumfields.

It was alleged before the Commission on the Kauri Gum Industry in 1914 that the wineshops in the gumfields, 'should not be allowed to continue in any shape or form, and that they were conducive to great immorality.'[26] The wine produced and sold in the North further aroused hostility against the Dalmatians.

It was widely believed that Dalmatians were trafficking in wines to the injury of the Maoris. 'A great deal of feeling against these men in the Far North is due to many of them being wine growers, and the belief that Maori women are able to get, through them, intoxicating liquors…' The Aliens Commission in 1916 thundered, 'Where young and vigorous men, attractive young women, free from conventional social restraints and abundance of intoxicating liquors are found together, debauchery will certainly result…'[27]

Anti-Dalmatian sentiment intensified during the First World War and in 1918 many Dalmatians were put in prison camps, or pressed into state service building roads and railways, and scrub-cutting. After the war the financial return from gum digging was on the decline. The decision of many to settle permanently and take up other occupations was a development of much significance in this generally unhappy period for Dalmatians in New Zealand.

Although Dalmatians are known to have grown vines at Pahi in north Kaipara as early as 1896, the most successful attempt at settlement in the North was at Herekino, south of Kaitaia, where vines were first planted in 1901. By 1907, fourteen tiny vineyards were producing about 2000 gallons (9092L) of wine per year. 'It is a curious fact', observed *The Auckland Weekly News* in May 1906, 'that although men of British blood were the first to prove that the vine would flourish in New Zealand, and even now have the largest and most up-to-date vineyards, the expansion of vine-growing is due at the present time largely to the efforts of foreigners.'[28]

Pride of place among Yugoslav wine makers in this period belongs to the Frankovich brothers, established on the Whangaparaoa Peninsula north of Auckland in 1899. They had eleven acres (4.5ha) of vines planted by 1913 and each year produced about 4000 gallons (18,184L) of wine. As more Dalmatians chose to settle after the war, and small vineyards spread across Northland and Auckland, the immediate future of the wine industry in New Zealand became, largely, whatever the Dalmatians would be able to make of it.

Looking back, what style of wine had been made in New Zealand in the colonial era? What, if any, were its virtues?

The best of the wine was vastly superior to many of the overseas wines available in New Zealand. *The Daily Southern Cross* saw fit in December 1875 to call upon settlers 'to enter largely into the culture of the grapevine ... as a means of placing in the market a description of wholesome beverage free from any of the deleterious adulterations so freely used in some of the imported wines.'[29]

Public preference, however, provided no incentive to wine growers to produce high quality table wines. At the close of the century the *New Zealand Farmer* observed that 'natural uneducated British taste, when it calls for wine, craves something that is red and sweet and strong. Good wine of a lighter kind might be better for the average drinker, but the ascent to that better state of affairs seems long and slow.'[30]

Some early wines must have been of low quality. Many growers, including Levet, used the Isabella grape to make wine. Most American *labrusca* grapes, including Isabella, produce strongly perfumed wine with little depth of flavour and a very weak 'finish'. Although growers of the era were much divided on the merits of *labrusca* varieties, Bragato's opinion was quite firm. Isabella was 'a very inferior grape from whatever point of view it may be regarded ... for winemaking its "foxy" flavour, lack of sugar and excess of acidity make it most unsuitable.'[31]

Vineyards had successfully been established on a small scale in the North so far as growing grapes was concerned, declared the *New Zealand Mail* in October 1882, 'but the wine, though considered good by some persons, has in no case acquired a character such as to render it an article in steady demand.'[32] Charles Levet, successfully growing wine on the Kaipara, disagreed. Nevertheless, in 1896 William Beetham strongly opposed suggestions that New Zealand should provide samples of wine for analysis by a leading London authority. 'Where are the vineyards? Where is the natural wine? A concoction of a little grape-juice and sugar that is called by some people wine, is not a wine of the country.'[33]

Beetham himself had cultivated mainly Pinot and Hermitage vines and produced a wine praised by Bragato in 1895 as 'Hermitage wine 6 years old, and certainly of prime quality.'[34] Soler's Wanganui wines were principally derived from classic French and Spanish grapes, and, long before the memorable success in Christchurch, won awards at the Melbourne International Exhibition in 1880.

In a paper entitled 'On Vine-growing in Hawkes Bay' read before the Hawkes Bay Philosophical Institute in August 1890, the Reverend Father Yardin of the Meeanee Mission related how: 'When leaving New Zealand, Comte d'Abbans, the French Vice-Consul at Wellington, took with him some twenty bottles of 1885 to 1888 wine of different qualities, made at Meeanee ... the Comte subsequently obtained the opinion of some of the best wine merchants in Paris, who have unanimously pronounced it unmistakably superior to anything produced in Australia.'[35] Bragato found the Mission wines 'most exquisite', recalling 'the liqueur wine produced on the Greek Archipelago islands.'[36]

The Hawkes Bay vineyards were widely planted in quality vines. In 1915 the Mission had all classical varieties: Cabernet Sauvignon, Pinot Noir, Pinot Meunier, Pinot Gris, Palomino, Pedro Ximenes and La Folle Blanche. At the deceased Henry Tiffen's Greenmeadows Vineyard, the 1899 Claret was produced from Shiraz, Cabernet Sauvignon and Malbec grapes — a blend favoured these days by some leading Australian wine makers.

At the Franco-British Exhibition held in London in 1908, the experimental viticultural station at Te Kauwhata won a gold medal for a wine 'approaching the Bordeaux clarets in lightness and delicacy'[37] — final proof that high quality wine, albeit in small quantities, was indeed made during this obscure era of New Zealand wine growing.

WINE GROWING FROM 1900 TO 1960

Those who had endured the struggle to make wine in the generally adverse social climate of nineteenth-century New Zealand enjoyed in the early 1900s a notable rise in fortune.

In 1901 the Government recalled Romeo Bragato to recommend how New Zealand should attack the phylloxera problem. Bragato declared that wine growers had been wrongly advised by the Department of Agriculture – and repeated his earlier view that phylloxera could be controlled only by a complete replanting of vineyards on phylloxera-resistant rootstocks. In 1902 Bragato accepted the newly-created post of Government Viticulturist and took personal charge of the war on phylloxera.

The Government station at Te Kauwhata was promptly upgraded. Originally a wattle plantation where vines had first been planted in 1897, by 1905 the station possessed an eight-hectare vineyard and a small new winery. The original vines were ripped out and replaced with vines grafted on phylloxera-resistant American rootstocks. Vines from all over Europe were imported and tested for their suitability for grafting and adjustment to New Zealand growing conditions. Many vineyards were replanted in this period with vines supplied from Te Kauwhata and the second Government vineyard established in 1903 at Arataki in Hawkes Bay.

At Te Kauwhata, Bragato also embarked upon a programme of experimental wine making. The *New Zealand Herald* in December 1902 recorded that thirty fruitgrowers had visited Te Kauwhata, where they 'inspected the cellar and tasted the wines made by Mr Bragato from last year's vintage. A red Hermitage wine was the first submitted, and this was pronounced excellent... Wines from the Pineaus and from the Carbenet [*sic*] were also tried, being of undoubted high quality. Mr Bragato ... expressed the opinion, that in Auckland not only would the vine flourish magnificently and produce heavy crops of grapes, but that there could be produced from these grapes wines equal in quality to the best in the world.'[38]

Bragato's vineyard foreman at Te Kauwhata, T.E. Rodda, later described his boss as a man alienated from most of his staff by an impulsive and abrasive personality. Nevertheless, sometimes late at night during vintage 'Bragato would come to light with a supper of dry water cracker biscuits, sardines, pickled olives, and claret. I could eat the biscuits and sardines, but could never acquire a taste for the olives. Sometimes when Bragato was in a good humour he would give us a lot of information in respect of winegrowing in Dalmatia.'[39]

Under Bragato's tutelage – his handbook *Viticulture in New Zealand* sold 5000 copies – and with the aid of the Government research stations, the wine industry looked set to prosper. New people were drawn to the industry, especially the Dalmatians who planted vines and began to produce wine at Henderson.

The Dalmatians came to Henderson as gumdiggers, buying land at easy prices with money accumulated on the northern gumfields. When the gum ran out, many turned to agriculture, establishing small mixed holdings of fruit-trees, grapevines and vegetables. Small-scale wine making was often an integral part of these essentially peasant enterprises.

Wadier Corban, son of the great pioneer A.A. Corban, at the age of 90, stands in front of the historic depot used to sell Corbans wine during the peak era of prohibition influence.

In 1902, the same year that the Lebanese A.A. Corban established four acres (1.6ha) in vines at Henderson, Stipan Jelich at Pleasant Valley made the first wine at what has now become the oldest surviving Dalmatian vineyard in New Zealand. 'In this way', Bragato observed, 'many of these men, who were formerly looked at askance and regarded by some as undesirable immigrants, may now be counted as sober, industrious and thrifty settlers...'[40] By May 1910 *The Weekly News* enthused that 'the vineyards in the Henderson and Oratia districts ... stand out as [a] striking example of what may be accomplished in the way of converting the once despised gumlands into highly profitable country'.[41]

But the influence of the prohibition movement peaked in the second decade of the century — with disastrous consequences for the wine growers. Prohibitionists achieved their first victories in wine districts in 1908 when Masterton and Eden — an Auckland electorate including part of Henderson — voted 'no-licence'. Denied the right to sell, although not to make, wine within a no-licence area, many wine makers were forced out of business.

A change emerged in the Government's attitude towards the wine industry. The minimum area in vines required before a wine maker could operate a still was raised in 1908 from two to five acres (0.8 to 2ha). Then cheap South African wines were imported on low preferential tariffs and made rapid inroads in the local market.

Bragato sought to counter the prohibition threat by arguing that wine contributed to the sobriety rather than to the drunkenness of a nation. 'As an agency in the cause of temperance the viticultural industry operates powerfully... It is a fact beyond contention, except by the bigot, that in wine-drinking countries the people are amongst the most sober, contented, and industrious on the face of the earth.'[42]

Bragato's vision of a thriving wine industry, which underlay his proposals for the training of viticultural cadets at Te Kauwhata and the publication of periodic technical bulletins, now encountered resistance even within the Department of Agriculture. A letter published in the Evening Post in December 1907 referred to 'a curious difference of opinion between Signor Bragato, Government viticulturist, and his chief, Mr J.D. Ritchie, who "doubted whether the wine grape will receive much attention in the near future".'[43] The vineyard areas at Te Kauwhata and Arataki were restricted and in 1908 Bragato lost control of both stations. Frustrated, and severely disillusioned, he resigned his post in 1909 and left the country for Canada. Eventually he was to commit suicide there, following a domestic crisis.

The Viticultural Division of the Department of Agriculture was disbanded and research at Te Kauwhata shifted to horticulture. Public interest in wine making waned; by 1909 Te Kauwhata had available a large amount of grafted vines, for which there were few buyers.

Late in 1911 a new organisation surfaced to defend the wine growers against the prohibitionists. The New Zealand Viticultural Association promptly petitioned the Government for help 'to save this fast decaying industry by initiating such legislation as will restore confidence among those who after long years of waiting have almost lost confidence in the justice of the Government. Through harsh laws and withdrawal of Government support and encouragement a great industry has been practically ruined.'[44]

Bragato had noted in 1903 that the sale of cheap fake wines was damaging the reputation of all New Zealand wine. Stories such as that appearing in the New Zealand Times, describing an incident at Don Buck's camp near Henderson, were not unusual. In November 1912 the camp was 'the scene of a drunken orgy, culminating in the death of a man called Harry Whiteside... A woman volunteered the statement that there had been considerable carousing, and yesterday a two-gallon keg of wine was brought to the camp... Some time before it had been reported that a wine highly fortified with some cheap spirit was being sold to gumdiggers, mill hands, and others. Austrian winegrowers received the blame.'[45]

The Viticultural Association publicly condemned the widespread practice of wine adulteration and called for the licensing of wine makers and regular checks on wine making standards. Soon after, the whole issue of wine adulteration came to a head.

During debate on the Licensing Amendment Act of 1914, Prime Minister W.F. Massey launched a sweeping attack on 'the manufacture and sale of what is called Austrian wine. I do not know whether the name is a misnomer or not [Dalmatia was then a reluctant part of the Austro-Hungarian Empire] but it is a liquor that is sold in the district north of Auckland. I have never seen the stuff, but I believe it to be one of the vilest concoctions which can possibly be imagined. I do not know what its ingredients are, but I have come across people who have seen the effects of the use of Austrian wine as a beverage, and from what I have learned it is a degrading, demoralising and sometimes maddening drink...'[46] Massey's sentiments towards wine in general are only too clear in this statement. An amendment subsequently introduced by Massey tightened Government control of the industry through the creation of a new system of wine makers' licences and a string of accompanying restrictions.

The close of war brought no respite for the harassed vintners. The Licensing Amendment Act of 1918 determined that, if national prohibition were carried, the liquor trade should receive no financial compensation for its losses. The wine industry would simply be forced to close down.

When Eden electoral boundaries were altered, all of Henderson became a no-licence area, forcing wine growers to erect depots away from their vineyards, in 'wet' areas, from which to sell their wine.

Then in 1919 New Zealand voted in favour of national prohibition. Only the crucial, primarily anti-prohibition votes of returning servicemen tipped the balance and rescued the wine growers from economic oblivion.

The 1920s and 1930s witnessed a slow, but definite, expansion in the wine industry. Support for prohibition at the polls gradually slumped. The failure of prohibition in the United States turned opinion against the movement in New Zealand, and the prohibitionists' refusal to accept the efficacy of reforms that fell short of complete prohibition hastened their decline. The prohibition tide had been stemmed; there then came a long period of stalemate between 1918 and 1939 during which there was no significant legislation on liquor. The New Zealand Viticultural Association wound down its activities and slipped into recess.

With wine making once more a feasible proposition, new vineyards were planted and wine production increased. This was the period of the main settlement

Corbans counter-attack the prohibitionists at the Auckland Spring Show before the key 1919 liquor poll.

of Yugoslavs in West Auckland, bringing to the area, according to the *New Zealand Herald* in July 1935 'something of the charm of a home industry with simple apparatus and unpretentious sheds.'[47] The influx was reflected in the rapidly rising numbers of licensed wine makers. There were forty in 1925; seven years later there were a hundred.

Hawkes Bay lacked cheap land and close markets of the size that made Auckland attractive to European immigrants. The trend there was to fewer and larger vineyards, and specialisation in wine making was more advanced. Friedrich Wohnsiedler established a vineyard at Waihirere near Gisborne in 1921; Tom McDonald bought his first land in 1927; and in 1933 Robert Bird founded Glenvale Vineyards at Bay View.

The Government continued to treat the industry in an apathetic and frequently hostile manner. Legislation passed in 1920 prevented any further issue of wine bar licences. Since the hotels and merchants selling imported wine regarded the local industry as a competitor, to be obstructed in every way possible, growers were forced to rely heavily on door sales, hunting prospective buyers on foot through the 'wet' areas of Auckland.

The laws regulating the industry were harsh and in a mess. The Customs Department supplied wine makers with brandy to fortify their wines; the Health Department prosecuted its use. Some of the first regulations drawn up for the control of wine making in 1924 would have forced many growers out of business had they had rigidly enforced. Government

Pioneer Dalmatian wine maker Josip (Joe) Babich, who died in 1983 aged 87, and his wife Mara who survives him. A man of voracious reading habits and infectious wit, he arrived in Auckland in 1910, having travelled half way round the world at the tender age of 14. Had he arrived a single year earlier, he could have crossed paths with a departing Romeo Bragato.

insensitivity was further demonstrated when a fresh wave of cheap imported wines was allowed in to threaten the local market.

The outcome was the emergence of a new organisation destined to shape the course of New Zealand wine history. Formation of the Viticultural Association of New Zealand — not to be confused with the earlier New Zealand Viticultural Association — was a response by wine growers to the several adversities facing the industry. The major problems appear in the minutes of a meeting of wine makers held in Henderson in July 1926: 'The industry is likely to be ruined by importation of wines from abroad which are at present practically coming in duty free, and also by the sale of non-genuine grape wines which are being sold, thus prejudicing the public against the genuine grape wines.'[48]

Wine adulteration remained a common practice. A customs officer who called on John Vella at Oratia in 1926, inspected his vineyard and found only 'four rows of a little over a chain each in length. He admitted frankly that he used raisins in making wine, using the wine so made for blending with wine made from grapes... He labels his wine as being made from the best of grapes.'[49] In the same year, Fred Sherwood at Henderson was prosecuted by the Health Department and convicted for selling wine made from apple juice and coloured with aniline dye.

One of the biggest problems for the wine industry lay in its own vineyards. Most *vinifera* vines were in a very low state of health. Blight and viruses had left the vines so weakened that it was widely believed that the *vinifera* varieties could not successfully be grown in New Zealand.

Oidium, according to Government Viticulturist Charles Woodfin in 1928, was still 'well-known through the viticultural areas of New Zealand, where it causes losses in both vineyards and vineries [glasshouses]. Few of the European vines are proof against the attacks.'[50] Grafting onto phylloxera-resistant roots had also hastened the deterioration of classical varieties. The imported rootstocks were infected with virus. Grafting enabled the virus to infiltrate the scion wood and sap the energy of the vines.

Bragato's decision to import native American rootstocks also backfired when many growers chose not to graft onto *vinifera* vines and simply planted the American varieties. These, according to Bragato's successor S. F. Anderson in 1917, were very inferior for wine making, 'owing to a peculiar black-currant or ... "foxy" flavour... The American class of vine is, moreover, deficient in the natural saccharine for wine making. Owing, however, to their hardiness in resisting fungoid diseases they are grown very largely in the north of New Zealand.'[51]

At the turn of the century, fear of prohibition had encouraged many growers to search for a dual purpose grape that if necessary could be sold as a table variety. When one of the American Isabella vines on George Pannill's property at Albany near Auckland produced exceptionally bountiful fruit, growers flocked to procure cuttings. Although the 'Albany Surprise' proved to be exceedingly productive and disease-resistant, its wine proved to have less admirable qualities.

In the 1930s F. E. Hewlett of the Maungatapu Vineyard near Tauranga planted out two acres of vines 'recommended by Te Kauwhata as being a variety from which nearly all New Zealand wines were made. From the time of planting the cuttings, it takes three years to get any grapes at all; and four years for the yield of even a small crop. Thus it took four years for us to find out that the Albany Surprise grape produced excellent crops of pleasant tasting grapes which, when fermented, produced a very poor quality wine.'[52] In 1960 Albany Surprise was still the most widely planted grape variety in New Zealand.

Another contribution to the declining standards of the national vineyard came in 1928, when Franco-American hybrid vines were imported and distributed from Te Kauwhata. The hybrid vines had been developed during the fight against phylloxera. By crossing European with American varieties, French scientists had endeavoured to produce vines coupling the disease-resistant qualities of the American varieties with the superior wine-making characteristics of *vinifera* grapes. Unfortunately, the coarse *labrusca* flavours emerge strongly in most hybrid wines, and eventually the hybrid vines were banned from all of the best French wine-growing regions.

Government Viticulturist Charles Woodfin was well aware of the inferior wine-making characteristics of the hybrids, but considered that they 'should prove valuable for cultivation in the districts where humid climatic conditions are favourable to the development of fungous diseases'.[53] The hybrids proved popular, and by 1945 the Department of Agriculture was strongly urging the cultivation of Seibel and Baco hybrid varieties in Henderson and the Waikato. Gone was the attention devoted in Bragato's time to the low-yielding *vinifera* varieties. Government policy now encouraged the production of cheap ordinary wine from the high-yielding hybrid vines, a switch that suited the struggling wine makers of the 1930s by making wine making a more attractive commercial proposition, but left growers stranded when the call went out for higher quality table wine in the 1960s.

The Depression failed to arrest the slow progress of the wine industry during the inter-War period, but certainly no one had very high hopes of it, and on the eve of Labour's ascension to power in 1935 there was little hint of future prosperity for the impoverished growers. In Tom McDonald's words, they were forced 'to sell the grapes to get the money to buy the sugar to make the wine'.[54]

In fact, Labour's long tenure in office was to prove of great benefit to the wine growers. Rex Mason, M.P. for Auckland Suburbs and then Waitakere, was appointed Minister of Justice in the new Government, and was thus ideally positioned to advance the interests of his wine grower constituents. Labour's determination to aid the wine industry became clear from 1938. Te Kauwhata received an injection of additional funds to upgrade facilities and expand its research activities, and a new viticultural inspector, B.W. Lindeman, was appointed.

Then—at the request of the wine makers—the Government raised the duty on Australian and South African wines, enabling New Zealand wines to compete on a price basis with imported wines, which previously had dominated the market. From 1938 the quantities of wines and spirits that could be brought in were slashed, and for several years import licences were held at fifty percent of their former value.

Sales of local wine soared. Merchants required by the Department of Industries and Commerce to buy two gallons of New Zealand wine for every gallon they imported, suddenly found themselves forced to clamour for local brands that they had long held in disdain.

An influx of American servicemen in 1942 on leave and in search of liquor—any liquor—further excited the demand for New Zealand wine. As one grower put it: 'I sold some wine to an American serviceman for ten shillings a gallon—he was very happy. Then a fortnight later I heard that wine was being sold for thirty shillings a gallon. So I bought a distillery, put in a cellar, and planted five or six acres in grapes. In 1943 in went another five acres...'[55]

With wine selling easily and at top prices, the financial position of wine growers rapidly improved. Brick wineries supplanted tin sheds, concrete vats replaced wooden, and many sideline wine-making operations emerged as profitable small businesses. Wartime conditions created a spring climate for wine growers, and they sank deep roots.

Unfortunately, quality took a back seat in the wartime rush for easy profits. With demand for wine exceeding the supply, growers made up the difference less from grapes than from sugar and water. There is ample contemporary evidence to show that huge amounts of 'plonk' were made and sold in the name of wine during the War. In 1946 the Royal Commission on Licensing was scathing in its criticism of New Zealand wine. 'Most of this New Zealand wine ... has been far inferior to that which could be imported. The Department of Agriculture states that more than 60 percent of the wine made by the smaller winemakers is infected with bacterial disorders ... [and] a considerable quantity of wine made in New Zealand would be classified as unfit for human consumption in other wine-producing countries.'[56] In the same year Mr F. Langstone, M.P. for Mt Roskill, told Parliament that 'most of the wine in New Zealand today is a concoction; it is not wine. There are no more grapes and grape-juice in a lot of it than there are in my boot.'[57]

Records deposited in National Archives show that although the Food and Drug Act prohibited the use of water in wine making, and limited the addition of sugar to grape juice to a maximum of two pounds per gallon (1kg per 4.5L), most New Zealand wines of this period—when they were made from grapes—were vinted from the Albany Surprise variety, contained at least twenty-five percent added water and three and a half to four pounds of added sugar per gallon (1.75 to 2kg per 4.5L).

The law itself was partly responsible for the low overall standard of wine making. Growers with less than two hectares of vines, prevented from operating their own stills, were unable to properly fortify their wines. New Zealand sherries and ports contained only fifteen to sixteen percent alcohol by volume, compared with nineteen percent for their imported equivalents. According to Lindeman, 'the fact of the wines not being fortified to a sufficient strength leaves them open to infection from various wine diseases which produce in the wine, through bacteria, acetic or lactic acid and various other elements which when absorbed by the system have a very deleterious effect'.[58]

The Department of Agriculture moved to tighten its control over wine-making practices, by drawing up a set of proposed regulations that caused much resentment amongst small-scale wine makers. The small growers argued that the regulations would force them to make major structural alterations to their wineries and, in the words of the Royal Commission on Licensing, 'prevent them from using water and certain colouring, flavouring, and sweetening substances which they had always used ... and ... from using a still unless they had 25 acres [10.1ha] of fully bearing grapes'.[59]

The smaller wine makers were convinced that the Department of Agriculture was in league with the larger wine companies. The proposed new regulations—which were never implemented—and the actions of the Government instructor, Lindeman, were correctly perceived by the smaller growers as favouring the large companies at their expense.

In July 1943, at a meeting of the Viticultural Association held at Henderson, the swelling ill-feeling between large and small-scale growers came to a head. Several non-Dalmatian members, notably the Corbans, broke away to form the New Zealand Wine Council and (for geographic reasons) the Hawkes Bay Grape Winegrowers' Association. From then until the formation of the Wine Institute in 1975, the internal politics of the wine industry were dominated by an extreme divisiveness rooted in the contrasting economic fortunes of large and small-scale growers. When the Viticultural Association on the one hand— composed mainly of small-scale growers of Dalmatian origin—and the Wine Council and Hawkes Bay Grape Winegrowers' Association on the other—representing primarily large-scale non-Dalmatian companies—were not pursuing individual paths on matters affecting the wine industry, they spent rather less time in co-operation than at each others' throats.

A separate splinter group was led by a Slovenian of independent vision, Paul Groshek. During the Depression Groshek established two acres of Albany

A collection of old New Zealand wine bottles unearthed a few years ago at Eastern Vineyards, Henderson. Only the Babich company name survives today. Note Paul Groshek's Muaga bottle, carrying for all to read the declaration: 'New Zealand Can Do It.'

Surprise and Isabella vines at Muaga Vineyards in Henderson, and those who came to inspect the maze of cellars he tunnelled into the hillside, and stayed to support his pleas for greater consumption of table wine, swore that he gave away more than he ever sold.

Groshek's reputation has lingered as an unorthodox industry spokesman. He used to write poetry in praise of wine, and was in the habit of flourishing before-and-after photographs of sickly animals miraculously restored to health by the healing qualities of Muaga wine. Until his death in 1964, Paul Groshek made a unique contribution to the wine industry's long fight against public indifference and Government restriction.

The sale of wine in restaurants, and tax adjustments to encourage the production of light table wines were among far-sighted recommendations made to improve New Zealand wine standards by the Royal Commission on Licensing in 1946. However the main part of the Commission's 'Report' recommended nationalisation of the breweries, a course that failed to commend itself to a Labour Government in decline at the polls, and the 'Report', including the potentially valuable section on the wine industry, was shelved.

A first step towards making New Zealand wine more freely available to the public was taken in 1948, when the wine reseller's licence was created, and tailored to meet the retail marketing needs of the wine makers. The licence opened up a whole new avenue of sale, by allowing growers, and others, to establish retail outlets for New Zealand wine throughout the country.

The wartime wine boom collapsed in the late 1940s after the easing of import restrictions when another wave of Australian wine entered the local market. The nation's political leaders certainly appear to have preferred overseas wines; when Walter Nash asked someone to 'go to Bellamy's and bring up a bottle of New Zealand wine the person sent returned with one half-pint bottle, which represented all the New Zealand wine that Bellamy's cellars could produce.'[60]

The market for local wines tightened and by 1949 prices had fallen appreciably below wartime levels. Then industry fears of competition from overseas wine companies venturing into the New Zealand market were aroused when between 1947 and 1950 McWilliam's Wines of Australia established vineyards and a winery in Hawkes Bay. Wine growers viewed the intrusion of foreign wine interests with such concern that the three principal growers' organisations came together in a shaky alliance to form the Wine Manufacturers' Federation, a body that lasted five years until it was torn apart by its own internal feuds.

At mid-century the industry was still failing to capitalise on New Zealand's potential for the production of world-class table wine.

A new impulse was felt when George Mazuran was elected president of the Viticultural Association in 1950. Convinced early that the future prosperity of the wine industry hinged on relaxation of the country's restrictive licensing laws, Mazuran subsequently carved out a long career for himself as one of the most

George Mazuran, regarded with amusement by some MPs for his 'quaint' ways, nevertheless carved out a career for himself as one of the most successful lobbyists New Zealand politics has known.

successful political lobbyists that New Zealand has known. The efforts of Mazuran and the Viticultural Association yielded an impressive string of legislative concessions from successive Governments that laid the foundation for the industry's phenomenal growth rates of recent years.

The early 1950s under a new National Government brought a series of measures designed to boost the ailing wine industry. The wartime forty percent sales tax was halved. Then in 1953 separate licences were created for the manufacture of grape and fruit wines — and no person or company was allowed to hold both. The idea was to prevent the sale of fruit wines masquerading as genuine grape wine.

The wine growers' annual dinner and field-day for Parliamentarians and Government officials was launched in 1952 and subsequently brought the wine industry to the favourable attention of a host of politicians. The field-day transformed the traditional European harvest celebrations into a superbly effective public relations exercise. MPs gained the background knowledge, and industry leaders the social contacts that together assured the wine industry of an accessible and responsive legislature.

Mazuran's assiduous lobbying soon paid off. A crucial breakthrough came in 1955 when Parliament reduced the minimum quantities of wine that could be sold by wine makers and wine resellers, from two gallons to a quart for table wines and — temporarily — to a half-gallon for fortified wines.

An even more important contribution to the resurgence of interest in the wine industry was made by the Winemaking Industry Committee, set up in 1956 to investigate all aspects of the manufacture and sale of New Zealand wine. For several years the breweries had succeeded in preventing the spread of wine resellers' licences, on the grounds that such outlets were unnecessary where New Zealand wine could already be bought from hotels. In a decision of cardinal

Walter Nash, Prime Minister during the Labour administration, 1957-60, here addresses an early Viticultural Association field-day. On his left sits the Hon. H.G.R. (Rex) Mason, a teetotaller who nevertheless promoted the interests of West Auckland wine makers for a period spanning thirty-seven years. Behind, standing, are Peter Fredatovich Snr of Lincoln Vineyards, Mate Selak and Mate Brajkovich of San Marino Vineyards.

significance, the Committee recommended that the existence of other forms of licence should not affect the spread of wineshops and that wine resellers' licences should be more freely granted. The outcome was the doubling in number of New Zealand wineshops by 1965.

Encouraging the spread of wineshops across the nation was the 1957 Committee's essential achievement. There were other useful proposals. The Committee suggested the formation of a Viticultural Advisory Committee consisting of wine growers and departmental officials; that restaurants should be licensed to serve New Zealand (and no other) wine; and that the provision allowing the sale of dessert wine in half-gallon quantities should be made permanent. Together, the recommendations received widespread legislative support.

The incoming Second Labour Government rendered further assistance to the wine growers. Imports of wines and spirits dropped in 1958 and 1959 to half their former volume. Another shot in the arm came with the high taxes slapped on beer and spirits in the 'Black Budget' of 1958. *The Weekly News* in September 1958 declared that the beer drinker 'was rocked on his heels by the sharp bump upwards in beer tax that came with the Nordmeyer Budget. Today, New Zealanders who wend their way homeward after 6 p.m. with brown parcels under arm will often have a bottle of wine as well as the traditional nut-brown brew.'[61]

The effects of Labour's moves are well described in the 1959 Annual Report of the Department of Agriculture. The tax and licensing adjustments had 'created an immediate and unprecedented demand for New Zealand wines. The market position for New Zealand wines changed from one of difficult and competitive trading to a buoyant market capable of absorbing all the wine that producers could supply.'[62] Shortly after, the law was eased to remove restrictions on wine sales in no-licence districts and allow single bottle sales of fortified wine.

WINE GROWING FROM 1960 TO 1983

Our southern outpost of the earth's millions of hectares of vines presently covers an area fifteen times larger than that in 1960, when there were 387 hectares planted. By 1983 the national vineyard covered nearly 6000 hectares. This rapid growth rate has involved the New Zealand wine industry in a number of drastic changes.

One outstanding feature, especially of the 1960s, has been the heavy investment by overseas companies in New Zealand wine. Foreign interests often staked their claims through investment in previously family-controlled wineries. McWilliam's led the way, establishing vineyards and a winery in Hawkes Bay between 1947 and 1950. In 1961 McWilliam's joined forces with McDonald's at Taradale to form what then became the largest wine-making group in the country.

Takeovers soon became commonplace. Like McWilliam's, Penfolds of Australia decided that the establishment of vineyards in New Zealand would best serve their interests in the local market. In a new company, Penfolds Wines (NZ) Ltd, founded in 1963, the parent company in Australia owned sixty-two percent of the capital and local brewers and merchants held the rest. Later Gilbey's moved into Nobilo at Huapai and Seppelt's of Australia became involved with Vidal at Hastings.

All three companies reverted to New Zealand ownership in the 1970s as foreign investors pared their overseas operations. Control of Nobilo's passed to a triumvirate of the Public Service Investment Society, Reid Nathan Ltd and the Development Finance Corporation; George Fistonich of Villa Maria acquired Vidals; and Penfolds was bought by Frank Yukich, formerly head of Montana. Meanwhile, Rothmans entered the wine industry through the purchase of a controlling share in Corbans.

The greatest impact by foreign capital on New Zealand wine has been made through Montana. Montana was established during the second world war by a Dalmatian immigrant, Ivan Yukich, as a one-fifth hectare vineyard high in the Waitakere Ranges west of Auckland. A subsequent crash expansion programme culminated in 1973 when Seagrams of New York acquired a 40 percent share in Montana. American finance and expertise has since enabled the company to emerge as the dominant force in the New Zealand wine industry.

Having failed to prevent the emergence of an indigenous wine industry, local wine merchants and brewers have recently taken a more positive attitude towards New Zealand wine. Hotel bottlestores throughout the country stock and promote the products of the vineyards in which the breweries have a financial stake. Their involvement in wine can be incestuous; in 1980, for example, two-thirds of McWilliam's shares were held by New Zealand Breweries, Ballins and Dominion Breweries between them.

With a view to the establishment of a brandy industry in New Zealand, in 1964 Government gave permission for wine growers to carry out experimental brandy distillations. Despite the production of several sound brandies and the discovery of suitable grape varieties—notably Baco 22A—nothing eventuated. The Government, not convinced that a brandy industry would be economically viable, hedged on the allocation of licences. Also the short supply of grapes for processing into wine left none to spare for brandy.

The wine industry derived greater benefit from a proliferation of new forms of liquor licences. From the 1960s the trend towards liberalisation of the licensing laws evident since 1948 grew much more decisive. Restaurants were licensed in 1960 and taverns in 1961. Theatres, airports and cabarets became licensed between 1969 and 1971, offering new avenues for wine sales. The creation of a permit system in 1976 gave belated legislative recognition to the BYO wine phenomenon by allowing the consumption of wine in unlicensed restaurants. Another amendment that year introduced vineyard bar licences, to enable the sale of wine by the glass or bottle at vineyards for consumption on the premises.

The emergence, quite recently, of contract grape growing has reshaped the structure of the viticultural industry in New Zealand. Traditionally, wineries had grown all of their own grape requirements. Viticulture and wine making formed integral parts of each winery's activities. This pattern altered in the late 1960s when several companies, seeking to avoid the heavy capital expenditure required to establish new vineyards, persuaded farmers to plant their surplus acres in grapevines. The wine companies provided vines, viticultural advice and assistance with financial arrangements in return for guaranteed access to the fruit of the new vineyards.

Vineyard acreages tripled between 1965 and 1970 as contract grape growing swept the Gisborne plains. An average winery bought in four percent of its grape requirements in 1960. Today contract grape growers produce and sell in excess of two-thirds of the country's grape crop.

Since 1970 Auckland has lost its former pre-eminence as New Zealand's major grape growing region. Auckland's share of the national vineyard area

André Simon, the legendary wine writer, is pictured here with George Mazuran. Most of the dessert wines he tasted during his 1964 tour of New Zealand vineyards, he later wrote, lacked 'any trace of bouquet or breed'.

dropped between 1970 and 1982 from nearly fifty per cent to 7.7 per cent. Shifts occurred within the province in this period as many Henderson wineries developed new vineyards further'north, in the more rural Huapai-Kumeu area.

Although vineyard expansion was slow in Auckland and the Waikato, further south in Marlborough, Hawkes Bay and Poverty Bay the pace has been hot. Corbans' plantings, for example, spread from Henderson to Kumeu and Taupaki and then to the East Coast and finally Marlborough. Cooks in the late 1960s established vineyards and a winery at Te Kauwhata, later contracted growers in Poverty Bay and then acquired vineyards at Riverhead (Auckland) and in Hawkes Bay. Montana planted at Mangatangi south of Auckland before contracting large acreages in Poverty Bay and pioneering the spread of viticulture to Marlborough.

Poverty Bay has narrowly emerged as the most heavily planted region in New Zealand, with 1922 hectares under vines in 1982. Hawkes Bay with 1891 hectares is well ahead of Marlborough's 1175 hectares, Auckland's 455 hectares and the Waikato with 336 hectares. This marked concentration of vineyards on the east coast of the North Island has shaped New Zealand's wine future. Given the fertility of the Gisborne and Hawkes Bay regions, by 1986 these two regions will produce around eighty-five per cent of the nation's grape crop. New Zealand wine, therefore, will primarily be of Hawkes Bay and Poverty Bay origin.

According to the then Viticultural Association chairman, George Mazuran, quoted in the *Weekly News* in April 1971, the wine boom of the 1960s 'was achieved at the expense of quality.' During the 'Cold Duck' era 15 years ago an undiscriminating and unsuspecting public snapped up large quantities of cheap adulterated sherries and table wines. Charged Mazuran: 'Some growers have been getting away with blue murder.'[63]

The 1970s brought an overall improvement in wine quality and heavy emphasis on the production of table wines. Wine production rose between 1960 and 1983 from 4.1 million litres to 57.7 million litres. This, said Alex Corban, means that New Zealand had 'probably the fastest growing wine industry in the world.'[64] The growth area is table wines, which captured twelve percent of the market in 1962. Today that figure stands at 73.7 percent and slightly sweet, fruity white table wines dominate the market.

Their predominance reflects the sweeping changes in the composition of New Zealand vineyards. Twenty years ago less than one-third of the vines planted in New Zealand were of classical European varieties — the most common varieties were Baco 22A and Albany Surprise. As a Cooks publication has noted: 'The first is prohibited in most European winemaking districts. The second would be if anyone proposed to plant it.'[65]

By 1983 the classical Müller-Thurgau variety was four times as heavily planted in New Zealand as any other variety. Cabernet Sauvignon is now the major variety for red wine. Classic varieties now constitute over ninety-five percent of all vines in New Zealand.

Twenty years ago we each drank an average of two bottles of wine annually — today we drink seventeen bottles. This increase in wine consumption reflects the much greater awareness of wine in the community.

Lindeman had observed back in 1939 that New Zealanders showed 'not only a lamentable ignorance of wine, but also a very conservative attitude toward it.'[66] Soon after, thousands of New Zealanders stationed in European wine districts during the second world war had their first, fumbling encounters with wine. An anonymous 'Kiwi Husband' writing in the magazine *Here and Now* in January 1952 recalled that most New Zealand soldiers made their first acquaintance with wine only when the supply of beer ran dry. 'It was a rough and ready meeting, and many of us dealt with wine in the manner to which we had become accustomed. We drank it from the bottle, and by the bottleful, often with sad results to ourselves and a total absence of respect for the vintage... It was consumed in quantities that horrified the inhabitants and tortured our stomachs. We drained the countryside of mature stocks and caught up with the harvest. We collected our wine in water carts that held some hundreds of gallons and imparted a taint of chlorine and foul lime sediments; we dispensed it in jerrycans designed for petrol and drank it from the mugs we used for hot tea. And we abandoned it for beer whenever we had the chance...'[67]

Some, like 'Kiwi Husband', later developed a more appreciative understanding of wine. The migration of thousands of continental Europeans to New Zealand introduced large groups of Italian, Yugoslav and Greek wine drinkers into our midst. Countless New Zealanders passing through Europe during the post-war boom in overseas travel were exposed to the traditional European enthusiasm for wine.

Rising affluence at home encouraged many New Zealanders to seek new experiences in food and drink. The mushrooming restaurant trade very profitably promoted wine as an essential aspect of 'the good life'. No longer, as in Groshek's day, was wine viewed as 'plonk', to be consumed in shame 'behind hedges and bullrushes.' Wine has become fashionable. The industry's own marketing efforts, the improved availability of quality wine and the emergence of wine columnists, wine competitions and wine clubs have combined to raise the level of public wine awareness in New Zealand to new heights.

Yet the turmoil in the wine industry in the 1970s produced a number of casualties. To switch from the manufacture of fortified wine to the production of classical table wines required heavy expenditure. While some companies acquired the necessary technical and marketing abilities derived from access to new capital, others fell behind in the race to expand and improve.

The failure of Western Vineyards, Spence's and Eastern Vineyards to lift their wine-making standards beyond those prevailing twenty years ago contributed to their demise in the late 1970s. Other old-established wineries in the Henderson Valley have suffered drastic declines in production. Vineyards seeking a permanent place had to acquire the sophistication necessary in an increasingly competitive market or face an uncertain future.

A labyrinth of many years' negotiations finally achieved in 1975 the formation of a single, united wine organisation to represent all New Zealand wine makers. It was agreed that the industry had grown too large, its problems and aspirations too complex, to allow the pursuit of sectional interests to jeopardise development.

Management of the new Wine Institute was vested in a seven member executive consisting of the elected representatives of three categories of wine makers grouped according to annual levels of production. The formula agreed upon — two representatives each of the small and medium-sized growers and three representatives of the big companies — ensured that, at least initially, a majority of executive members would belong to the Viticultural Association. The large companies were relying upon their belief that the wine

Eastern Vineyards, now vanished, was established by George Antunovich in Sturges Road, in the foothills of the Waitakere Ranges, in 1939.

Eastern Vineyards winery, rear view showing concrete storage tanks.

industry fell 'into three definite categories rather than two, and that the kind of representatives who would emerge from the middle group would tend towards the view of the larger companies rather than the smaller growers.'[68] Under newly-elected chairman Alex Corban, several sub-committees were created to investigate such areas of special concern as viticulture, public relations, wine making, tariffs and legislation.

The Wine Institute encountered sustained criticism in 1979 when it became widely known that the illegal practice of wine-watering was common in New Zealand. Many wineries had taken advantage of the continuing shortage of wine in the market place to 'stretch' their products. Several scientific studies yielded evidence suggesting that consumers annually had been paying for up to 15 million litres of tap water masquerading as wine.

Amendments to the Food and Drug Regulations in 1980 dropped the previous prohibition of water addition and set a scale of minimum grapejuice levels: ninety-five percent for premium or varietal wines, eighty percent for non-premium table wines and sixty percent for dessert wines. A pledge by the Health Department to tighten its surveillance of the regulations led to a marked lift in the quality of 1980 vintage wines.

Yet the whole issue flared again in 1981 when several firms released large volumes of 'flavoured wine', especially in casks. 'Flavoured wine' by law was able to contain as low as forty percent grape juice. Confronted by a heavy barrage of adverse publicity — and an impending grape glut — the wine growers finally agreed in 1982 to support moves to prevent watering. Amendment No. 7 to the Food and Drug Regulations dropped altogether the 'flavoured wine' category. From 1983 table wines may contain only fifty millilitres of water per litre of wine, where the water has been used as a processing aid for legal additives. In effect, table wines of any description must now be produced almost wholly from grape juice, although the sixty percent juice level for dessert wines remains.

For over a century, various enthusiasts have predicted a buoyant overseas trade in New Zealand wine. Walter Brodie, for instance, ignoring the almost total absence of wines in the Colony, declared in 1845 that 'New Zealand in a few years, will export much wine.'[69] Brodie was wrong. The British newspaper the *Daily Mail* enquired nearly one hundred years later, in 1934, whether there were any 'New Zealand or West Indian wines that could be offered in this country?' Observed the paper generously: 'We Englishmen are prepared to try anything once.'[70]

A small, steady overseas trade in New Zealand wine has been plied since 1963. Corbans until recently dominated activity with their sales of medium sherry to the western provinces of Canada. Although New Zealand sold only $720,000 worth of wine overseas in the year ending June 1980, exports are climbing slowly and reached a value of $1,243,000 in the year to June 1983.

The prevailing crisp and fruity New Zealand white wine style is well-suited to the demands of the international wine market. But only recently have there been sufficient quantities of premium table wines for the wine industry to think seriously of export. In the past far too many hybrid-based table wines and adulterated sherries have been shipped abroad. Now, potential exports are subjected to both analytical and sensory evaluations. There is no doubt that our top wines possess the quality to compete on world markets.

Already, small footholds have been established in Britain, the United States, Canada, the Pacific Islands and Australia. Increasingly Government looks to the wine industry for export action, rather than words.

In 1979 the wine industry was referred for study to the Industries Development Commission as part of the Government's policy of economic 'restructuring'. In its 'Wine Industry Development Plan to 1986' the Commission sought to 'assess the potential of the wine-producing industry to contribute to the future growth of the economy, taking into account the interests of the wine-producing industry, consumers, and the distributive trades and recommend a strategy for future development.'[71]

The Commission's essential conclusion was that the wine industry deserved special encouragement. The industry employed 3000 people and turned out a product with eighty-five percent domestic content. Nevertheless, the IDC strongly criticised the price of most New Zealand wine as being too high for the future welfare of the industry. Soaring costs were threatening to push the price of a bottle of wine beyond most New Zealanders' reach.

The IDC produced a series of recommendations designed to contain escalating costs through the encouragement of stiffer competition in the market. In the Commission's view, over-protection of the local industry from imported wine had placed a burden on the consumer unjustified by the wine industry's 'poor' export performance. Distortion of competition in the wine market also derived from the commercial dominance of a select cluster of wineries, merchants and resellers described by the IDC as 'a highly cartelised group characterised by their oligopolistic influence in the market.' The lack of real competition had encouraged an unhealthy 'cost-plus attitude to escalating costs ... to a point where consumer resistance to price shows incipient signs of developing into a major constraint upon consumption...'[72]

Several, although not all, of the IDC's recommendations won Government acceptance. Foreign wines were freed from import licensing in 1981, although not from tariff restrictions. In an effort to stimulate greater competition in the wholesale distribution of wine, a new class of wine distributor licence was created. And sales tax on wine was altered from a value basis to a volume rate (in 1984, fifty-four cents per bottle on table wine, $1.05 per bottle on fortified wine), producing a drop in the retail prices for the better class wines.

Yet as early as 1982 serious doubts arose about the successful achievement of the aims of the Wine Industry Development Plan. The plan had projected an annual per capita consumption of New Zealand wine of fifteen litres by 1986, but consumption fell from 12.5 litres in 1981 to 12.1 litres in 1982, then to an estimated 11.56 litres in 1983 (Source — Wine Institute Annual Report 1982/83). The drop in sales, largely linked to heavier imports and consumer price resistance, proved a serious setback to an industry geared to rapid growth.

Heavy overplanting of new vineyards in the early 1980s helped raise the spectre of a wine glut. Although the Development Plan had suggested that vineyards should total 5550 hectares in 1986, by 1983 5876 hectares of vines were already planted out. With a gradual phasing-out of tariffs on Australian wines due to commence in 1986, the coming surplus brought consternation to some contract growers and wine companies.

1983 involved much speculation about mergers and takeovers. Brierley Investments' proposal to merge three major companies, Cooks, McWilliam's and Penfolds, was judged by the Examiner of Commercial Practices to be likely to be contrary to the public interest. Later, discussion centred on a possible Penfolds-McWilliam's merger. Cooks announced plans late in 1983 to severely *reduce* its production.

The rationalisation needed at this stage in the industry's development need not necessarily involve company takeovers. Greater co-operation, based on a more efficient use of existing resources, may be an answer. Penfolds and Corbans, for example, possibly could shelve plans to build their own wineries in Marlborough and process their South Island grapes on contract at Montana's Marlborough winery. As Mate Brajkovich, chairman of the Wine Institute, has put it, 'boom times need not be a good thing for an industry which must keep improving its quality. Tougher times determine who measures up and who doesn't.'[73]

Samuel Marsden observed over 160 years ago that 'New Zealand promises to be very favourable to the vine.'[74] That distant prediction has only lately been fulfilled by the rapid advances made in viticulture and wine making in the past decade.

The greatest scope for future progress lies in the vineyards. Some of the best grape varieties are still in short supply and too many unsuitable vines remain. Our knowledge of which grape varieties are best suited to the various viticultural regions is very incomplete. And the prime locations for grape growing in New Zealand have yet to be fully defined.

Nevertheless, the eminent German viticulturist Dr Helmut Becker predicts that New Zealand should emerge after the necessary viticultural experiments and refinements as 'one of the top wine countries in the world in terms of quality... Your winemaking technology is as good as any other in the world. You have the right equipment and the skilled wine makers. Also you have the climate and the soil.'[75] Abundant supplies of fine quality grapes hold the key to New Zealand's acceptance in the 1980s as a southern hemisphere producer of fine table wines.

NOTES FOR CHAPTER ONE

1. Barrington, A.J. 'Diary of a West Coast Prospecting Party' in Taylor, N.M. (ed.) *Early Travellers in New Zealand*, Oxford 1959, p.402.

2. Rawson-Elder, J., *Letters and Journals of Samuel Marsden*, Otago University Council, 1932.

3. *Report from the Select Committee on New Zealand*, House of Commons, London, July 1844, p.6.

4. Quoted in Scott, D., *Winemakers of New Zealand*, Auckland, 1964, p.16.

5. Wright, Olive, *Voyage of the Astrolabe 1840*, Wellington 1955. See Thorpy, F., *Wine in New Zealand*, Auckland, 1st edn 1971, p.20.

6. See Scott, D., *op.cit.*, p.16.

7. Petrie, H.W., *An Account of the Settlements of the New Zealand Company*, London, 5th edn 1842, p.59.

8. The Annual Report of the Agricultural and Horticultural Society of Auckland, quoted in *The Southern Cross* newspaper, 25 November 1843, p.4.

9. *The New Zealander*, 7 March 1849, p.3.

10. Quoted in Thorpy, F., *op.cit.*, p.26.

11. Petrie, H.W., *op.cit.*, p.60.

12. Bragato, R., *Report on the Prospects of Viticulture in New Zealand*, Department of Agriculture, 1895, p.6.

13. *The Daily Southern Cross*, 31 March 1875, p.3 and 27 March 1876, p.3.

14. The Flax and Other Industries Committee, Report on the Wine and Fruit Industry, Appendix to the Journals of the House of Representatives, 1890, (I-68), p.9.

15. Report of the Industries Committee, A.J.H.R. (I-12), p.233.

16. *The New Zealand Graphic*, 8 July 1899, p.45.

17. Beetham, W., The Flax and Other Industries Committee, *op.cit.*, p.18.

18. *Ibid.*

19. Bragato, R., *op.cit.*, p.3.

20. Beetham, W., in *Conference of New Zealand Fruit Growers and Horticulturists*, Dunedin, June 1901, p.75.

21. Hanlon, L., in *Proceedings of The Conference of Australasian Fruitgrowers*, Wellington, May 1896, p.90.

22. Bragato, R., *op.cit.*, pp.8-10.

23. Anderson, S.F., 'Grape Culture', *New Zealand Journal of Agriculture*, 20 May 1914, p.507.

24. *Auckland Star*, 1 December 1898, p.32.

25. Kosovich, A., 'Uzdisaj Za Danovini' ('Longing for Home') 1908. Translation by A. Batistich, made available by S. Jelicich.

26. Report of The New Zealand Commission to Inspect and Classify the Kauri Gum Reserves in the Auckland Land District, 1914, A.J.H.R. (C-12), p.20.

27. Quoted in the *Auckland Star*, 19 September 1916, p.8.

28. *The Auckland Weekly News*, 31 May 1906, p.47.

29. *The Daily Southern Cross*, 14 December 1875, p.3.

30. Quoted in Thorpy, F., op.cit., p.20.

31. Quoted in Thorpy, F., *op.cit.*, pp.52-3.

32. *New Zealand Mail*, 21 October 1882, p.17.

33. Letter, William Beetham to J.D. Ritchie, Secretary of Agriculture, 30 September 1896, National Archives, Wellington.

34. Bragato, R., *op.cit.*, p.7.

35. Yaldin, Reverend Father, 'On Vine-growing in Hawkes Bay' in Transactions and Proceedings of the New Zealand Institute, vol.23, 1890, p.530.

36. Quoted in Scott, D., *op.cit.*, p.25.

37. Thorpy, F., *op.cit.*, p.36.

38. *New Zealand Herald*, 12 December 1902, p.7.

39. Rodda, T.E. 'Recollections of an Early Pioneer of the Department of Agriculture, New Zealand', Auckland Historical Society Miscellaneous Manuscripts, Auckland Institute and Museum, M.S. 808 76/28-31.

40. Quoted in Scott, D., *op.cit.*, p.57.

41. *The Auckland Weekly News*, 5 May 1910, p.26.

42. Bragato, R., *op.cit.*, p.12.

43. *Evening Post*, 13 December 1907.

44. Quoted in Thorpy, F., *op.cit.*, p.38.

45. *New Zealand Times*, 19 November 1912.

46. New Zealand Parliamentary Debates, 1914, Vol.168, pp.829-30.

47. *New Zealand Herald*, 12 July 1935.

48. Quoted in *Wine Review*, Winter 1966, Vol.3 No.2, p.21.

49. Thomas, W.C., Memorandum, 20 December 1926, National Archives.

50. Woodfin, J.C. 'Control of Vine Diseases and Pests Occurring in New Zealand', New Zealand Department of Agriculture, Bulletin No. 134, 1928.

51. Anderson, S.F., 'Outdoor Culture of the Grape Vine in New Zealand'. *New Zealand Journal of Agriculture*, February 1917, p.101.

52. Hewlett, F.E., 'Historical Background to the Establishment of the Maungatapu Vineyard', Journal of the Tauranga Historical Society, No.8 October 1957, p.11.

53. Woodfin, J.C. 'Grape Vines for New Zealand Conditions', New Zealand Journal of Agriculture, 20 February 1928, p.106.

54. McDonald, T.B., quoted in *Wine Review*, Vol. 8, No. 1, Autumn 1971.

55. *Wine Review*, Vol.12, No.4, Summer 1975.

56. The Report of the Royal Commission on Licensing, 1946, p.255.

57. New Zealand Parliamentary Debates, 8 October 1946, vol. 275, p.712.

58. Lindeman, B.W., letter to the Government Analyst, 15 March 1943. National Archives.

59. The Report of the Royal Commission on Licensing, 1946, p.262.

60. New Zealand Parliamentary Debates, 1955, p.3461.

61. Bolster, T.N., 'Lucky Break for New Zealand Winemakers', *The Weekly News*, 24 September 1958, p.3.

62. Annual Report, Department of Agriculture and Fisheries, 1959.

63. *The Weekly News*, 5 April 1971, p.4.

64. Corban, A., address to an International Wine Symposium, Auckland, 1978.

65. Company Brochure, 1979.

66. Lindeman, B.W., Report on the Possibilities of Expansion in the Wine Industry of New Zealand, 3 March 1939. Unpublished. National Archives.

67. 'Observations at the Shrine of Bacchus' *Here and Now*, 2, No.4, January 1952, p.2.

68. Minutes of a Meeting of the New Zealand Wine Council, 16 July 1974. See Cooper, M. 'The Wine Lobby: Pressure Group Politics and the New Zealand Wine Industry'. University of Auckland M.A. Thesis, 1977, p.150.

69. Brodie, W., *Remarks on The Past and Present State of New Zealand*, London, 1845, p.105.

70. Quoted in the *New Zealand Herald*, 12 July 1935.

71. Report of the Industries Development Commission: The Wine Industry Development Plan to 1986. 1980.

72. *Ibid.*

73. *The Auckland Star*, 1983.

74. Rawson-Elder, J., op.cit.

75. Quoted in The Wine Report, March 1980.

CLIMATE AND SOILS

Several basic factors influence the emergence of all wine styles—climate, the soil, grape varieties and the wine maker.

Grapes are more responsive to climate than most other fruits, and during the growing season the amount of rainfall, hours of sunshine and degrees of heat all have an eventual effect on the quality of the crop. Variations in soil types also influence the character and quality of wine: although vines grow in a wide variety of soils, heavy clays and poorly drained soils are less suitable than gravelly or sandy soils.

But the careful selection of soils and climatic zones must be matched by the planting of suitable grape varieties. In New World wine countries, the selection of grape types involves a very considered judgement about grape quality, hardiness and yield. And, although wines are often said to be produced in the vineyard rather than in the winery, the wine maker's equipment is important too, as well as his mastery of the skills of harvesting, crushing, pressing, fermentation, clarification and maturation.

Climate

Over the years some curious notions have flourished about the suitability of New Zealand's climate for viticulture. Last century, despite the labours of many wine growers, it was widely believed that vines would not perform well outdoors. Bragato encountered — and rejected — the popular assumption that grapes could be cultivated only in 'vineries' (glasshouses).

The early colonists worried, not without reason, about vine diseases and the difficulty of ripening grapes fully in our temperate climate. Certainly, no one appears to have argued that New Zealand is too hot for wine making. S.F. Anderson, Government Viticulturist, in February 1917 stated in the *New Zealand Journal of Agriculture* that a natural sweet wine cannot be made in our temperate climate: 'The long dry autumn where the grapes can hang without injury until partially desiccated is not met within our climate.'

In the viticultural sense New Zealand has a cool climate ideal for the production of light table wines. If you compare New Zealand with the European wine areas, the climate most closely resembles grape growing conditions in the north of Europe: Bordeaux, Burgundy, Alsace, the Rheingau and the Moselle. Germany lies further north of the Equator than any other quality wine producer: New Zealand lies the furthest south. Both are cool-climate grape growing regions noted for their elegant white wines.

Latitude

Precise parallels cannot be drawn between the latitudes north and south of the Equator that offer the best prospects for making wine. The moderating influence of the Gulf Stream in Europe allows vines to be grown closer to the polar regions than in the southern hemisphere. Alone in vast seas, New Zealand encounters cooler temperatures than regions at comparable latitudes in the northern hemisphere. Hawkes Bay has a climate similar to Bordeaux, yet Bordeaux lies in latitudes parallel to Timaru in the south of New Zealand.

Temperature

Heat and rain are the two essential climatic influences on grapevines. To fully ripen, grapes must receive a certain amount of heat during the growing season. Research in the United States has demonstrated that the single most important aspect of climate for viticulture is temperature.

Heat summation, an empirical tool designed to evaluate the potential for viticulture of various parts of California, measures the amount of heat received during the growing season, above the minimum required for active growth. 'Region One' climates accumulate 2001-2500 'degree days', which is the sum of the mean daily temperatures above 50°F (10°C), the temperature at which the sap rises in the vine. Region One climates are characterised by moderately cool weather under which ripening proceeds slowly.

Such areas, including Bordeaux and Burgundy, the Rhine and the Moselle, produce the world's finest table wines. Sugars can be a problem and acidities tend to be high. The cool weather brings to the fruit optimum development of its aroma and flavour constituents.

The major wine regions of New Zealand possess Region One climates for grape growing. Bragato recognised that 'so far as the temperature and the brightness of the sun's rays are concerned, no fear need be entertained but that the greater part of New Zealand will adequately satisfy the demands of the vine.' He was right. Blenheim averages 2070-2250 degree days, Hawkes Bay 2160-2250, Gisborne 2250-2340, Te Kauwhata 2250-2340 and Henderson 2340-2430.

The heat summation method of analysis proven successful for California may not apply equally well to all other viticultural regions of the world. In the Hunter Valley of New South Wales, for instance, fine red and white wines are produced in a consistently warm climate, defying assumptions to be derived from the heat summation method about the suitability of that area for making wine. New Zealand, in time, may develop its own climatic recipes for successful viticulture.

Rain

The frequent rainfall that characterises our maritime climate creates favourable growing conditions for an enormous variety of plants. Rain, however, is the villain of the New Zealand climate so far as making wine is concerned.

Heavy rains frequently descend on the wine regions during the ripening and harvesting periods of the year. Sometimes abundant rainfall is viewed by the wine maker as an asset; summer rains, for instance, enhance the low-alcohol, fruity elegance of German white wines. The vine, however, needs a dry autumn. In New Zealand it rarely gets one.

On deep, well-drained soils, vines prefer a winter rainfall of about 381mm (15in), followed by another 304.8mm (12in) during the October-April growing season. From a low level in early spring, the water demands of the vine climb to a mid-summer maximum as the vine achieves its peak of vegetative growth. As vintage nears in New Zealand, the best conditions are moderate rains in January followed by very light rain for the rest of the season.

Heavy rains late in the season can damage most grape varieties and cause severe losses. Downpours in the month before vintage dilute sugar levels and split the berries. In Auckland the high humidity and rainfall combine to cause problems with wet weather diseases such as botrytis and downy mildew. Ripening is delayed and the bunches rot.

Although chemical sprays can reduce some of the problems associated with autumn rains, in the past many growers simply preferred to pick their crop early, before the rains arrived. Amelioration with sugar and water was the inevitable result, to supplement low natural sugars and reduce the high levels of acidity.

In respect of rainfall some areas of New Zealand are much more fortunate than others. The principal wine regions range in average rainfall from a low of 655mm (25.8in) in Blenheim to a high 1577mm (62.1in) in Henderson. By overseas standards the rainfall in Henderson and Te Kauwhata, 1176mm (46.3in) is excessive. Gisborne is borderline for acceptance as a quality region with 1010 mm (39.8in). Hawkes Bay at 737mm (30.6in) and Blenheim are ideal.

On the basis of rainfall during the critical February-April ripening period, again Blenheim with 137mm (5.4in) and Hawkes Bay with 182mm (7.2in) emerge on top. Henderson's 355mm (14in) is most unfortunate.

Heavy rains sometimes descend in Hawkes Bay during the ripening period, as shown in this flooded vineyard scene.

Hail-damaged grapes, left vulnerable to fungus problems and birds.

Frosts

Heavy frosts in early spring are hazardous for young vine growth. Temperatures below freezing damage the fruit-set and ruin the size and condition of the eventual crop.

Severe spring frosts occasionally occur in New Zealand. Screen frosts, recorded in ventilated screens about 1.2 metres (4ft) above the ground are the most likely to damage the vine's shoots and buds. Auckland, Te Kauwhata and areas north are largely frost-free, but the risk increases in the south. Screen frosts afflict Gisborne in the spring on average about once every three years, and Hawkes Bay and Blenheim every second year. Nowhere, however, in the major grape-growing areas is the threat of frost so severe as to deter future expansion.

Micro-climates

Wine makers often try to convince you that their own particular vineyards enjoy 'micro-climates' superior to neighbouring sites. Disregarding the propaganda element, it is true that local conditions of wind and rain, frosts and drainage, soils and exposure can greatly affect grape quality.

In regions considered generally unsuitable for grape growing, it is not uncommon to find small areas where local conditions of climate and soil combine to allow the vine to flourish. Factors present at the micro-level can result in a marked variation in heat readings between vineyards and the local meteorological station. The sunny, sheltered slopes of the vineyards at Geisenheim, Germany, are said to accumulate 15-20 percent more 'degree days' during the growing season than the surrounding districts.

Planting vines on a sunny slope facing north considerably increases heat readings. Dr Becker has stressed that New Zealand 'should pay more attention to gently sloping land, rather than flat land, because the slopes allow for better drainage and higher concentration of sunlight and heat.' The tendency, however, has been to develop flat land that is easier to work and yields grapes in profusion. Apart from localised sites in Auckland and Te Kauwhata most vines have been planted on flat to gently undulating terrain. On the Gisborne plains, for example, the average gradient is about 1 in 2000.

In extremely marginal climates for wine making such as Canterbury and Central Otago, attempts to establish vineyards will rely heavily on the discovery of sites with favourable micro-climates.

Soils

The Germans have a saying that where the plough can go the vine should not. Usually, vines planted in rich soils and allowed to crop heavily yield mediocre wine. If the vines are stressed by being planted in relatively poor soil, the smaller crop will be concentrated in flavour and produce better wine.

The outstanding attribute of the soil in the most famous vineyards is its poverty. Vines flourish on chalk in Champagne, on slate in the Moselle and on sandy gravel in Bordeaux. An extensive root system

The flat Marlborough vineyards are planted in silty-alluvial loams over gravelly subsoils.

Fertile, alluvial loam soils are characteristic of the Gisborne plains at Poverty Bay.

The heavy clay soils in the Henderson region have poor natural drainage.

that thrusts far into the ground in pursuit of water and other nutrients enables the vine to perform well in soils where often nothing else will grow.

Immensely adaptable, the grapevine will grow in soils ranging from heavy clays to gravel sands, of low or high fertility, deep or shallow. Bragato noted that 'the vine displays no epicurean instincts as regards soil but has been found to luxuriate in all classes...'

The least suitable soils for quality wine making are heavy clays and shallow or poorly-drained soils. Californian viticulturist Dr Harold Olmo claimed after a 1978 visit that heavy waterlogging of the soil in the months prior to harvest was causing excessive vegetative growth in New Zealand and preventing the berries from fully ripening. Olmo called upon viticulturists to plant more heavily in soils that can rapidly drain away excess water supplies. The most desirable soils are well-drained, of low-to-moderate fertility, rich in the minerals that yield subtle nuances in the flavour of wine.

The soil pattern of New Zealand is complex, varying with the parent rocks, the climate that weathers the rocks, the topography and the covering vegetation. Most Auckland vineyards are on heavy clay land that requires deep ploughing and tile-draining to reduce waterlogging of the soil. In Gisborne the poor natural drainage promotes high fertility. The lighter soils of Hawkes Bay range from shingle to alluvial sand to silt and clay loams. At Blenheim the stony soils reflect the sun's rays and allow water to penetrate deep into the ground. The emergence of regional wine styles and the reputations of the various wine areas hinge to some extent on these variations in soil type.

Climate and Wine Styles

Cool-climate grape growing countries such as New Zealand are blessed with natural conditions ideal for producing premium table wines. In any region, the style of wine produced is largely determined by the composition of the grapes at harvest, which in turn is heavily influenced by the local climate. The more rigorous the climate, the more subtly intriguing the wine.

The wine industry in New Zealand has finally realised its climatic potential. The strong emphasis placed, not long ago, on producing fortified wine styles has declined. The industry's ambition is now to win acceptance as one of the fine table wine producers of the world. The climate and the soils are there to do it.

Debate often centres on whether New Zealand possesses a red or a white wine climate. Some point to the similarities of climate between Hawkes Bay and the red and white wine producing districts of Bordeaux and Burgundy. Others argue that New Zealand has a cool white wine climate and cannot produce good reds.

We are currently producing worthwhile white wines from several grape varieties and promising reds from Cabernet Sauvignon and Pinot Noir. The overall standard of the whites is higher, yet some of the recent high award-winning wines are reds. Probably, as in other countries, we can succeed with both.

THE GRAPES

Ordinary wines were long produced in New Zealand without special consideration of the merits of different grape types. Only recently have the wine makers fully appreciated that excellent wine can be made only from a limited range of premium grape varieties. Good wine comes from good grapes.

Although several thousand varieties of grapes have been recorded worldwide, fewer than twenty are grown much in New Zealand. Grapes belong to the genus Vitis *(the Latin word for vine). There are dozens of grape species classified in the genus and almost all are useless for wine making.*

Grape varieties can loosely be divided into table (eating) and wine types. Apart from the Muscatel and Chasselas varieties, few grapes are well-suited to both table use and wine making. The large, pleasantly-flavoured berries of the table varieties typically yield wine that is dull and thin. By contrast, the small-berried varieties used in the best wines seem all seeds and skins when you eat them.

Vitis Vinifera

The outstanding species of *Vitis* is *Vitis vinifera*, a species almost solely responsible for European wines. Originating in the area of the Caspian Sea, *Vitis vinifera* has been cultivated for at least five thousand years and featured prominently in the ancient agricultures of Phoenicia, Egypt, Greece and Rome. During the modern era of exploration and colonisation *Vitis vinifera* travelled as seeds, cuttings and rooted plants west to the Americas and south to South Africa, Australia and New Zealand.

Vitis vinifera is by far the most important wine species around the world. Despite their vulnerability to insect pests and fungous diseases, *vinifera* grapes without exception form the basis of all fine wines. Twenty years ago only one-third of vines grown in New Zealand were *vinifera* varieties; today they dominate plantings to the extent of over ninety-five percent.

Vitis Labrusca

The profusion of wild-growing grapevines in the New World led the early explorer Leif Erikson to call his discovery 'Vineland' — or so legend has it. The first European settlers in America found several native species flourishing. *Vitis labrusca*, known in America as the 'fox' grape, is the most important.

Despite the assertive, unpleasant flavour of its wine *Vitis labrusca* has played a vital role in modern viticulture. The wild-growing *labrusca* vines developed a powerful resistance both to the endemic threat of phylloxera and the severe climate of the mid-Atlantic states. After phylloxera crossed the Atlantic last century, the European vineyards were reconstructed with classical *vinifera* vines grafted on to phylloxera-resistant native American rootstocks.

The Hybrids

French grape breeders also made countless crossings of *vinifera* and *labrusca* varieties, seeking to create new vines that could produce good wine and yet still grow on their own roots in phylloxera-infested soils. However, despite the labours of Seibel, Baco, Oberlin and others the ideal hybrid never eventuated. Vines that were highly resistant to pests and disease yielded poor quality grapes; if the wine proved satisfactory the vines proved vulnerable. And as the problems associated with grafting suitable phylloxera-resistant American rootstocks on *vinifera* vines were solved, the phylloxera-resistant qualities of the hybrids — often suspect — became obsolete.

The major hybrid varieties in New Zealand were imported by Government Viticulturist Charles Woodfin in the late 1920s. Among the more prominent are Baco 22A and Baco No. 1, Oberlin 595, Gaillard Gerard 157 and numerous Seibels. Some hybrids have acquired local names, for instance 'Seibouchet' and 'Tintara' for Seibel 5437.

In New Zealand wine circles 'hybrid' has become a rather dirty word. The grapes when picked are often high in acid and low in natural sugars. Owing at least partly to the presence of methyl anthranilate, the unpleasant flavours of *labrusca* grapes are often easily detectable in hybrid wines. In Europe the planting of all except a few hybrids has been prohibited, and in New Zealand plantings are not expanding.

The hybrids nevertheless made some positive contributions to New Zealand viticulture. When few New Zealanders were interested in table wines those hardy, high-yielding vines made wine making far more economic than cultivating the shy-bearing *vinifera* varieties. Hybrids once dominated the vineyards, comprising sixty-six percent of total plantings in 1960; now they comprise less than five percent. The best hybrid wines can offer sound, straightforward drinking.

Vineyard Surveys

Every five years since 1960 the Ministry of Agriculture and Fisheries has conducted a survey of New Zealand vineyards. The surveys reveal drastic changes in the varietal composition of our vineyards.

In 1960 the total vineyard area of 388 hectares was most heavily planted in Albany Surprise (sixty hectares), Baco 22A (forty-five hectares) and Seibel 5455 (twenty-nine hectares): these were all hybrid or *labrusca* varieties, offering limited scope to the wine maker in pursuit of quality.

By 1965 Baco 22A (sixty-eight hectares) had outstripped Albany Surprise (sixty hectares) to become the main grape variety in New Zealand. Palomino, the Spanish sherry grape, moved into third position with fifty-eight hectares.

The rush of hybrid and *vinifera* plantings in the late 1960s, showed up in the survey conducted in 1970. Palomino topped the list with 243 hectares, heading Baco 22A, at 217 hectares still in its ascendancy, and Müller-Thurgau rising from obscurity to third place with 194 hectares.

In 1975 Müller-Thurgau emerged well on top, at 649 hectares far ahead of Palomino (338 hectares) and the resilient Baco 22A (208 hectares). Other major plantings included, in fourth place, Cabernet Sauvignon (179 hectares), Seibel 5455 (129 hectares), Chasselas (126 hectares) and Pinotage (106 hectares). Plantings of Chardonnay and Pinot Noir were also rising.

Vine plantings more than doubled between 1975 and 1980, from 2351 to 4853 hectares. The 1980 vineyard survey also revealed that an astonishing 50 percent of all vines planted were less than two years old, and not yet bearing. Müller-Thurgau had maintained its ascendancy with a 200 percent increase in plantings to 1819 hectares — 38 percent of the total vineyard area. Chenin Blanc (289 hectares) and Gewürztraminer (247 hectares) had enjoyed a rapid emergence.

Then Cabernet Sauvignon rose, between 1980 and 1983, from the relative obscurity of sixth place, to become New Zealand's second most heavily planted vine, pushing Palomino into third place. According to the Ministry of Agriculture and Fisheries/Wine Institute Survey conducted in November 1983, the ten most widely planted grape varieties are:

Other varieties covering at least 100 hectares are Rhine Riesling (148 hectares), Pinot Noir (139 hectares), and Pinotage (100 hectares). Hybrids together cover 256 hectares, or 4.4 percent of all plantings. The 1983 survey also records the smaller presences of Sémillon (eighty-six hectares), Flora (seventy hectares), Breidecker (fifty-one hectares), Grey Riesling (forty-four hectares), Merlot (forty-three hectares) and Pinot Gris (26.5 hectares).

Overall, vines covered 5876 hectares in 1983.

Müller-Thurgau

	Hectares at 31/10/83	% of Total Plantings
Müller-Thurgau	1873	31.9
Cabernet Sauvignon	414	7.1
Palomino	408	7.0
Chardonnay	402	6.8
Chenin Blanc	372	6.3
Muscat varieties	331	5.6
Gewürztraminer	284	4.8
Chasselas	236	4.0
Sauvignon Blanc	200	3.4
Gamay Beaujolais	157	2.7

BACO 22A

Baco 22A is a widely-planted hybrid primarily used in cheap quaffing white wines, in a role similar to Seibel 5455 for bulk reds.

The vine is a cross between a coarse *labrusca* variety called Noah and Folle Blanche, one of three grapes used in the production of Cognac. Baco 22A features prominently in the vineyards of Armagnac, where it is used for making brandy, and in other countries where adverse weather conditions demand a stalwart vine. In New Zealand the grape has been concentrated in Auckland and to a lesser extent in Gisborne.

Baco 22A won popularity in New Zealand for its impressive cropping abilities, up to twenty tonnes per hectare, and its resistance to wet weather. The grapes ripen in April, late in the season, which is a disadvantage, but this is offset by their ability to hang well on the vine until fully ripe. The berries are medium-sized with tough, transparent whitish-yellow skins.

Trials to assess the brandy-making potential of Baco 22A achieved promising results, but the quality of its table wine ranges from harsh to ordinary. The wine is often excessively acid with a detectable *labrusca* coarseness. Nevertheless, many people find the wine acceptable and although Baco 22A is now principally used in cheaper bulk wines, the best versions such as earlier vintages of Babich Dry White and Collard Private Bin Dry White attained good flavour in a straight-forward, no-fuss style.

> 1970 plantings: 217 hectares
> 1980 plantings: 157 hectares

CHARDONNAY

Oak-aged, complex, with superbly sustained flavours, the Chardonnays of Burgundy and the Napa Valley in California rank among the greatest dry white table wines in the world. In New Zealand, after years of neglect, this variety is rapidly coming to the fore.

Although Chardonnay is often referred to as Pinot Chardonnay, it is not a true Pinot. There has even been doubt as to whether the variety known traditionally in New Zealand as Pinot Chardonnay is the same vine as the Chardonnay grown in Burgundy. The clones imported in the late 1920s never grew well and the vines languished. In the late 1960s the Department of Scientific and Industrial Research discovered that all Chardonnay vines in New Zealand were virus-infected.

Recently, new virus-indexed clones promising a better vineyard performance became available and Chardonnay has been established in all the major wine regions. The grapes ripen mid-season in small bunches of thick-skinned yellow-green berries. Yields are low: only five tonnes per hectare off virused vines and, off healthy vines, seven to ten tonnes.

New Zealand Chardonnays are typically medium-bodied, with good varietal character. As better quality grapes come on stream and growers experiment with various methods of wood treatment, the standard of Chardonnay is improving all the time. The top wines, from McWilliam's, Delegat's and Cooks, develop after two or three years the full, earthy flintiness for which Chardonnay is renowned.

Some vintages produce exceptional wines. McWilliam's for instance, in 1974, 1978 and 1980 have produced world-class Chardonnays: perfectly balanced, with lovely depth of flavour.

> 1970 plantings: 35 hectares
> 1983 plantings: 402 hectares

GEWÜRZTRAMINER

The highly aromatic and spicy Gewürztraminers of Alsace are among the most distinctive white wines in the world. New Zealand, too, handles this grape with marked success.

Pronounced Ge-vertz-truh-meen-uh, with the stress on the 'meen', the name of the wine is sometimes shortened to Traminer. 'Gewürz' means spicy. In Germany it was customary to call the wine Gewürztraminer if it was spicy; Traminer if it was not. In Alsace the current practice is to label all the wines Gewürztraminer. New Zealand uses both names.

The vine had an inauspicious start here. In 1953 the Department of Agriculture imported a strain called Roter Traminer. McWilliam's established a plot at Tuki Tuki which bore poorly and produced disappointing wine. As a result, many growers believed that Gewürztraminer could not successfully be cultivated in New Zealand.

Recently, healthier vines have been planted in most districts.

Gewürztraminer ripens mid-season in New Zealand with plenty of sugar, but its characteristic poor set of the berries produces low yields of five to eight tonnes per hectare. The bunches hang well on the vine, with reasonable resistance to disease, the small, pink-skinned grapes become juicy and sweet, with a strong, spicy aroma.

New Zealand Gewürztraminers capture well the unique character of this grape. Less ebullient perhaps, than the assertive Alsatian wines, New Zealand versions nevertheless possess in good measure the spicy essence of the variety and are much sought after by wine enthusiasts. The wine is usually made slightly sweet, to mask the slight bitterness typical of Gewürztraminer.

The best producer is Matawhero Wines at Gisborne. The typical Matawhero Gewürztraminer is drier and more pungent than most, with intense varietal character.

1983 plantings: 284 hectares

CHASSELAS

Variously known as Chasselas, Golden Chasselas, Chasselas d'or and Chasselas Doré, Chasselas is widely cultivated overseas as a table grape. As a wine grape it achieves some prominence in cool-climate regions, where its low-acid, early-ripening qualities are of value. In Switzerland Chasselas is the major grape variety and its wine is also known in Alsace, the Loire, Germany and Austria.

Chasselas is one of New Zealand's principal white wine grapes with plantings especially heavy in Gisborne and Hawkes Bay. Maturing early, at about the same time as Müller-Thurgau, Chasselas produces about fifteen tonnes per hectare of large, greenish yellow, low-acid grapes.

The grape is versatile. As a white table wine, Chasselas has a light bouquet and pleasant, low-acid flavour. Soft and fresh when young, it is easily mistaken for Müller-Thurgau in a blind tasting. When aged, it sometimes develops a fuller, earthy flavour in a light white-burgundy style.

The sales response to Chasselas wines marketed as varietals was slow in New Zealand and increasingly the wine is sold under brand and generic names. The grape is also often used as a base in sparkling wines and as an ideal low-acid variety for blending purposes.

1970 plantings: 129 hectares
1983 plantings: 236 hectares

CHENIN BLANC

Although a relative newcomer to the New Zealand wine scene, Chenin Blanc is a major variety in France. There, in the middle Loire, the vine yields fresh, fruity white wines such as Vouvray, typically with an acid finish in cooler years. Chenin Blanc also produces soft, full, easy-drinking wines in California and South Africa.

In New Zealand the wine industry is divided on the merits of this variety. Although Chenin Blanc ripens early in warm climates, here it tends to ripen late, with very high acidity. Yields are high for a premium variety, at twelve to fifteen tonnes per hectare. Nevertheless, the grapes are vulnerable to wet weather and to botrytis. Some growers have recently discarded their vines and replanted with other varieties.

Chenin Blanc makes a light-bodied, fresh, fruity wine in New Zealand with true varietal bouquet and fuller flavour than Müller-Thurgau. The wines are almost invariably made slightly sweet in an effort to balance the high acidity.

Corbans established this variety as a quality wine. Their much acclaimed 1976 Chenin Blanc developed from a full-flavoured, fruity wine at six months old into an earthy, dry rather white burgundy style after three years.

1983 plantings: 372 hectares

GREY RIESLING

This grape is not a Riesling at all, but is probably related to a French variety called Chauché Gris. In California, where the vine is well-known, it produces only pleasant vin ordinaire.

Grey Riesling has been grown commercially for a few years in New Zealand. In Auckland, where it has been viewed as a potential replacement for Müller-Thurgau, the vines grow strongly, cropping thirteen tonnes per hectare of dull, reddish-tan grapes. (To avoid colour transfer, the juice is immediately separated from the skins after picking.) The berries ripen early, with higher acids and sugars than Müller-Thurgau.

Matua Valley has pioneered this variety in New Zealand and latterly Cooks entered the field. Both produce attractive, fragrant wines, fairly sweet, with body somewhere between Müller-Thurgau and Chenin Blanc. The wine lacks interest in its first twelve months, then with age the flavour builds up and the distinct slightly earthy varietal character appears.

1983 plantings: 44 hectares

MUSCAT

Muscat varieties form a large, instantly recognisable family of white and red grapes notable for their almost overpowering musky scent and sweet grapy flavour. The vines grow all over the Mediterranean and in the New World wine regions, yielding a diversity of styles ranging from delicate dry whites in Alsace through to sweet Asti sparklings in Italy and, most commonly, sweet fortified wines such as those of Portugal and Australia.

The vines crop well in New Zealand, producing large fleshy berries with a pronounced Muscat aroma and flavour. Sometimes, following the German practice, Muscat is blended with Müller-Thurgau to add aroma to the wine; it also appears in 'Asti' type sparklings, in sweet fortified Muscats, and recently in light-bodied, fruity, sweetish varietal white wines.

1983 plantings: 331 hectares

MÜLLER-THURGAU

Imagine a pair of white wines: the first pale straw in colour, light-bodied, with a delicate scent and crisp dry flavour; the second softer and more mouth-filling, tasting distinctly fruity, with a refreshing balance of sugars and acids. In New Zealand both styles often carry the stamp of the Müller-Thurgau grape.

Müller-Thurgau is often called Riesling-Sylvaner, in the belief that the variety is one of many crossings between the true Riesling vine and the Sylvaner. In fact the genetic origins of this grape have not been established beyond all doubt. To avoid assertions about the vine's ancestry, the Germans wisely prohibit the use in official circles of any name other than Müller-Thurgau.

The vine was bred late in the nineteenth century at Geisenheim in Germany, by Professor Hermann Müller, a native of the Swiss canton of Thurgau. Müller-Thurgau was originally regarded as a bulk producer of low merit. Later, growers unable to ripen Rhine Riesling grapes on less favoured sites discovered that the new vine could produce large quantities of attractive wine, with less susceptibility to weather conditions. The early-ripening Müller-Thurgau offered growers the prospect of a reasonable crop every year, and in poor years better quality wine than Rhine Riesling.

According to German viticulturist Dr Helmut Becker, 'no other variety has ever spread so rapidly in so few decades ... up until 40 years ago,

opponents wanted to strictly prohibit it. Now the critics of this strain are subdued, but not yet silent.'

The drawback is that Müller-Thurgau as a wine cannot match the body, intensity of flavour, or longevity of Rhine Riesling. German Müller-Thurgaus are described by one authority, S.F. Hallgarten, as 'mild, aromatic and pleasant with a slight Muscatel flavour.' In Dr Becker's view the wines are 'elegant, palatable, harmonious and mild, although Rhine Riesling drinkers often find them too mild.' Clearly, the Müller-Thurgau lacks the greatness of Rhine Riesling.

Nevertheless in 1980 the vine ranked, in terms of acreage, as the number one variety in Germany, covering 25,028 hectares—twenty-eight percent of the total vineyard area. Müller-Thurgau has made least impression in the most famous regions, especially in the Rheingau.

Elsewhere, Müller-Thurgau has spread to other cool wine growing regions such as Austria and Switzerland, Hungary, Yugoslavia, Alsace, Liechtenstein and England. In the 1930s Government Viticulturist Charles Woodfin imported the vine into New Zealand.

The commercial value of Müller-Thurgau became apparent much later, when the demand for white table wines escalated in the 1960s. Then, the vine spread rapidly, prized for its early-ripening ability and high yields. A rush of plantings in the early 1970s rapidly established Müller-Thurgau as New Zealand's leading grape variety. In 1975, almost one-half of all vines aged one to four years were of this single variety. The wine industry had gone overboard for Müller-Thurgau, and plantings since then have expanded rapidly.

Müller-Thurgau grows vigorously in New Zealand and on most soils yields good crops of ten to twenty tonnes per hectare. The berries, yellow-green and flecked with small brown spots, ripen early, and Müller-Thurgau is generally the first variety to be picked. The grapes are susceptible to wet weather at vintage and to fungous diseases, although careful spray programmes reduce the risks.

Müller-Thurgau is well-established in all the major regions. The vines crop most heavily on the more fertile East Coast soils and less economically in Auckland and the Waikato. Distinct regional wine styles are beginning to emerge: Auckland produces Müller-Thurgau with greater depth of flavour and more pronounced aroma than the lighter Gisborne wines; Hawkes Bay versions display a good balance of ripe fruit and crisp acidity; the Marlborough wines are more earthy and Alsatian in style.

New Zealand Müller-Thurgaus vary from dry to very sweet. As a dry wine Müller-Thurgau tends to lack body, needing slight sweetness to fill out the flavour and balance the crisp natural acids. Most Müller-Thurgaus are therefore backblended with a small amount of unfermented grapejuice to produce an elegant, fruity style that is very similar to most German commercial white wines and often better.

The name Müller-Thurgau on the label usually—but not always—implies that the wine has been made slightly sweet. Wines labelled Riesling-Sylvaner are generally drier. It is advisable to read the small print.

The best New Zealand Müller-Thurgaus are of a high standard. Among a wide array several wines stand out as having been consistently satisfying—Robard and Butler, Delegat's, Babich, Collards and Montana Marlborough Riesling-Sylvaner.

Nevertheless most of our Müller-Thurgau is simply clean, straightfoward wine—good vin ordinaire. The prestige of this grape has steadily been usurped by such up-and-coming varieties as Chardonnay and Sauvignon Blanc. Hence, increasing amounts of Müller-Thurgau are emerging as bulk wine in casks and carafes.

Müller-Thurgau offers good short-term cellaring prospects. In the first six months the wines are typically fresh and lively, highly aromatic and grapy in flavour. With age a more interesting, developed character emerges. Sweeter versions occasionally acquire an oily consistency and honied perfume reminiscent of the finer German whites.

1970 plantings: 194 hectares
1983 plantings: 1873 hectares

43

PALOMINO

Palomino is the leading New Zealand 'sherry' variety. The grape is traditionally used to produce the famous sherries of the Jerez region of Spain and at first glance would appear ill-suited to New Zealand's cooler climate. The vine was largely unknown in New Zealand until comparatively recently. The Palomino's ability to produce large crops was first demonstrated at Te Kauwhata in the early 1950s and thereafter the vine spread rapidly through all the wine districts. Palomino emerged by 1970 as the main grape variety in the country, with its heaviest concentrations in Auckland and Hawkes Bay.

The vine grows with much vigour, yielding twenty to thirty tonnes per hectare of large, thick-skinned, fleshy yellow-green grapes that make good eating. The grapes ripen late to mid season with a relatively low acidity and without the high sugars achieved in warmer climates. Palomino withstands wet weather reasonably well, but if there are persistent rain and high humidities as vintage approaches, the grapes are susceptible to botrytis.

Palomino grapes feature in the better New Zealand sherries, dry and sweet, and the best of these can rival their Spanish counterparts. Flor sherries such as Montana Private Bin Pale Dry Sherry and mature sweeter styles like Mazuran's Old Mellow Sweet Sherry are excellent drinking—although difficult to purchase.

The strong sherry character inherent in the Palomino renders the variety unsuitable for producing any other style of wine. Blends of Palomino and other varieties to which the Palomino contributes a dull, earthy, lifeless character are, unfortunately, still found in the quaffing range of white table wines.

1970 plantings: 243 hectares
1983 plantings: 408 hectares

PINOT GRIS (not illustrated)

Pinot Gris belongs to the Pinot family of vines and is cultivated in Central Europe, Germany and various regions of France. In Alsace—where it is also known as Tokay d'Alsace—Pinot Gris produces good wine, dry, full-flavoured and flinty.

Although Bragato praised the variety in 1906 ('in the far north [it] bears heavily and produces an excellent white wine'), Pinot Gris later fell out of favour with most growers because of its tendency to crop erratically.

The vines grow with moderate vigour, bearing a light crop of seven to ten tonnes per hectare of small, thin-skinned, pinkish-brown berries. The grapes mature early with fair acidity and high sugar levels.

Cooks Pinot Gris and Mission Tokay d'Alsace deserve attention: the Mission wine typically slightly sweet and full-bodied; the Cooks version drier and more delicate to taste.

1983 plantings: 26 hectares

RHINE RIESLING

Rhine Riesling is the greatest and most famous grape variety of Germany. Although surpassed now by Müller-Thurgau in acreage terms, Rhine Riesling is still dominant in the best areas—the Rheingau and the Moselle. There, its wine is strongly scented, the flavour a harmony of honey-like fruit and steely acid. Rhine Riesling also performs well in Alsace, Central Europe, California, Chile, South Africa and Australia and recently this grape has made its presence felt in New Zealand.

The proper name of the variety is Riesling. In New Zealand it is called Rhine Riesling to avoid the confusion that could arise out of the common spoken practice of abbreviating Riesling-Sylvaner (Müller-Thurgau) to Riesling.

Obtaining a reasonable yield from Rhine Riesling has long been recognised as a difficulty in New Zealand. Bragato declined to recommend the vines of this variety, 'being only fair bearers.' The 1975 vineyard survey revealed the scarcity of Rhine Riesling vines in the country; eight hectares in Hawkes Bay and half a hectare in Auckland. Since then planting has gathered momentum, especially in Marlborough.

The Rhine Riesling is a shy bearer, yielding only six to eight tonnes per hectare. The grapes ripen late in the season but hang on well, resisting frosts and cold. Harvested late, the small, translucent yellow-green berries produce luscious sweet wines.

Although Collard's 1978 Rhine Riesling—an earthy, raisiny wine—won many accolades, the best examples of this variety to date in New Zealand have been Montana's Marlborough Rhine Rieslings, which have a strongly-flavoured rather Germanic style, with fine, elegant fruit and crisp underlying acid.

1983 plantings: 148 hectares

SAUVIGNON BLANC

The highly distinctive, capsicum/grassy flavour of Sauvignon Blanc contributes to the best Bordeaux whites, from the dry wines of Graves to sweet Sauternes. In the Loire and California, it produces crisp, flinty whites comparable to those emerging in New Zealand.

Sauvignon Blanc, pioneered by Matua Valley at Waimauku, near Auckland and established commercially by Montana at Marlborough, is a relative newcomer to this country. The vines, although vigorous, crop lightly at five to ten tonnes per hectare of small, yellow-green berries. The grapes ripen mid-season with high sugars and good acidity. Tough stems make the bunches difficult to harvest mechanically and in wet weather the grapes are prone to split, causing rot.

Sauvignon Blanc has a fruity herbaceous aroma coupled with an intense, flinty flavour and a fine, lingering finish. A superb example of how well this grape can perform in New Zealand is Montana's Marlborough Sauvignon Blanc 1980. This variety seems assured of a very prominent role in the future.

1983 plantings: 200 hectares

SÉMILLON

Sémillon gives rise to a diversity of styles ranging from the fine dry whites of Graves and Australia to the sweet, late-harvested wines of Sauternes and Barsac. Sémillon imparts softness to its blend with Sauvignon Blanc in Graves, and in Sauternes, infection of Sémillon grapes with *Botrytis cinerea* brings a distinctive, 'noble rot' character to the best wines. Although in Europe the variety is invariably blended with other grapes, Australia makes excellent varietal wines from Sémillon, especially the soft, complex 'white burgundies' of the Hunter Valley.

Small commercial plantings of Sémillon have recently been made in New Zealand with encouraging results. The vines display vigorous growth and yield 10 to 17 tonnes per hectare. The tough-skinned, greenish-yellow berries mature in mid-season with good weather resistance.

The Matua Valley and Villa Maria Sémillons offer early indications of the New Zealand style of this grape—crisp and firm, with a very stalky bouquet and green, grassy flavour distinctly similar to Sauvignon Blanc.

1983 plantings: 86 hectares

SYLVANER (not illustrated)

Sylvaner is a major white variety of the Rheinhessen region of Germany, where it produces pleasant, soft, unobtrusive wines, mostly sold as Liebfraumilch. The vine also appears in Alsace, Austria and Switzerland and small quantities of Sylvaner have recently been established in New Zealand.

The grapes ripen earlier and crop more generously than Rhine Riesling, but cannot be expected to yield wines of comparable distinction. The most appealing versions produced so far have been Weingut Seifried's soft, fruity wines.

1980 plantings: 42 hectares

ALBANY SURPRISE (not illustrated)

The most widely grown table grape in New Zealand, Albany Surprise was traditionally pressed into service as a grapejuice and wine-making variety. The vine, a clonal selection of the black American variety Isabella, was discovered and propagated by George Pannill at Albany, near Auckland. With its larger berries and better-formed bunches, Albany Surprise superseded Isabella and spread rapidly through New Zealand at the turn of the century. The grapes weather well and the thick skins resist splitting. The yield, up to 18 tonnes per hectare, encouraged Bragato's 1908 observation that: 'As to a vine for producing the cheapest grapes, it is doubtful if there are many varieties to equal the Albany Surprise.'

Unfortunately, as a wine grape Albany Surprise ripens late in the season with excessive acid, low sugars and the pronounced 'foxy' flavour characteristic of *labrusca* varieties. Its wine is undrinkable. By 1970, growers who traditionally had sold their crops of this grape to wine makers had trouble finding buyers.

1970 Plantings: 81 hectares
1980 Plantings: 67 hectares

CABERNET SAUVIGNON

The full-flavoured, complex red wines of the Cabernet Sauvignon grape, together with the vine's successful adaptation to a diversity of grape growing environments, have created for this variety a world-wide reputation as the finest red wine grape of all. In New Zealand, as elsewhere, the best red wines often reflect the superb wine making qualities of Cabernet Sauvignon.

Cabernet Sauvignon—often abbreviated to Cabernet—has a long history in New Zealand. The chances are high that the vine first arrived with Busby or with the French settlers at Akaroa. Last century the vine was well-known in New Zealand and in 1906 Bragato pronounced it to be 'one of the best varieties grown here ... the wine produced is of an excellent quality.'

Nevertheless, interest in Cabernet Sauvignon slumped during the wasted years of cheap 'plonk' manufacture. The current revival dates from the early 1970s, when Cabernet came to be regarded as the ideal grape to upgrade the overall standard of red wines. The vine spread rapidly through all of the major wine regions; in 1975 nearly eighty percent of all Cabernet vines in New Zealand were less than five years old. Cabernet Sauvignon now is firmly established as our most popular red grape variety.

In cool climates Cabernet Sauvignon ripens late in the season. Despite their susceptibility to fungous diseases, with proper spray protection the grapes hang well on the vine. Often labelled a shy bearer, Cabernet produces between six and twelve tonnes per hectare of small, blue-black tough-skinned berries tasting astringent even when fully ripe. In New Zealand the grapes are usually picked last, in April, with high levels of acid and tannin.

Cabernet Sauvignon yields wine in New Zealand that is generally superior to that obtained from any other red variety. Nevertheless, the best reds are always made from ripe fruit and New Zealand Cabernets can emerge from poor seasons tasting thin and green. Also, many Cabernet vines have recently had to be replanted because they were from diseased stock. The new virus-indexed plantings coming into production are producing wines of a much higher standard.

At their best, New Zealand Cabernets display the cool-climate characteristics of lightness of body coupled with true varietal flavour. Aged for from one to two years in small oak, the wines develop a style and subtlety similar to Bordeaux, although lacking the heavy French tannin.

By itself, Cabernet can be too austere for some palates and a search is currently under way for a variety to blend with Cabernet to produce a softer style. Pinotage has been used with only moderate success. Merlot, blended with Cabernet in Bordeaux and California, and recently established here, offers better prospects.

Scores of New Zealand Cabernets have fuelled my enthusiasm for this grape. Three memorable wines that have become personal favourites are McWilliam's Cabernet Sauvignon 1970, Nobilo's Cabernet Sauvignon 1976 and Babich Cabernet Sauvignon 1978; all three possess the lovely, sustained flavour and delicacy of style that identifies the finest New Zealand reds.

1970 plantings: 39 hectares
1983 plantings: 414 hectares

PINOTAGE

Pinotage is a black South African grape variety, obtained by crossing Pinot Noir with a vine known in South Africa as Hermitage, but which is really the more humble Cinsaut grape of French and Algerian origin. As a commercially grown wine variety Pinotage is unique to South Africa and New Zealand, where it yields soft, rounded reds that are often under-rated.

Pinotage was established in New Zealand during the late sixties and early seventies, during the rush to replace hybrids with *vinifera* material. The vine grew prolifically, ripening reasonably early with good yields of medium-sized, thick-skinned berries. The variety was widely planted in Auckland, owing to its ability to withstand humid conditions, to a lesser extent in Gisborne and the Waikato—and more recently in Marlborough.

Pinotage has had a rather turbulent career in New Zealand. Once heralded as a premium variety capable of producing the 'great New Zealand red', it has since been much criticised. Some claim that Pinotage is coarse in the mid-palate and the wine has failed to impress such overseas authorities as John Avery and Len Evans.

The criticism has derived partly from the fact that many so-called Pinotage wines used to include substantial amounts of hybrids, ostensibly to improve the wine's colour. A straight Pinotage is much more worthwhile. Also, the quality of the wine has varied with the clone and the extent of virus infection.

A well-made Pinotage is a soft, burgundy-style wine, less tannic than Cabernet Sauvignon, peppery, with a pleasant berry-like flavour and smooth finish. Twice, when the variety has looked in danger of eclipse as a prestige red, Nobilo's have scored gold medals at the national wine competition. The company regularly vies with Montana for top honours with this grape.

Pinotage is now also appearing in the quaffing wine range, to the overall improvement of our carafe and cask reds. The production of rosés from Pinotage is another trend: the wines are light-bodied, fresh, pinkish, varying from dry to sweet and make excellent lunchtime drinking.

1970 plantings: 61 hectares
1983 plantings: 100 hectares

GAMAY BEAUJOLAIS

Gamay Beaujolais is the major grape of the famous French district of Beaujolais, renowned for its light, fruity red wines best drunk within a year or two of the harvest.

In California and New Zealand, where in recent years the vine has become popular, there is doubt as to whether the variety known as Gamay Beaujolais is really the genuine grape of Beaujolais or a clone of Pinot Noir.

The vines yield about ten tonnes per hectare of small, early-ripening grapes. The wine is straightforward, to be valued for its fruitiness and popular appeal. McWilliam's produced the first significant release of Gamay Beaujolais in New Zealand and small wineries like Korepo at Ruby Bay and Victory at Richmond, both in the South Island, are collecting medals for their wines. The best that I have drunk is Abel's Gamay de Beaujolais 1979, an appealing brick-red wine with a soft, fragrant nose and supple body. The Beaujolais Nouvelle Zélande 1984 from the same vineyard, however, lacks charm and freshness.

1983 plantings: 157 hectares

MERLOT

Merlot is widely cultivated in Bordeaux, where it imparts softness and roundness to the Médoc red wines based on Cabernet Sauvignon. The grape also grows in Italy, Switzerland, Eastern Europe, Chile and California and in the late 1970s became established in New Zealand.

The vine displays moderate vigour producing eight to ten tonnes per hectare of blue-black, thick-skinned berries in large bunches. Ripening is late in the season, about the same time as Cabernet, and the grapes resist wet weather well.

Hopes are held that Merlot can enhance the quality of New Zealand reds by adding its characteristic fullness and suppleness of flavour to the middle-palate of Cabernet Sauvignon. Cabernet/Merlot blends, or straight varietal bottlings of Merlot, will soon establish a presence on our wine-shelves. Babich Merlot 1981 and Collard Cabernet Sauvignon/Merlot 1981 are positive indications of the good wines to come.

1983 plantings: 43 hectares

PINOT MEUNIER   (not illustrated)

Pinot Meunier is most widely known as a major variety of the Champagne district of France.

In New Zealand, Pinot Meunier was the mainstay of the early wine industry. S.F. Anderson wrote in 1917 that: 'Fully two-thirds of the vines grown for winemaking in the Dominion are of this variety. It is the hardiest of all our wine producing grapes. It is the most regular and consistent cropper, contains the largest amount of saccharine... [and] ripens well within our grape season...' According to Bragato, Pinot Meunier produced 'a good crop of high class wine.'

Pinot Meunier lost its lead position because of degenerative virus diseases which sapped the vines' strength and reduced the quality of their grapes. Some plants survive, especially in Hawkes Bay, but for many years Pinot Meunier has been confined to a role as a low-acid variety suitable for blending. It is rare to find the wine marketed as a straight varietal—Cooks Pinot Meunier was an exception—and I have yet to drink a worthwhile red from this historic grape.

1983 plantings: 8 hectares

PINOT NOIR

Pinot Noir is one of the great red wine grapes, responsible for the softly flavoured, elegant, yet mouth-filling reds of Burgundy. The vine, however, is temperamental in its choice of soil and climate and does not readily adapt to regions outside northern Europe. Pinot Noir performs without real distinction in Australia and California, and in New Zealand until recently its wine has generally disappointed.

Although the first vines in New Zealand were virus-infected, healthier vines have been available since the early 1970s. Pinot Noir ripens ahead of Cabernet Sauvignon, producing seven to ten tonnes per hectare of small, thick-skinned berries. Several clones are being cultivated, notably Bachtobel and the higher-yielding 10/5.

Lately, plantings of this variety have been quite energetic in the belief that the soft, velvety flavour of well made Pinot Noir is more likely to appeal to New Zealanders than Cabernet Sauvignon. Better wines are emerging. Nobilo's in 1976, Babich in 1981 and St Helena in 1982 have captured the true varietal aroma and flavour of Pinot Noir.

1970 plantings: 21 hectares
1983 plantings: 139 hectares

SEIBELS

These are red and white hybrid varieties once popular for their heavy crops of weather-resistant grapes.

The white grapes such as Seibel 5408 and 5409 are not much grown in New Zealand. Many of our bulk reds, however, used to include substantial proportions of the black varieties Seibel 5437 and 5455.

Seibel 5437

Also known as Seibouchet and Tintara, Seibel 5437 was renowned for its brilliantly-coloured purple-red juice, useful for blending with wines lacking in colour intensity, such as virused Pinotage.

The long, dark-blue grapes ripen in mid-season with high acids and an aggressive hybrid flavour.

1970 plantings: 66 hectares
1980 plantings: 62 hectares

Seibel 5455

Known also as Cinqua and Moya, Seibel 5455 is one of the more highly

regarded hybrids grown in France as a bulk wine producer.

The grape ripens in mid-March in New Zealand with very heavy crops of small, tough-skinned dark blue berries. The variety is still quite widely planted, especially in Auckland and also in Hawkes Bay and Gisborne.

The fruit when fully-ripened is capable of making a surprisingly pleasant red wine, with a soft, quite fruity flavour. Seibel 5455 is usually found in New Zealand as the base material for cheap reds, sometimes blended, sometimes not. The moderate hybrid flavour is not sufficiently pronounced to be offensive. A few wines, usually produced from selected pickings, have deservedly attracted attention, most notably earlier vintages of Abel's Reserve Dry Red and of Collard's Private Bin Claret.

1970 plantings: 111 hectares
1980 plantings: 98 hectares

SHIRAZ

Shiraz is the principal black grape of the Rhône Valley of France and is also heavily planted in Australia. In the Rhône it is called Syrah and sometimes in Australia, Hermitage. Regardless of the name of the vine or the location of its vineyard, Shiraz typically yields robust, richly-flavoured reds, peppery in character and with a heady perfume.

Shiraz has a long history in New Zealand. Bragato was a fervent supporter, declaring in 1895 that: 'The Hermitage will, in your colony, give heavy yields and wine of first quality ... [it] should compose at least one half of the vineyard...' Good wines were made, but in many areas the grapes failed to ripen, lacking sugar and colour and remaining overly-acid. S.F. Anderson wrote in 1917 that Shiraz was being 'grown in nearly all our vineyards [but] the trouble with this variety has been an unevenness in ripening its fruit.'

After decades of eclipse, Shiraz is being re-evaluated. New clones and virus-indexed vines show an improved ripening performance. A few blends have appeared, notably Matua Valley Cabernet/Hermitage and Collard Pinotage/Cabernet/Shiraz. In both of these wines Shiraz had a real impact, adding deep colour, fullness to the middle palate and a soft finish. Nevertheless, this variety has traditionally flourished in warmer grape-growing climates and the future Shiraz in New Zealand remains uncertain.

1980 plantings: 1 hectare

THE SEASONAL CYCLE IN THE VINEYARDS

The peaceful routines of vineyard labour are fixed by the passage of the seasons, each of which has its own special appeal. Perhaps the most spectacular is autumn, after the harvest, when green turns to gold and russet, making bold patterns of colour over vine-covered landscapes. The viticulturist's year really begins with the first cold spells in autumn, when the vines are green and still active and the bunches have been gathered in. Then the weather cools further, and in a flaming shower of crimson, yellow and rust-brown, the leaves drop from the vines.

In winter the vines rest, building their resources for the burgeoning of growth which will take place much later in the year. The vineyards soon lie barren and silent, the vines dormant and bared to the winter rains. Now is a useful period for cleaning up the vineyard — for clearing debris away from drains and the ends of rows, and for replacing posts and wires.

In June, pruning begins and dominates vineyard activity through to the end of August. Left alone, the vines would spread along the ground and climb vigorously, pouring energy into vegetative growth, to the detriment of the fruit which will come later. Through trellising and pruning, the viticulturist is able to achieve greater ease of cultivation and produce a superior crop. In New Zealand, most vines are planted about two metres apart in rows three metres wide and trained along a low trellis a metre or so high, although higher trellises up to two metres are becoming increasingly common.

The art of pruning requires a knowledge of the needs of different varieties as well as swift judgement of the strength of each individual vine. If too few buds are left on the canes after pruning the crop will be small; if too many remain, the vine will be unable to ripen all its fruit. Once the pruner has decided on the correct balance the canes are cut, bent to the wire and tied in place. The bearing arms are laid along the bottom wire and later the season's new foliage will be trained above.

When spring comes, sap rises and nudges fragile buds out from the gnarled canes that have protected them through winter. Shoots and flower-clusters emerge, and tiny leaves unfurl. Several weeks later the flowers 'set' as small, hard green berries. From now until the vintage the vines need constant care.

To arrest weed growth the vineyards are cultivated several times during the growing season. Kikuyu grass, paspalum, blackberry and other weeds create pockets of stagnant air conducive to disease, and compete with the vines for moisture and nourishment. The strip of earth directly under the vines is therefore either sprayed with herbicides, hand-hoed, or ploughed with a manoeuvrable hydraulic blade attached to the side of a tractor.

In spring, cover crops such as lupins and clover, which supply the vines' nitrogen needs, are turned under. Soil which was ploughed onto the vines in autumn, in order to channel winter rains away from

Flaming leaves in the Babich vineyard at the peak of autumn.

In winter pruners remove 90 percent of the previous season's canes.

The remaining canes are twisted around the wire and tied securely at the end.

Botrytis cinerea, shown here infecting Grey Riesling grapes, is the most serious wet weather rot in New Zealand.

the roots, is now cleared away. The rows are disced or rotary-hoed until the earth is well broken-up and aerated. Spray programmes commence too, and run through to the harvest.

The sprays protect the vines against fungous diseases and insect pests such as oidium, black spot, botrytis, downy mildew and mealy bugs. Since the sprays protect the vines, rather than eradicating the pests, up to ten to fifteen applications may be necessary during the season to shield new growth and replace sprays washed away by rain.

Botrytis is the worst problem. Late in the season warm, wet weather encourages grapes to swell up with moisture and split open. Botrytis, which appears as a grey, fluffy mould on the leaves and bunches, causes the grapes to rot on the vines. Fine dry autumn weather can allow botrytis-infected grapes to develop an intense concentration of flavour and sweetness. In New Zealand's generally wet autumns, however, botrytis can severely damage the grapes, oxidising the juice and tainting the flavour of its wine.

Birds are another menace. Sparrows, blackbirds, starlings, mynas and thrushes feast on the ripening grapes, splitting the skins and paving the way for an onslaught of fungous diseases. The wine growers use a variety of defences: wire netting, scarecrows, shotguns, raucous motorcycles, bird-repellent sprays and compressed air explosives.

In summer the vines reach their peak period of growth. The tangled canes are trimmed back, tucked and tied. As ripening proceeds, a waxy white 'bloom' of yeasts develops on the skins of the grapes. Soon, as the bunches approach their optimum level of ripeness, the harvest can begin.

When grapes ripen, two crucial changes occur. The amount of sugar is progressively enriched and the natural acids decline. Prior to the main ripening period, which begins a few weeks before the vintage, the grapes grow rapidly, yet remain hard and acid. At the point of 'turning'—the real beginning of the ripening period—black varieties develop colour and white grapes change from green to their characteristic white or yellow.

The berries soften and the changes in sweetness, acidity and flavour gather momentum. Sugar, almost all at this point of 'turning', is swiftly built up in the leaves and transported to the fruit. Acids fall, the greener malic acid more steeply than the soft tartaric acid. In the very last stages of ripening these changes decelerate. For a few days, when the berries are at their maximum size, sugar enrichment is slow, and on cooler days may even waver, the sugar retreating back into the stalks.

To set the precise day on which the harvest should start, the wine growers usually rely on the ratio of sugars and acids in the grapes. These are the two major constituents of grapes and two of any wine's primary taste factors. For several weeks before the vintage, therefore, berries are randomly selected from the top, middle and bottom of bunches on both sides of the vines and analysed for their sugar and acid contents.

Grapes are often picked with an eye to obtaining

Colour changes in red wine grapes are particularly noticeable in the rapid growth phase prior to maturity. Cabernet Sauvignon grapes, shown here, ripen late in the season.

the best possible yield. A growing trend, nevertheless, with premium varieties, is to delay the harvest in order to achieve higher sugar levels, even at the cost of weight loss through the evaporation of water in the fruit.

The vintage is the most demanding part of the wine grower's year. Considerable skill is needed if the grapes are to be picked at the right moment and arrive at the winery in sound condition. This first, vital step in the making of the new season's wine begins in New Zealand late in February and lasts until May.

A decade ago the entire grape supply was picked by hand, in the traditional manner. The arrival, however, of the first mechanical harvester in New Zealand in 1973 soon forced the hand-pickers into retreat.

The hand-pickers now survive only in the smaller, steeper vineyards. The grapes, cut from the vines in bunches, are left in boxes under the vines for other vineyard workers to collect. These boxes are then either poured into cavernous, tractor-towed trailers in the field or simply stacked on a flat trailer and sent to the winery. Speed is crucial, especially for white varieties. If the grapes are delayed in the vineyard or roughly handled, the juice of any berries with broken skins can oxidise and lose its more delicate aromas and flavours. The wine suffers accordingly. To eliminate such oxidation, the grapes are sometimes crushed and destemmed in the field, and then pumped into a sealed tanker under a layer of inert gas — such as CO_2 or nitrogen — before despatch to the winery.

Many small wineries, like Pleasant Valley, still pick the grapes by hand.

During the vintage, boxes of grapes in the vineyard should be kept in the shade, to reduce the danger of oxidation in any damaged berries.

Mechanical harvesting has destroyed much of the traditional conviviality and social atmosphere of the vintage. Nevertheless, its economic advantages are beyond dispute. One machine can harvest grapes at the same rate as seventy to eighty hand-pickers. The speed of the mechanical harvesters, which can operate twenty-four hours a day, also allows the grapes to be left longer on the vines and so achieve a more advanced stage of maturity.

The harvesters straddle the vines and lumber up and down the rows, beating the grapes off with fibreglass rods. The fruit is then carried by conveyer belts to a large hopper, being towed by a tractor in an adjacent row. Any leaves and twigs are separated by a blower and discarded on the ground. After the machine has passed, some grapes lie strewn on the ground. Since individual berries rather than whole bunches are removed, the bare stalks are still attached to the vines. It is time for the cold days of autumn, seemingly barren but nonetheless full of promise, to set in again.

Mechanical harvesters do not fit the traditional romantic image of the grape harvest but on large vineyards like Cooks at Te Kauwhata they drastically reduce picking costs.

Mechanical harvesting at Matua Valley, with company director Bill Spence at the tractor wheel.

Hand-pickers remove whole bunches from the vines, but the mechanical harvesters leave the stalks intact, although stripped.

RESEARCH

Formal research into viticulture and wine making was from the beginning the responsibility of the Department of Agriculture and Fisheries. The Department still retains responsibility for viticultural field work in the grape-growing regions.

In 1981, however, overall charge both of viticultural and oenological research passed to the Department of Scientific and Industrial Research (DSIR). Industry participation in research is primarily channelled through VORAC, the Viticultural and Oenological Research Advisory Council, which comprises representatives of the DSIR, MAF, Health Department, the Grape Growers' Council and the Wine Institute.

1901 marked the first vintage at Te Kauwhata Viticultural Research Station.

Te Kauwhata

The Te Kauwhata Viticultural Research Station has vitally influenced the development of the commercial wine industry. Practically every grapevine in the country has at one stage or another originated from Te Kauwhata. The station, nevertheless, has often encountered intense criticism from wine makers.

Vines were first planted at Te Kauwhata in 1897 on land described by a contemporary observer, Gerald Peacocke, as 'an expanse of poor clay hills, interspersed with a succession of miserable-looking rush swamps.' The site was originally considered by the Department of Agriculture to be suitable only for growing wattle trees. Vines were eventually established not in the belief that Te Kauwhata was an ideal location for a viticultural research centre but in order to demonstrate the agricultural possibilities of that region. The department recorded in 1899 that 'a small area has been set aside as an experimental nursery... If these vines and fruit trees do well it will serve as an object lesson to surrounding settlers.'

The vines including Shiraz, Chardonnay, Cabernet Sauvignon, Pinot Noir and Rhine Riesling, thrived. Peacocke related that 'the way the vines throve on this

originally unsuitable-looking land surprised everyone. Not only did the vines grow, but they bore and ripened heavy crops of grapes...' This success led to the erection of a small winery completed in time for the 1901 vintage.

Four years later, under Bragato, there was 'a splendid vineyard of 18 acres, a nursery of two acres and a modern cellar', complete with 3000 gallons of wine. Special trainloads of visitors journeyed from Auckland to inspect progress including, in 1902, Assid Abraham Corban.

The flourishing research activity at Te Kauwhata was cut short by the spread of sympathy for prohibition. A slump in official support, followed by Bragato's departure in 1909, led to the station's viticultural efforts being restricted to essential vineyard maintenance. Experiments ceased.

The revival of interest in wine making after World War One, coupled with the declining economic importance of wattle bark (a source of tannin for treating hides), led eventually to the resumption of research work at Te Kauwhata. In this period Charles Woodfin imported the new hybrid varieties and planted them out on trial. Then at the worst period of the Depression the National Expenditure Commission recommended that the station should be sold ('A saving of £350 would result'). But there were no buyers.

The Te Kauwhata station took full commercial advantage of the shortage of wine during the second world war. Official policy was to produce and sell sufficient wine to cover the station's operating costs. The cellar was upgraded and the vineyard extended; apple wine was made and water used to stretch the wine supply. Little emphasis was given to research.

After the war a much-needed change of direction was made. Commercial wine production was scaled down and resident scientific officers, such as Denis Kasza, conducted various research projects. These, however, were performed more on individual whim than as part of a properly controlled research programme. Explicit recognition of the shifting emphasis in Te Kauwhata's activities came in 1965 when control of the station was transferred from the Horticultural to the Research Division of the Department of Agriculture.

In the 1970s scientific staff including a viticulturist, an oenologist and a microbiologist conducted studies in vine spacing and trellising, vine nutrition and disease control. Basic data was collected on varietal yields and ripening patterns. Experimental wines – 150 in 1976 – were made to evaluate different varieties and to combat wine-making problems.

None of this has saved Te Kauwhata from frequent and quite forceful criticism. One sore point with wine growers was the station's physical isolation from the traditional wine areas at Henderson and Hawkes Bay. Because of this remoteness, research performed at Te Kauwhata often had to be duplicated in the major wine districts. Such delays caused considerable frustration to wine makers anxious to identify and establish promising new vines. To overcome this problem, evaluation trials are now established in all the principal wine regions simultaneously with those at Te Kauwhata.

The station has also been attacked for selling its wine to the public in direct competition with the commercial wine industry. From Romeo Bragato's era onwards Te Kauwhata acquired a reputation for producing good wine. For decades its commercial wine supply was sold out on a pre-order system before release.

The Wine Manufacturers' Federation charged in 1954 that Te Kauwhata was 'gathering the vulgar propensity of a commercial winery.' Te Kauwhata, however, never produced more than three percent of New Zealand's total wine output – the real competition lay more in the field of quality. This issue was finally resolved in 1975 when the station ceased bottling wine for public sale.

Another plunge in the rollercoaster history of Te Kauwhata was narrowly averted in 1980. The Department of Agriculture proposed to close the station down – to save funds – and transfer the basic vine collection to a site near Ruakura. The Wine Institute vigorously opposed the Department's plan, and won.

Te Kauwhata subsequently was retained and upgraded, and its valuable research continues. Amongst other things, researchers are able to investigate several problems connected with viticulture, six of which I shall now mention.

The mildly sloping vineyard at the research station is planted in heavy loams over clay subsoils, typical of the Waikato region.

Grapes and Regions

Urgent priority has been given in New Zealand to the discovery of the grape varieties that perform best in the various viticultural areas.

Over many centuries the Old World wine countries have sorted out the most suitable vines for each district and discarded the rest. In the newer wine countries this process of discovery is still underway — and sometimes just beginning. Australia, for example, has found that although Rhine Riesling vines adapt well to cooler parts of the Barossa Valley, the warmer Hunter Valley of New South Wales is better suited to producing full-flavoured white wines from the Sémillon variety.

In New Zealand many vineyards consist of a dozen different grape varieties planted side by side. Few vines, however, can be expected to adapt equally well to regions with such a diversity of climates and soils as Auckland, Gisborne, Hawkes Bay and Marlborough. New Zealand wine makers can be expected in future to concentrate on a reduced range of varieties proven suitable for local conditions.

New Grape Varieties

Many wine makers have complained of the slow trickle from Te Kauwhata of new vines suitable for New Zealand conditions.

In the past, imported vines were quarantined for at least two growing seasons before being added to the collection at Te Kauwhata. After several years the vines bore fruit which was then assessed for its wine-making potential. By the time they became available to wine makers, the new vines had often been in the country for a decade.

Reichensteiner is a relatively new crossing from Germany of Müller-Thurgau with Madelaine Angevine and Caladreser Fröhlich. It yields pleasant but unmemorable wines.

Sometimes valuable material was neglected. Six new varieties bred at Geisenheim Research Station in Germany arrived at Te Kauwhata in 1963. Among the collection were the Reichensteiner and Breidecker varieties, presently attracting interest for their heavy yields of early-ripening grapes. These vines were overlooked for more than ten years.

An effort has recently been made to speed up the evaluation of new varieties. Instead of growers having to wait for Te Kauwhata's findings, the vines are now simultaneously given field trials in the principal growing areas. Californian viticulturist Dr Harold Olmo has emphasised how important it is for New Zealand to establish as many new varieties as possible on a trial basis. The goal is to find the vines that are best suited to our grape-growing environment.

Virus Diseases

Viruses have sapped the strength of vines in New Zealand (and overseas), reducing yields and preventing ripening.

Leafroll and fanleaf are the two virus diseases known to exist in New Zealand. Leafroll virus — the main problem — is easily recognised by its distinctive downward roll of the leaf margins, coupled with premature autumn colouring of the leaves.

These viruses appear to have originated from Te Kauwhata. The rootstocks used in the war against phylloxera in the early years are now known to have been symptomless carriers of virus diseases. Most of the country's vines have been bred from these early Te Kauwhata plants and the viruses have simply been passed down from one generation to the next.

The surge of vineyard plantings in the late 1960s was based on the propagation of these diseased vines. Unfortunately, once a virus has entered a vine it is there for the rest of the plant's life. The only solution for the wine industry is to rip out the infected vines and replace them with healthy ones.

The outcome of this procedure must be better wines. A survey of healthy and virus-infected Cabernet Sauvignon vines at Henderson showed how far viruses can weaken a plant's performance. The healthy vines, cropping twice as heavily, ripened their fruit two weeks earlier with superior skin colours, lower acids and a twenty percent increase in sugar levels.

Clonal Selection

Elimination of viruses offers one way to improve our vineyards. Clonal selection offers another.

Sometimes vines of the same variety, planted side by side, show different characteristics. Often one is visibly superior to the other, with a heavier crop, finer fruit quality, or both. The selection and propagation of these individual clones — or strains — is called clonal selection. In New Zealand it is the superior clones which are being freed from viruses.

As a general rule, the European wine countries improve their vineyards by upgrading their established varieties. Through a painstaking selection of vines over many years, a clone may be obtained that is outstandingly well adapted to a particular area. The

Viruses reduce the vigour of a vine, reduce the crop, retard ripening and cause premature autumn colouring. This is a badly virused Pinotage vine.

A virus only rarely kills the vine; instead, it heavily reduces the plant's efficiency. No sprays or vineyard practices will control a virus infection.

The phylloxera aphid lives on the roots of grape vines but above ground infected vines can often be recognised by their weak growth. Imported Austrian vines at the Te Kauwhata Viticultural Research Station.

Germans, for instance, claim since 1920 to have improved by clonal selection the yield of Rhine Riesling vines by up to 400 percent.

Sometimes superior clones afflicted with viruses can even out-perform lesser strains freed from virus. In New Zealand, the two procedures of clonal selection and virus eradication are being carried out jointly.

Phylloxera

Almost a century after Romeo Bragato's identification of phylloxera and his sound advice on its treatment, New Zealand is still highly vulnerable to the pest. 'I don't want to sound an alarmist,' declared Dr Becker in 1980, 'but you have quite a big problem with phylloxera.'

Phylloxera was discovered in Hawkes Bay in 1964, negating a long-standing belief that the aphid was confined to areas north of the Waikato. The pest was found in 1970 in Gisborne and by 1982 about ninety percent of all Gisborne vineyard blocks were afflicted. In early 1984 phylloxera was confirmed in Marlborough.

The plants most vulnerable to phylloxera are *vinifera* varieties grown on their own roots. American *labrusca* vines have strong resistance to the aphid and are used widely throughout the world as phylloxera-resistant rootstocks on which to graft the classic *vinifera* vines.

In New Zealand, too many growers have sought to avoid the higher costs and greater effort involved in planting grafted plants, and have opted for the easier alternative of simply establishing cuttings on their own roots. Most of our vines—eighty-three percent in 1980—are ungrafted. The phylloxera aphids attack by swarming over the roots and sucking on the vine's sap. Tumours develop on the damaged roots and the vine weakens and eventually dies. Massive replanting with grafted vines is the only answer.

Rootstocks

Viticulturists initially became interested in grafted plants as a means of combating phylloxera. Later it became obvious that rootstocks can also influence the size and quality of a vine's crop.

Rootstocks display wide variations in their resistance to phylloxera, affinity with different varieties, adaptation to various soil types and ability to promote yields. It is important, therefore, to match a variety with the right stock and the stock itself to the local soils and climate. New Zealand has been far too dependent on the single rootstock Mourvedre x Rupestris 1202.

This stock became popular both for its ready adaptation to Henderson's clay soils and as an early stock capable of bringing grapes to a reasonable level of ripeness before the onset of autumn rains. The problem, however, is that powerful rootstocks like 1202 produce heavy vegetative growth at the cost of full ripening of the fruit. Recently, New Zealand wine makers have switched away from 1202 in favour of weaker stocks, capable of bringing the grapes to a more advanced level of maturity.

CHAPTER THREE
Wine Making in New Zealand

The wine grape is unique: most fruits can be made to produce an acceptable alcoholic beverage, but only a few classic grape types can yield wine of real distinction.

Grapes are the usual and most natural source for making wine. Ripe grapes contain an unusually high level of sugar, sufficient to produce by fermentation the level of alcohol necessary in wine. The yeasts needed to activate the fermentation are conveniently located in the 'bloom' on the surface of the berries. Grapes are also more juicy and possess more complex flavours than other fruits, and it is these qualities which have made 'wine' synonymous with 'grape wine'.

The basic potential of a wine is set by its fruit quality. Beyond this, the skill of the wine maker and the quality of his equipment become important. With modern technology, it is more likely that the potential inherent in the fruit can be carried forward into the finished wine. Recent research into the finer details of juice handling, fermentation and aging has brought new winery methods and equipment. An outstanding example is refrigeration, a late arrival on the New Zealand wine scene now widely used to stabilise wine, hold back unfermented grape juice and control fermentation.

Many of the old established wineries in New Zealand were slow to appreciate the advantages of modern technology, because ancient traditions of peasant wine making stood in the way. Most wineries were technically ill-prepared when public demand switched from heavy dessert to white table wines. It is a fortunate irony that New Zealand's late development of interest in wine science has allowed the wine industry to avoid other countries' mistakes and to adopt only the established best. The present level of sophistication of our wine technology compares well with overseas regions.

Before entering into the particulars of white and red wine making, it is useful to know the general techniques that are common to both. I shall briefly describe these below.

Grapes consist of three basic elements: the 'bloom' on the surface of the skins, carrying yeasts and other micro-organisms; the skins, which contain colouring and flavouring substances; and the inner pulp and juice, which consists basically of water and sugar along with acids and other flavour components. For the wine maker the skins and the juice are the items of real interest.

Good wines are not easily made. Nevertheless, the myriad tasks of a modern winery are simply elaborations of a basic process.

When grapes are crushed, the yeasts present on the skins enter the juice and convert the grape sugars into alcohol and carbon-dioxide. The seething of the juice during fermentation is caused by the evolution of CO_2 as a gas. When the sugar supply is exhausted, the wine is made and the yeasts sink to the bottom of the tank. The newly made wine is then pumped off its sediment, clarified, stabilised, and either bottled immediately or stored away in casks and tanks to mature.

A box of hand-picked grapes arriving at the Mission winery.

Although it is usual to make a swift separation of white wine juice from the skins, this is not a hard and fast rule, as the period of contact depends on the style of wine being made. Where the goal is a light, delicate white or a white wine produced from black-skinned varieties, the juice is removed immediately. If a more substantial style is sought, a trend emerging in New Zealand is to allow, say, twenty-four hours of skin contact, in an effort to step up the colour and flavour of the finished wine. Another alternative is to ferment the juice briefly on the skins, before removing the skins and continuing to ferment the juice alone.

Clarifying the Juice

After pressing, the juice contains a turbid accumulation of organic matter — particles of skin and pulp and broken-down yeast cells. These are prone to produce off-flavours (especially hydrogen sulphide) during fermentation. Fermenting a clear juice is more likely to produce sound wine.

Sometimes the must is allowed to settle for a day or two after pressing and then pumped off the sediment. In New Zealand, a centrifuge is more often used to reduce the handling time. The centrifuge — looking like a cream separator and operating on the same principle — employs centrifugal force to throw the solids to the outer reaches of spinning discs, and the polished juice goes down the centre.

Then sugar and acid levels are adjusted, where necessary, to prepare the juice for its fermentation.

Centrifuges are commonly used to clear the must after pressing and prior to the fermentation.

Sugar

Sugaring in New Zealand wine has been a controversial issue. Wine makers in the past have undeniably made much use of sugar relative to the gallonage of wine produced. For the 1967-68 season, for instance, Frank Thorpy calculated that the wine industry used nearly four pounds of sugar for every gallon of wine.

More of this 'Chelsea sunshine' was used to produce alcohol than for sweetening. When there is insufficient sugar in the juice to achieve through fermentation a stable level of alcohol (nine to eleven percent) in the finished wine, the wine maker usually adds a sugar and water solution, which dilutes the juice, but is more practical than adding crystal sugar. Sugar added to the must before fermentation has little discernible effect on the flavour of wine.

Lately the fruit has come on stream from new, earlier-ripening varieties and from healthier vines of established varieties, so that the natural sugar content of the grapes has risen. Nevertheless 'chaptalisation' (raising the level of sugar in musts) will always be needed with certain varieties and in poorer years. New Zealand is hardly unique in this: all the cooler wine regions in 'lesser' vintages find it essential to supplement their low natural grape sugars. In Germany, for example, wine makers often add sugar to the must: up to fifteen percent for the lowest grade, Tafelwein, and up to ten percent in the middle category, Qualitatswein. Superior (Qualitatswein mit Pradikat) wines are by law not allowed to be chaptalised, although that does not necessarily prevent its happening.

Crushed and pressed grapes after removal of the juice. This residue is discarded.

Acidity

Acidity is vital to the colour, preservation and flavour of white wines. In its correct balance, acid imparts the desirable qualities of freshness and firmness, but too much acid leaves the wine sharp and sour. Temperate regions such as New Zealand often harvest grapes with a high natural acidity, sometimes too high.

Various options are available to the wine maker to de-acidify a high-acid must before the fermentation, including the simple addition of $CaCo_3$, known as 'chalking'. High and low acid musts can also be blended together. Well-ripened early varieties may even arrive at the winery deficient in acidity, and here tartaric acid will be added to prevent the finished wine tasting flabby.

A crisp and lively acidity is normally one of the more engaging and instantly recognisable hallmarks of New Zealand whites.

Water in Wine

Adding water, which is the most obvious way to reduce acidity in wine, has been only too well known in New Zealand. 'Oenological amelioration' was the official jargon for the practice of adding water to wine (or more accurately grape juice) in an effort to improve its quality, and it was illegal in New Zealand until 1980. Nevertheless its use was unofficially tolerated, since it enabled wine makers to combat low sugars and high acids and reduce the coarse flavours of hybrid wines. Even government agencies were deeply involved in the practice of wine amelioration (or adulteration — it depends on your point of view). During the second world war, for instance, the Department of Agriculture sanctioned the addition by wine makers of up to one-third water to their wines.

Wine watering, although rarely discussed outside industry circles, was routine procedure in most wineries. In 1971 an analysis by the DSIR found that about eighty percent of the sixty-eight white wines had been watered. A later study of 123 white wines entered in the 1977 national wine competition revealed a big improvement: the percentage of samples illegally diluted with water had dropped to twenty-seven percent.

Cask wines and fortifieds were nonetheless still heavily adulterated. In 1979 a Health Department investigation into the quality of cask wines found that half of those surveyed had 'indisputably' been stretched, some of them by more than fifty percent. In the same year the issue was brought to a head when Montana Wines introduced into the market casks of 'Brother Dominic'.

'Brother Dominic' was packaged and labelled like wine, and with massive promotion soon captured a lucrative slice of the bulk wine market. In terms of the Food and Drug Regulations, however, 'Brother Dominic' was an 'alcoholic beverage' made with limited assistance from grapes. The product aroused the ire of competing wine companies and the ensuing scrap soon riveted the attention of the media on the question of water and wine.

The Government hastened to change the regulations on wine making prior to the 1980 harvest. On the grounds that a total ban on wine-watering would be impractical, the previous prohibition against water addition was dropped. Under the new regulations, all table wines were now required to contain a minimum eighty percent of grape juice, and the juice in wines named by a grape variety or as 'premium' or 'private bin' had to reach ninety-five percent. This allowed wine makers to add up to twenty percent water (where necessary) to table wines to aid de-acidification, chaptalisation and other winery procedures such as racking and fining.

To legalise what had once been illegal struck some critics as an odd way to reduce the water content of New Zealand wine. The paradox was resolved, however, by the Health Department's intention to firmly enforce the new rules. In reality the threat of official action resulted in a substantial reduction in use of the water-hose.

Since our grapes do not always ripen fully, legislative provision for the tightly controlled addition of water to some of our lesser wines was simply realistic. Regulations must be such that responsible growers are able to live with them. However, since better fruit is now becoming available from new and improved grape varieties, the 1983 change to the regulations, that set a ninety-five percent minimum grapejuice level for *all* table wines, should ensure that future New Zealand vintages genuinely deserve to be called wine.

Yeasts

Yeasts are single-celled micro-organisms that grow and multiply during fermentation, using the sugar in the juice as a source of energy. Yeasts occur naturally on grapeskins and are also present in cellars, in the air, and on equipment.

Ruakura scientist Dr Jack Parle investigated the yeasts responsible for the natural fermentation of wine in New Zealand. The species of most interest to wine makers, *Saccharomyces cerevisiae* is present only in small numbers. *Kloeckera apiculata,* the dominant type, yields a low level of alcohol and imparts an unpleasant flavour to wine. Yeasts such as this can also ruin wine by producing acetic acid and hydrogen-sulphide.

Since some yeasts have these bad fermentation characteristics, most wineries inhibit natural yeast growth by adding sulphur to the must after crushing, and later initiate the fermentation with a selected 'pure' wine yeast.

'Cold fermentation' yeasts are now widely used in New Zealand. These yeasts are better able to tolerate high levels of sugar, alcohol and carbon-dioxide during fermentation, the bouquet is improved, and the wine tends to be more constant in character and quality. By selecting individual yeast strains, the wine maker is also able to influence the secondary flavours produced during fermentation.

Fermentation

After inoculation with a selected yeast culture, the first bubbles of CO_2 gas appearing in the juice signal that the fermentation has begun.

The process of fermentation is essentially the conversion of sugar to alcohol and so of grape juice to wine. The basic reaction can be shown thus:

Sugar + Yeast → Ethyl Alcohol + Carbon Dioxide + Energy. Alcohol is the primary end product, but other taste components also emerge that have a bearing on the final flavour of the wine. And as the acids in the wine combine with the alcohol the elements that comprise the bouquet develop.

Usually the wine is fermented through to dryness, although sometimes the wine maker will act to stop the fermentation so as to retain a little residual sweetness.

Until about fifteen years ago most New Zealand wineries used open fermenting vats made of wood or concrete. Wood, an easy material to shape, was the usual means of wine storage for our pioneer wine makers, and for them a knowledge of coopering was essential.

Later, wooden vats were replaced by concrete vats lined with a neutral surfacing material. Open concrete vats coated with polyurethane are still seen, but they are rarely used today for the fermentation of white wines; to avoid the loss through air contact of elements crucial to the development of the bouquet and flavour, almost invariably white wines are fermented in enclosed stainless steel tanks.

Pressure builds up inside the tank during fermentation from the evolution of CO_2 gas. By means of pressure dials and a special release valve the wine maker is able to modify this pressure, and so to slow the rate of fermentation. The higher the pressure, the slower the fermentation. Wines fermented in a sealed tank often retain a small amount of CO_2 after bottling – leaving a 'spritzig' tingle in the mouth.

Cold Fermentation

An uncontrolled, hot fermentation is prone to yield a spoiled wine. Overseas, control over the build-up of heat during fermentation is sometimes achieved by fermenting wine in cool underground cellars. Until twenty years ago in New Zealand, however, the fermentation was slowed by simply adding heavy doses of sulphur.

Corbans introduced cold fermentation techniques to New Zealand in the 1960s. It was apparent immediately that white wines which were fermented at a low temperature were noticeably more fragrant and fuller in flavour than those made by traditional methods. Cold fermentation allowed the wine maker to trap some of the aroma and flavour components that would otherwise escape with the gas.

Today it is customary to ferment white wines at 15°C or below. Sometimes water is passed through coils immersed in a fermentation tank or allowed to spill down the outside of the tank. Usually more sophisticated refrigeration methods are used. A coolant is run through a pipe spiralled between the inner and outer jackets of the tank, the heat generated during fermentation is dissipated and the ferment slows from a few days to three weeks or more.

Clarification

After the fermentation there is usually no sugar left. The yeasts are now inactive and gradually sink to the bottom of the tank where, with other sediment, they are known as 'lees'. At this stage the new wine is essentially unstable. Clarification involves the removal of these remaining solids in the wine by racking, fining and filtering.

Racking is the removal of a wine from its lees by pumping it from one container to another. The first racking takes place as soon as possible after fermentation, to prevent off-flavours – especially hydrogen sulphide – developing through the decomposition of yeast cells.

Although most of the solid material in a new wine settles naturally in the lees, a fine haze of proteins and yeast particles tends to remain in suspension. Fining materials such as bentonite (a type of clay) and gelatine are sometimes used as a kind of net to draw the suspended solids to the bottom of the tank.

Fining, a time-honoured method of clarifying wine, is rapidly being replaced by advanced filtration processes. Filtration is the removal of particles by pumping wine through progressively finer filter pads. Compared with the traditional combination of racking and fining, filtration allows the wine maker to clean the wine rapidly and more efficiently.

Water-cooled tanks at Penfolds. Low temperatures (10-15°C) are especially important for white wines, both during fermentation and storage.

The danger is that excessive fining and filtering can rip out the body and flavour of a wine along with its waste materials. This problem is particularly acute in countries like New Zealand that produce naturally light wines. Sediment found in a bottle can often be a positive indication that the wine has its flavour and aging components intact.

Occasionally crystals of tartaric acid can be seen in a bottle; this acid becomes insoluble in the alcohol produced during fermentation and tends to precipitate out as the wine matures. The wine in this case comes to no harm but sales may do, so to prevent this happening most companies chill the wine before bottling to reduce the solubility of the tartrates. These precipitate out and the wine is filtered and bottled cold. 'Cold-stabilised' wines are unlikely to throw any deposits in the bottle.

Aging

The young wine can now either be stored away to mature or be promptly bottled.

A heavy majority of white wines made in New Zealand spend only a few months in steel tanks before bottling. Wood aging of whites is still in its infancy; few go into oak and then only for short periods. The obvious candidate for this is Chardonnay, and some New Zealand Chardonnays display the complexity to be gained from slight oxidation through the pores of the cask and the acquisition of oak flavours. A few 'white burgundies', Sauvignon Blancs and Chenin Blancs also receive wood treatment.

Sweetening

Traditionally New Zealand's sweeter white wines were sweetened simply by adding cane sugar. Unfortunately, sugar added as a sweetener late in the wine-making process imparts a cloying, slightly sickly, artificial flavour to wine.

Natural grape sugars blend in much more harmoniously. The two techniques — 'back-blending' and 'stop-fermentation' — now used to produce most of the better medium whites, both involve the capturing of a natural sweetness.

Back-blending is the addition of unfermented or concentrated grape juice to a wine prior to bottling. The technique was launched commercially in New Zealand in 1974, by Montana with Bernkaizler (now Benmorven) Riesling-Sylvaner.

The style immediately caught on, and has since been responsible for a vast improvement in the standard of our sweeter whites. Müller-Thurgau responds especially well to back-blending. Made in a dry style this variety can be rather thin and sharp; back-blending relieves this austerity and brings out the elegance inherent in the fruit. Wines that have been back-blended are generally more full-bodied — since grape juice is thicker than wine — lower in alcohol and, of course, sweeter.

Stop-fermentation is a more complicated process that requires the fermentation to be interrupted. The wine is chilled to a temperature that renders the yeasts inactive before all the grape sugars have been converted to alcohol. The yeasts are then removed by centrifuging and sterile filtration; the resulting wine is slightly sweet and often contains trapped CO_2 along with the residual sugar. Hence the slight tingle on the tongue of many stop-fermented whites.

Some outstanding, more expensive sweet white wines are produced in New Zealand by a third method — freeze concentration. By freezing out a proportion of the natural water content of grape juice, a rich, extremely sweet juice can be obtained that, when fermented, can produce wine of great intensity.

Bottling

Generally white wines are ensconced in bottles within a few months of the harvest. Light, delicate wines need little time to mature. By early bottling the wine maker is also able to preserve the fresh grapy character that appeals so strongly to many New Zealanders.

To ensure sterility, everything with which the wine comes into contact during bottling — hoses, bottling-lines, corks and bottles — must be sterilised. Final checks are made for spoilage and stability. At no stage must the wine be exposed to air.

RED WINES

The preparation of red wines departs from that of whites in two crucial ways. First, fermentation takes place with the skins in contact with the juice; secondly red wines are often matured in oak for long periods before bottling.

An accomplished wine maker can stamp his individual style on a quality red in a way that is rarely possible with a white. Red wines are more robust and flavoursome than whites, so that in a way the processing of red wine is hedged about by fewer precautions; oxygen for example, in small amounts, has a highly beneficial effect on reds. You could say white wine making depends a lot on science, while making reds depends on art.

Red wines are made from so-called 'black' grapes which in reality are of varying shades from deep blue to purple. The juice itself is usually pale, while the skins contain the colouring material and other components vital to the fuller character of a red wine. Fermenting the juice on the skins thus gives red wine its full colour and flavour.

Fermentation

Red wines are fermented in open containers as well as steel tanks, since oxidation is less of a problem.

During fermentation the evolution of CO_2 gas causes the skins to rise to the surface and form a dense cap. If this layer of warm, dry skins remains unbroken, air and acetic acid bacteria may be trapped, resulting in off-flavours and a high level of volatile acidity in the wine; colour extraction will also be impeded if there is a barrier of CO_2 gas between the juice and the skins. Therefore the cap is periodically mixed with the juice, by plunging the skins under by hand or by drawing off the juice below the cap and pumping it back over the skins.

Red wine fermentations are usually warmer than whites; 20°C is adequate to ensure a generous

The release of carbon dioxide gas in this red wine fermentation at McWilliam's Taradale winery shows that the yeasts are still active and the fermentation is still under way.

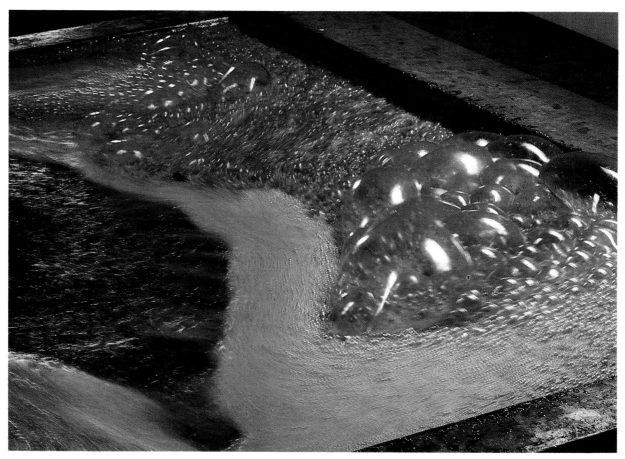

extraction of colour. As the ferment seethes along, the alcohol draws out the colour from the skins and the juice gradually turns red. Tannin from the pips and skins dissolves into the juice, contributing body, flavour and aging potential to the wine. Depending on the amount of colour and tannin desired, the yeasts will have consumed at least half of the natural sugars before the juice is removed from the skins.

Choosing the right moment to draw off the juice is important. Few consumers age their reds these days and light, early maturing styles are most in demand. So to reduce tannin levels, most wine makers cut down on the period of skin contact. When sufficient colour has been picked up, the juice is drained from the skins and completes its fermentation alone. Pressed juice can later be blended back as required.

Malolactic fermentation

A major aspect of red wine making is the malolactic fermentation. This secondary fermentation – based on the bacterial conversion of malic acid to lactic acid and carbon dioxide – occurs in dry red wines after the initial alcoholic fermentation; a young red held on its lees with a low sulphur level will usually 'go malolactic'.

New Zealand red wines gain immensely from this process because the wine becomes more palatable: malic acid imparts a harsh, sour taste to wine, whereas lactic acid is a soft, warm acid that enhances red wine. There is also a decline in total acidity – an advantage with most cool-climate wines. Biological stability is a third factor: a dry red which has not undergone a malolactic fermentation may later have it in the bottle, producing a gassy wine with sediment and an unpleasant 'nose'.

Many leading red wine regions – France, northern Italy, the cooler zones of Australia – regard the malolactic fermentation as a desirable, indeed essential part of the red wine making process. Other warmer areas with lower natural acidity in their wines – southern Italy, most of Australia – prefer to avoid it. New Zealand falls into the first group.

Methods of clarification, stabilisation and bottling for red and white wines are almost identical. After the completion of the fermentation process the other prime difference consists in aging.

Wood Maturation

Reds for everyday drinking in New Zealand are generally aged in steel tanks and bottled around twelve months after the vintage. Reds with any aspirations to quality, however, have at least a short spell in oak.

Wood has a dual effect on wine. Originally, casks were regarded simply as a convenient container in which to store wine. After a while, it became clear that certain timbers enhanced the flavour and character of the wine they housed. Oak flavours, tannin, colouring and aromatic substances pass from the wood and elevate the wine to greater complexity.

The second crucial point about wood aging is that the grain structure of oak allows a leisurely passage of air into the wine. From this slight oxidation, a red wine emerges vastly improved. There is another method quite widely practised in New Zealand for swiftly and cheaply securing some of the flavouring effects of oak: a muslin bag filled with oak chips is steeped in the wine for a brief period. A most unromantic process, which cannot rival proper aging in barrels, yet the quality of the red wine is nonetheless improved.

The amount of wood character desirable is fixed by a wine's ability to carry oak in balance with its fruit. Small new casks provide strong oak flavours in a matter of months, while older and larger barrels act on the wine less hurriedly. As a rule the more fully flavoured reds go into smaller casks and spend a long period in wood before bottling. New Zealand Cabernet Sauvignon, for example, spends up to two years in oak.

Wood used for cooperage in New Zealand is almost entirely imported. Oak is the least porous of timbers and by far the best for wine making purposes; it is also a slow-growing tree much in demand and inevitably expensive. New Zealand wineries use several types: French Limousin or Nevers oak and American oak.

Few native timbers have proved to be of value for wine making. Totara has been widely used for tubs and vats; Te Kauwhata in 1937 reported 'full satisfaction' with both tawa and silver beech as cheaper substitutes for oak. But the art of barrel-making has almost vanished in New Zealand. The Auckland Coopers' Union was wound up in 1978 when its membership fell to fifteen.

Since maturing red wine is able to 'breathe' through wood, water and alcohol can in their turn evaporate out of the cask, causing an air space to develop. To prevent spoilage this 'ullage' must be kept topped up. About twice a year the wine is also racked to promote aging and clarification.

Tasted straight out of the wood, a red wine often has a strong oak flavour. To allow this wood character to marry with the fruit, and to permit the wine to develop, a conscientious winery will allow its reds to age for at least a year in the bottle before release.

Totara casks at the Ormond winery on the East Coast.

ROSÉS

SPARKLING WINES

Rosés vary in colour from pink to a slightly tawny shade like an onion skin. The wine should be light and fruity, straightforward in its appeal, and above all refreshing.

Rosés are prepared in much the same way as whites. The best method is to allow red grapes a short period of skin contact during, or prior to the fermentation, then to separate the skins and finally ferment the juice alone. The precise time the juice spends on the skins — routinely one or two days — holds the key to the wine's colour.

Other techniques include mixing red and white wines together. Oak aging is still uncommon since rosés are usually sold young.

'Lolly-water' was the old catch-cry for thin hybrid rosé wines with cane-sugar sweetness. But today a new breed of New Zealand rosé has appeared, drier and from better grapes. Leaders in the field include Cabernet rosés from Penfolds and Delegat's and a Rosé of Pinotage from Collard Brothers. All are crisp and lively with good flavour; very appealing wines.

A selection of rosés.

Traditionally many wineries have regarded 'bubbly' as an easy outlet for low-grade juice, obtained from pressings of Chasselas, Palomino or hybrid grapes. With the inherent fruit deficiencies masked by sweetening and carbon-dioxide gas, these wines, dressed to kill in fancy foil wrapping, sold to a largely uncritical public. Informed wine-drinkers gave them a wide berth.

Yet New Zealand has the potential to produce world-class sparklings. The country's basic wine style — crisp and delicate — is ideally suited to sparkling wines.

A major hindrance in the past has been the shortage of suitable grapes. The Champagne region of France, which like New Zealand has difficulty ripening its grapes, uses Pinot Noir, Pinot Meunier and Chardonnay to produce the crisp acid dry whites on which Champagne is based. Current efforts in New Zealand using Chardonnay and Pinot Noir promise to give our top sparklings a long-overdue lift.

Wine makers in New Zealand use three methods to place bubbles in wine. The most common technique, used in the medium-priced sparklings such as Corban's Première Cuvée or McWilliam's Marque Vue, is called bulk fermentation, or 'Charmat', after the Frenchman who developed it.

Here the bubbles are derived from a secondary fermentation carried out in a sealed tank. Yeasts and sugar are added to a dry base wine and a proportion of the gas, which is generated in the ensuing fermentation and trapped inside the tank, is bound to the alcohol. To achieve a sweet or dry style the wine maker simply halts the fermentation at the appropriate stage.

The wine is bottled cold. More bubbles are retained, because CO_2 is more soluble at low temperatures, and the reduced pressure makes for an easier bottling operation.

A great many excellent Spanish, French, German, Italian, South African and Australian sparkling wines are made in this way. The most popular sparkling in New Zealand, Penfold's Chardon, is bulk fermented. No gas is artificially introduced and the bubbles linger briefly in the glass after pouring.

Cheap sparkling wines are 'carbonated'. Here the base wine is chilled inside a sealed tank and CO_2 gas is simply pumped into it. Pressure builds up in the wine as the temperature returns to normal after bottling.

The drawback with this technique is that the gas fails to combine with the alcohol (there is no secondary fermentation) and the CO_2 remains in the wine as large undissolved bubbles. These race out of the glass when the wine is poured.

Bottle-fermented sparkling wine at Selaks. After the slow, second fermentation in the bottle, its position is gradually shifted from almost horizontal to upside down, which forces the sediment into the neck of the bottle, ready for the dégorgement.

Not so with 'bottle-fermented' sparkling wine: 'How it puns and quibbles in the glass' wrote George Farquhar about Champagne in Love in a Bottle, published in 1699. 'Méthode Champenoise' is the method used in the world's best sparklings where the bubbles are derived from a secondary fermentation that occurs not in an enclosed tank but in the bottle itself.

Here, sugar and yeasts are added to the base wine prior to its bottling. Sufficient sugar is added to ferment right out when the wine reaches its desired pressure; too much sugar would generate too much gas and the bottle would explode. At the end of the secondary fermentation in the bottle, the yeast cells decompose, conferring a yeasty character to the wine: this is welcomed in Champagne as an essential quality factor. Then the bottles are laid head down in special 'riddling' racks, and over several months the yeast is gradually shaken from the sides of the bottle down to

the cork. 'Disgorging' follows, where the bottle-neck is frozen to allow the cork and plug of sediment to be removed without losing too much wine. Finally the bottle is topped-up, sweetened if necessary, corked and wired.

Up to 1980 New Zealand wine makers' achievements with bottle-fermented sparklings had been few. Two companies, Mission and Selaks, had pioneered the method with mediocre results. Now, however, Montana, Selaks and Penfolds all have worthwhile, 'méthode champenoise' wines vinted from Pinot Noir, Chardonnay, or a blend of both.

SHERRIES

André Simon, wine author and legendary founder of the Wine and Food Society, gave a candid opinion on the sherries and ports he tasted in New Zealand. 'Very few of the dessert wines can claim to belong to the quality wine class' he wrote in *Wines of the World*, edited by Simon in 1967 'they are sweet, spirity, without any trace of bouquet or breed.'

Sherry first achieved popularity in New Zealand after the first world war. By the time of Simon's visit in 1964, sherries and ports dominated sales, and they still retain a significant twenty-seven percent share of the market. Nevertheless it is hard to enthuse about the majority of these wines.

The heart of the problem is that New Zealand's climate is ill suited to produce sherry or port or any other fortified wine style. The best fortified wines come from hot countries—Portugal, Spain, South Africa, Australia—where the grapes achieve a high natural level of sweetness. These plentiful sugars produce a natural lusciousness and strong alcoholic content in the wines. New Zealand wine makers have been forced to compensate for the lesser ripening of their grape material with heavy additions of cane-sugar, and as a result our fortified wines tend to lack the fruit character of true sherry and port; most are simply neutral fortified wines.

In the past many so-called 'sherries' and 'ports' were made from grape skins, yeasts, sugar and water with only minimal help from grapejuice. The common

Dry sherry matures in wood at McWilliam's Taradale winery.

A distillation wash, made from skins, pips, pulp, sugar and water, then distilled to produce fortifying spirit. Grape spirit has recently been displaced by whey alcohol in the production of New Zealand fortified wines.

PORT

Generally the standard of New Zealand port has paralleled that of sherry. Port used to be a concoction derived from the black skins which remained after a red wine had been made. Sweetened with heavy additions of cane sugar, coloured, and sometimes flavoured, such wines bore little resemblance to the famed dessert wines of the region surrounding Oporto in Portugal.

Port is properly made by fermenting red grapes on their skins until most of the sugar has been consumed. Then the fermentation of the sweet part-wine is halted by running it off the skins and fortifying to about eighteen to nineteen percent alcohol by volume. After fining and filtering, the wine is transferred to oak barrels for its vital maturation period in wood.

Ruby ports are bottled young, within a couple of years, and display a distinct ruby colour combined with a soft, fruity, relatively fresh flavour. Tawny ports show the effects of longer oak aging with a tawny-brown appearance and a more mature, complex palate.

The end result should be a rounded, fruity, not overly sweet wine. Two of the most consistently bemedalled ports at recent competitions, Babich Reserve Port and Montana Private Bin Tawny Port, both lean towards the Portuguese style of port, being fruity and fairly dry. Mazuran offers a different style, heavy, old and syrupy.

Vintage ports, based on Cabernet Sauvignon and made for cellaring are an important emerging wine style. Prominent among early releases are full bodied, firm ports from Matua Valley, Cooks, Penfolds, Babich and Corbans.

procedure was to drain off the best juice after crushing, and then to pump a sugar-water solution onto the remaining pulp. The ensuing fermentation produced a low-quality 'wine'. Then perhaps another sugar solution was run over the original residue – by this stage there was very little grapejuice left – and the process might even be repeated a third time for distillation purposes. After the third ferment the resulting liquid was largely devoid of colour, aroma and grape flavour. If you then added further sugar to fill out the flavour, coloured it with caramel, fortified it, perhaps aged it in wood, you still had an eminently salable sherry.

A 1980 amendment to the Food and Drug Regulations reduced this level of adulteration by prescribing a sixty percent minimum grapejuice level for dessert wines. The level set is to allow for the diluting effects of additives like fortifying spirit and sugar solution.

Sweet old sherries can be surprisingly good. The best emerge after many years aging in barrels with a rich, full, mellow character that often wins high accolades from wine judges. Mazuran has been the leading specialist in this style.

Now that New Zealand has also perfected the 'flor' technique, a few dry sherries of outstanding quality have been developed. 'Flor' is Spanish for flower; in Spain the flor yeast 'flowers' as a creamy substance on the surface of sherry in a cask, living on the sugar and alcohol and imparting a nutty, yeasty flavour.

Sometimes in New Zealand flor sherries are made by this traditional method, although here the base wine has to be artificially inoculated with a flor yeast, whereas in Spain this occurs naturally. Larger wineries such as Penfolds and Montana use an alternative 'submerged flor' technique. This involves pumping a different type of flor yeast, and oxygen, into the sherry under pressure. The result is a faster and more pungent pick-up of flor character. Top versions – particularly Montana Pale Dry Sherry – are notably reminiscent of their Spanish counterparts and fine wines in their own right.

CHAPTER FOUR
The Principal Wine Regions

Wine growing is a strongly localised occupation. Hawkes Bay and Poverty Bay contained in 1983 almost two-thirds of the national vineyard area. If you add these provinces together with Auckland, Marlborough and the Waikato, you find ninety-eight percent of vines concentrated in five provinces. Scattered holdings also exist in Northland, Bay of Plenty, Taranaki, Wellington, Nelson, Canterbury and Central Otago, but there is no viticulture on a commercial basis elsewhere.

At various stages of our history, nonetheless, grapevines have been planted, with or without success, over most parts of the country. Bragato in 1895 encountered vines growing in Central Otago, Akaroa, Nelson, Wairarapa, Hawkes Bay, Bay of Plenty, Wanganui, the Waikato, Auckland and Northland. Such a widespread scattering of early grape growing and wine making reflected the isolated, far-flung nature of the first settlements. Although, ideally, considerations of climate and soil should have been uppermost in selecting areas to establish vines, in fact it was the influence of cultural traditions and the availability of cheap land which played leading roles in the early location of the industry in New Zealand.

The early exploitation of the Auckland region was due to the scale of the available market and the presence of Dalmatians and others eager to make wine, rather than to any climatic or physical advantages. Hawkes Bay, with ideal natural conditions for grape growing, was sufficiently distant from Auckland to compete for markets in the south. Auckland and Hawkes Bay thus remained the two centres of New Zealand wine for more than a half century. Then in the 1960s, when it became obvious that extensive new plantings would be necessary to cater for the rising demand for table wines, vineyards spread beyond the traditional grape growing zones into Taupaki, Kumeu, Mangatangi and above all Poverty Bay.

Poverty Bay, although sharing some of the climatic advantages of Hawkes Bay, is isolated by rugged terrain from the major wine markets. However, Corbans, Cooks and Montana encouraged contract growers there to establish sizeable areas in vines. The answer lay in the fertility of the Gisborne Plains soils; Auckland and the Waikato produce an average yield of eight and a half tonnes per hectare of *vinifera* grapes; Poverty Bay yields seventeen and a half tonnes.

The more recent move into Marlborough by Montana, Corbans and Penfolds was in pursuit of another objective. Crops there are relatively light at eight to ten tonnes per hectare — but scientific analyses have shown that the region is ideal for cool-climate table wine making.

Future plantings will probably be concentrated in the same areas that have shown the most recent expansion: Hawkes Bay, Poverty Bay and Marlborough. In 1978 the Wine Institute announced that surveys were being undertaken to assess potential new grape-growing districts. DSIR scientists have since claimed that parts of the eastern side of the Wairarapa and another area lying inland between Wanganui and Foxton, have potential for premium table wine making.

With the pronounced variations in soil and climate from Auckland to Marlborough, the challenge now facing wine makers is to sort out the best grapes for each region and then to produce the style of wine which fully captures the potential inherent in the fruit. Back in 1896 the Whangarei wine grower, L. Hanlon, stressed this point at a Conference of Australasian Fruitgrowers held in Wellington. 'As has been the case in other countries, so doubtless it will be the case here, that each district will produce one class of wine which will surpass all others in point of excellence... The absurdity of every man who has an acre or two of vineyard manufacturing so-called port, sherry, Bordeaux, Burgundy, Chablis, Tokay etc., need not be discussed. It cannot too forcibly be impressed upon the future wine growers of New Zealand the great importance of each district producing a class of wine of definite type.'

It seems that New Zealand wine growing is going in the direction indicated by Hanlon. It is true that sound reasons often exist for blending together grapes from a variety of regions, and it may not always be economically feasible to produce small batches of regional wines, but regionalism is nevertheless a strong trend.

Certain local strengths are already apparent; Hawkes Bay in Cabernet Sauvignon and Chardonnay; Auckland in Cabernet Sauvignon and Pinot Noir; Marlborough in Rhine Riesling and Sauvignon Blanc.

The formation of Hawkes Bay Vintners in 1979 offered further evidence of the growing emphasis on regional identification — all wineries in the district agreed to jointly foster Hawkes Bay's image as an area which produces quality wines. In 1983, the Winemakers of West Auckland started adopting the same aims.

THE WINEMAKING REGIONS
Acreages in vines 1982

NORTHLAND
18 ha.

AUCKLAND
455 ha.

WAIKATO
336 ha.

BAY OF PLENTY
9 ha.

POVERTY BAY/
EAST CAPE
1922 ha.

HAWKES BAY
1891 ha.

NELSON
39 ha.

WELLINGTON
7 ha.

MARLBOROUGH
1175 ha.

CANTERBURY
49 ha.

TOTAL AREA 5901 ha.

NORTHLAND

The northernmost region of New Zealand stretches out over 500 kilometres of rolling hill country. Its climate is almost subtropical, with warm humid summers, mild winters and abundant rainfall. Northland's main occupation is pastoral farming, yet from the Kaipara Harbour in the south to Ruawai in the north, there are ten or more vineyards.

Northland was the cradle of New Zealand wine: here Marsden planted the first vines and here, too, Busby made the first wine. After 1840 and the Treaty of Waitangi, however, the region was exploited mainly for its magnificent kauri forests and later for its gum. Descendants of Dalmatian gumdiggers and the sons and daughters of more recent Dalmatian arrivals almost alone have preserved the wine making traditions of Busby. Few depend on their vines for a living; with a total of eighteen hectares under vines, in fact, the region has a mere 0.3 percent of New Zealand's vineyard area. Only a rivulet of wine flows in Northland; the vineyards, averaging less than 2 hectares, are the smallest in the country and their wine is all sold locally. Milina, Continental, Whatitiri and Music's are not household names in the rest of New Zealand — or even in Northland for that matter.

The wines, predominantly sweet and fortified vin ordinaire, are reminiscent of the national wine style twenty years ago. In view of the moist climate, and the grapes grown, this is not at all surprising. In 1980 the three leading varieties were Albany Surprise, Baco 22A and Seibel 5455.

Continental

Continental Wines at Otaika, just south of Whangarei, with 4.3 hectares under vines is one of the largest growers in Northland. The vineyard was established in 1964 by Mate Vuletich who, as his widow relates, was born under a grapevine on the family vineyard in Yugoslavia. Vuletich planted Baco 22A and Niagara vines, but more recently plots of Grey Riesling, Breidecker and Reichensteiner have been established.

Today the founder's son Mario is one of the few full-time wine makers in the North. In a small well-equipped winery, 27,000 litres of wine are annually produced and sold at the gate. The wines I have tasted — Riesling-Sylvaner, Chasselas Hock, Sauternes and Dry Red — verged on thinness and were not entirely clean.

Milica Vuletich is actively involved in the company founded by her husband twenty years ago.

Whatitiri

West of Whangarei, at Poroti, Whatitiri Wines until 1983 made drinkable wines with strong hybrid flavours. This vineyard was established by a Frenchman in the 1920s. Surveyor Peter Boyes and his schoolteacher wife, Jan, bought the property, then called 'Nick's Wines', from Nick Krisinic in 1975.

The small two-hectare plot of American Diamond and Baco No. 1 vines yielded a wide array of wines: a rosé, three white table wines, three reds, sherry and port. About 9000 litres of wine were produced annually with the aid of minimal equipment. In 1983, however, Peter Boyes switched to kiwifruit and gave up the struggle to produce wine in Whangarei county.

Wine making was trimmed to the basics at the tiny Whatitiri winery.

Peter Boyes experimented with classic varieties like Cabernet Sauvignon and Grenache in Northland's heavy clay soils before he abandoned viticulture.

KUMEU/HUAPAI/WAIMAUKU

From Waimauku in the north-west to Riverhead in the east and southwards to Taupaki, this region surrounding the rural townships of Kumeu and Huapai boasts several noted wineries; Matua Valley, Nobilo, Coopers Creek and Selaks have all contributed to the area's strong reputation.

In 1960 Kumeu-Huapai accounted for only nineteen percent of all plantings in the Auckland province; by 1975 the figure exceeded fifty percent. Henderson wine makers of the 1960s, wishing to expand to meet increasing demand, faced a serious problem in the lack of cheap, reasonably large blocks of land in Henderson. Their options were threefold: to purchase the new grapes from contract growers, to relocate their wineries, or to buy new vineyard land away from their company headquarters.

With land at Henderson between 1965 and 1970 valued at $4500 per hectare, and land at Kumeu selling for only $1500 per hectare, expansion soon shifted to the Kumeu-Huapai area. Old established companies were able to plant new vineyards only fifteen kilometres away from their existing wineries.

Many companies—Delegat's, Lincoln, Soljans, Collard, Cooks, Corbans and others—established new vineyards here. Others, such as Nobilo and San Marino, have an extended history in the district. Matua Valley and Abel and Co. are relative newcomers who chose to base their entire operations there.

Red wines stand out as the best: Nobilo's Cabernet Sauvignon, earlier Abel and Co. vintages. Nobilo attribute their success with red wines partly to the complex soil pattern. In fact there is much variation in soil types throughout the area. Kumeu has mainly peat and silt deposits with areas of alluvial loam over clay subsoils; the fertile Riverlea soils range from loam over clay to heavier river silts.

The local climate, according to meteorologists, is one of the best for table wines in the Auckland region. The district's distance from the Waitakere Ranges produces a lower rainfall than at Henderson. Shelter belts of trees are nevertheless required to shield the vines from the cool and sometimes strong westerly air flow.

Family-owned Dalmatian enterprises are in a strong majority there.

Crushing grapes in the field at the Nobilo vineyard, Huapai.

Corbans planted, and more
recently sold, extensive vineyards
in the Kumeu and Taupaki districts.

Abel and Co.

Robert Schroder now directs operations in this visually appealing and compact winery.

Malcolm Abel, a soft-spoken wine maker who died in 1981 at the age of 38, owned the only winery in New Zealand that specialised entirely in a single wine style.

Abel purchased a four-hectare block at the back of Kumeu in 1970, erected a chalet-style winery and started buying in grapes. His first commercial release, Reserve Dry Red 1974, scored well in wine competitions, and silver awards for the 1975 and 1976 vintages soon established Abel and Co. as a leading 'boutique' winery.

In the belief — shared with Nobilo — that Kumeu is red wine country, he chose to concentrate on dry red table wines. To preserve the area style, grapes for the company's wines were drawn almost entirely from the surrounding locality — mainly the Watson and Nicholls vineyards acknowledged on the labels.

Two lines were regularly offered, Reserve Dry Red and Pinotage. Both were always very drinkable, reflecting the benefits of well-ripened fruit. The 1978 Reserve Dry Red, for example, was medium bodied, deeply coloured, with a big ripe bouquet. A trace of sugar was often retained to enhance the fruit character of these wines.

Abel Pinotage was an outstanding example of this variety. Both the 1977 and 1978 vintages were perfumed, zesty wines enhanced by careful oak handling. Similarly, a 1979 Gamay de Beaujolais was a supple, light red wine of strong appeal.

After the founder's early death, the Abel winery was sold to two science graduates in their late twenties, Danny Southee and Robert Schroder. The reds I have recently tasted, all from the 1980 and 1981 vintages, have proved disappointing — perhaps reflecting the protracted change of ownership.

Two white wines have also appeared under the Abel company's label. Weissherbst, a white wine vinted from Pinotage grapes, is a dryish, medium bodied wine of earthy aroma and hard finish. Abel Beaunois is a big dry white, over thirteen percent alcohol, a Gisborne Chardonnay that lacks delicacy.

Shortly after his move into wine making on a full-time basis, Malcolm Abel died, an untimely loss to the industry.

Coopers Creek

Randy Weaver released this fighting fund wine to publicise his vineyard's battle with local authorities.

Potter drainers, not very common in New Zealand, by draining the must through screens inside the tank, extract a very high percentage of the juice as free-run.

Coopers Creek, a small 'boutique' winery three kilometres north of Kumeu, is the latest arrival on the Kumeu/Huapai wine scene.

The company is the brainchild of two partners: Californian wine maker Randy Weaver, formerly of Penfolds and Montana; and accountant Andrew Hendry, also ex-Penfolds and responsible for this unique, limited liability partnership involving grower-partners and other investors. Although the home vineyard has 3.2 hectares planted in the red vines Cabernet Sauvignon and Merlot, grower-partners principally in Hawkes Bay supply most of the fruit intake.

Coopers Creek's path since the first vintage in 1982 was for a long time blocked by the local council. The regional development plan failed to make any provision for the use by new wineries of grapes from other areas. For two years, the partners fought to get local body permission to use their Kumeu winery. Wine maker Randy Weaver was even forced to make his 1983 vintage wines at six different wineries. Fortunately, the matter has since been largely resolved.

The company's declared intention is to produce wines that are compatible with food — dry, full bodied and with the ability to age. Certainly Coopers Creek Gewürztraminer is a big, high alcohol, mouth-filling style of real interest to the serious wine drinker. And the 1982 Chardonnay showed enough depth of fruit and careful oak handling to signal a promising future for this variety also. The 1982 Fumé Blanc was a restrained, wood-aged style that sought mellowness and complexity but which, in the end, was too subdued. From 1983, both a Fumé Blanc and a Fumé Blanc (Oak Cask) have been made.

Although Coopers Creek will produce largely white wine, a mediocre Dry Red blended from Pinot Noir and Pinotage has reached the market and in 1985 the 1983 Cabernet Sauvignon will be released.

Coopers Creek wines are sold in restaurants and some resellers, by mail-order and at the winery.

Glenburn

At its debut in 1974 at the national wine competition, this small vineyard aroused interest by gaining gold and silver medals for its sherry and port.

The origins of this winery go back to 1927 when Andrew Jelas, the present owner's father, planted a half-hectare in vines at Riverhead. He began to make wine and by 1935 was selling it commercially.

One of his sons, Michael Jelas, later took over part of the property and established Glenburn Wines in 1950. The original cellar remains at the rear of the present winery and until 1984 was used as a bottling area.

On peat and volcanic soils, six hectares of Baco 22A, Seibel 5455, Palomino, Müller-Thurgau, and Albany Surprise vines are grown. Of the wide range of wines produced, Glenburn's strength lies only in fortifieds. Blending sherries, aged for up to 15 years, contribute a mature mellowness to the company's top wines.

These old medium and sweet sherries, sold only at the winery, will soon be no longer available, for Glenburn in 1984 announced the decision to close the company down.

Glenburn has won the THC Trophy for sherry.

Markovina

Clean, basic wine at a very low price sums up the achievement of this small Kumeu winery.

Markovina means Mark of Wine — obviously there was a forebear who enjoyed a glass or two. Ivan Markovina Snr in his youth was active in the family vineyards on the island of Korcula, off the Dalmatian coast — but it was not until nearly forty years after his arrival in New Zealand, when his son chose to become a wine maker, that the present four hectare vineyard was founded in Old Railway Road.

Ivan Markovina Jnr (37), who also enjoys a glass of wine, now runs the company. The small vineyard, on peaty loam soils, has a range of both hybrid and classical varieties: Palomino, Baco 22A, Müller-Thurgau, Cabernet Sauvignon, black Seibels, Sémillon, Chardonnay and Pinot Noir.

A unique feature of this vineyard is the presence of Grk vines. Grk is a white wine with a highly individual aftertaste made principally on Korcula. At Kumeu the grapes ripen late and have proved vulnerable to botrytis, but, insists Ivan Markovina Snr, the tiny amounts of wine so far made have been reminiscent of the original. By 1985 Markovina hope to have a small supply of 'grk' for release.

Markovina wines are not widely distributed — most are sold from the gate or by a limited number of wineshops. Carafe wines are a specialty. The Dry White and Moselle, blended from Baco 22A and

Winemaker Ivan Markovina Jnr stands at his cellar door. 'Please toot horn for service', reads the handwritten sign.

Palomino are both ordinary quaffing wines, winners of an occasional medal and low priced.

The winery also markets a small range of well-matured 'private bin' lines. The top white, Pinot/Riesling is an 80/20 blend of Müller-Thurgau and Chardonnay: a dry, light-bodied wine with a touch of Chardonnay fullness. The best red I have sampled, the Classic Blend was blended from four distinct varieties, richly coloured, with a well-rounded palate and nice tannin grip. These are interesting wines — although nothing more than that.

Matua Valley

One of the most innovative wineries in New Zealand lies north-west of Huapai, about four kilometres from the village of Waimauku in the tranquil Waikoukou Valley. Here the Hunting Lodge Restaurant, in a house near the winery built in 1868, serves country style food, emphasising lamb, beef and game.

Matua Valley—named after the original vineyard in Matua Road, Huapai—is controlled by the Spence Brothers, Ross (41) who trained at the wine faculty of Fresno University of California and Bill (33) who studied agriculture at Massey. The venture began in a leased tin shed in Swanson, near Henderson, with the brothers holding down full-time jobs elsewhere and producing their wine in the evenings and at weekends. The first show entries won immediate acclaim and there were silver medals for successive vintages of Matua Valley Burgundy, a soft, flavoursome red then vinted from hybrid grape material. The spectacle of these two part-time wine makers outperforming the major established wineries in the hybrid red class won for the company an enthusiastic early following.

The tin shed lasted three vintages until an expired lease forced a change of premises. The present octagonal winery at Waimauku is designed to handle 40,000 cases of wine a year in due course, and its roof was still being built during the first vintage in 1978.

In the twenty-five hectare, undulating vineyard on sandy loam soils are a number of grape varieties rarely

The old country house, built by Auckland's Kerr-Taylor family in 1868, is today a gracious restaurant serving excellent food with Matua Valley wines.

seen elsewhere: Flora (a Gewürztraminer/Sémillon cross), Malbec, and Hermitage. There are also commercial quantities of Cabernet Sauvignon, Pinot Noir, Sémillon, Chardonnay, Sauvignon Blanc and Grey Riesling; they also use Müller-Thurgau and Chasselas grapes, most of which are bought from contract suppliers in Gisborne and Auckland.

Matua Valley specialises in relatively small batches of interesting and often quite high quality wines. Nevertheless, after the initial successes with hybrid reds, subsequent releases of classic red wines from this vineyard proved disappointing. The 1978 quartet of Pinotage, Hermitage, Gamay Teinturier and Cabernet Sauvignon, for instance, were light-bodied reds, lacking real depth of fruit. And the 1982 Pinot Noir only hints at the lovely sustained flavour of this variety at its best.

An occasional red has stood out; the Cabernet Sauvignon 1977 at five years old—at its peak—developed into an exquisite wine, and the 1982 blend of Cabernet/Hermitage is a pleasant, low tannin red softened by the inclusion of Hermitage in the wine.

But Matua Valley's major contribution has been its white wines. The Sauvignon Blanc is invariably

interesting. The memorable 1974 vintage opened up in 1978 in superb form; with perfect green/gold colour and a sustained finish. Since then the style has varied from year to year as the company experimented with oak aging and fermenting the juice on-and-off the skins. The 1983 Fumé Blanc version is again outstanding, perhaps more restrained than Montana's Marlborough Sauvignon Blanc, yet with an arresting, herbaceous aroma and big flavour.

Matua Valley has also pioneered in New Zealand the workhorse Australian white wine variety — Sémillon. The first vintage, 1979, was aggressive and finished sharply, and the 1982 Sémillon, slightly back-blended, has an unsubtle, strongly grassy flavour. Another grape championed by Ross Spence is Grey Riesling. Matua Valley make theirs slightly sweet; some years have developed after bottle aging into lovely, fruity wines with hints of Germanic character.

The Chardonnay is usually pleasant but not memorable, with light body and a touch of wood. But watch for the big 1983 vintage Waimauku Chardonnay. A blend, Chenin/Chardonnay developed since 1980 is another first for this winery, showing a predominantly Chenin Blanc bouquet and fruity palate enhanced by the presence of Chardonnay — one to cellar.

Matua Valley Muscat Blanc is a rather sweet, low-acid wine that does not attempt to scale any heights, but still appeals for the unique Muscat flavour — a refreshing change from Müller-Thurgau, and easy summer drinking. The recently named Breidecker — vinted from a German variety, CD 49/84, developed from Müller-Thurgau, with a white Seibel hybrid as a grandparent is also worth trying; the flavour, although reminiscent of Müller-Thurgau, has a slight musky character.

In the less exotic range, the company sells large quantities of Chablis, an unpretentious medium-dry wine blended in 1983 predominantly from Müller-Thurgau. There is also a Müller-Thurgau, a back-blended fruity style of variable quality.

A prestige fortified wine worth laying hands on is the Vintage Port, top-scorer in the port category at the 1980 national wine competition, and a regular gold medal winner since.

Most of these wines are sold at a very young age. Classic whites such as Sauvignon Blanc go on sale in the year of vintage, and premium reds at eighteen months. With this winery — as with many others — it is essential to lay the wines down.

The company has graduated from its humble origins in an old tin shed at Swanson.

Interior shot of Matua Valley's octagonal winery.

Nobilo

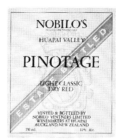
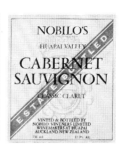

The Nobilo winery lies close to the rural township of Huapai.

Renowned for its Müller-Thurgau and respected for its trio of reds — Cabernet Sauvignon, Pinotage and Pinot Noir — Nobilo is one of the leading red wine companies in New Zealand with a proud success record in competitions.

At twenty-four, Nikola Nobilo arrived in New Zealand in 1937, from the island of Korcula in the Adriatic Sea. A stonemason by trade, Nikola (Nick Nobilo Snr) planted vines near the main highway just north of Huapai, while also tending chickens, cows and grapefruit trees.

The Nobilo operation was transformed in the 1960s when Nick Nobilo Jnr joined the company. Gilbey-Nobilo, formed in 1966, saw Gilbey's of England taking up a substantial shareholding, and providing the funds for an ambitious expansion programme based on classical grape varieties. When Gilbey's withdrew in 1974 — a move forced by shareholding transfers in Britain — Nobilos were established with the vineyards and wood aging facilities necessary to produce fine wines.

The reconstructed company, formed in 1975, brought the Nobilo family into partnership with distribution agents, Nathans and the PSIS — a liquor interest later acquired by Wilson Neill — plus the Development Finance Corporation. One outcome of these financial changes has been a loss of overall financial control by the Nobilo family. They retain,

however, charge of daily operations: Mark Nobilo concentrating on viticulture, Nick Nobilo Jnr on winemaking, and Steve Nobilo on sales and marketing.

Nobilo have sixty hectares of vines surrounding the winery at Huapai. Cabernet Sauvignon, Pinot Noir, Merlot, Pinotage, Chardonnay and Gewürztraminer are the major varieties. The vines, spaced only a metre apart — about twice the average density in New Zealand — are trained high above the ground on a 'T' bar trellising system.

Company policy is now to concentrate on red wines, in the belief that the Huapai area is especially suited to their production — red grape varieties flower later at Huapai and with a better fruit 'set'.

A major replanting and expansion programme, from 1981 to 1986 will see the white grapes phased out and the home vineyard extended to eighty-eight hectares entirely of red varieties. In future, white varieties like Müller-Thurgau, Chardonnay and Gewürztraminer will be bought on contract from the East Coast.

The finest achievement of this vineyard is the Cabernet Sauvignon — at its best a complex wine, showing a lovely balance of fruit and oak flavours. The 1976 vintage was one of the best New Zealand reds of the decade. The fruit, harvested late at the end of April, was field-crushed, fermented on the skins and then aged for two years in French oak puncheons. By 1980 the wine was superb — perfumed, deeply coloured, with subtle flavours very reminiscent of red Bordeaux.

Although the 1978 has a similar character, several recent vintages have disappointed: 1977 faded early, the 1979 and 1980 wines were sharp, light reds. It is hoped that the availability from 1983 onwards of virus-free grapes in quantity will restore Nobilo Cabernet Sauvignon to its place as a top New Zealand red.

Although other companies are producing fine Cabernet Sauvignons, Nobilo's Pinotage has fewer rivals. The 1976 and 1978 vintages are big wines with a soft, peppery flavour that reminds one of the Rhône wines of France. The 1977 vintage and 1979-80 vintage blend were of a lower standard.

Nobilo produce their Pinot Noir by the 'macération carbonique' method. The grapes, instead of being crushed, go straight into an enclosed stainless steel fermenter. With the pressure of the grapes on top of each other, juice gradually escapes and during the ensuing fermentation the berries disintegrate. After a week or so the juice is then racked off, with an apparently improved colour and flavour. Sometimes the Pinot Noir tends to be too austere, lacking the appealing softness of this variety. The 1978, however, was outstanding, with a penetrating and true Pinot bouquet and a combination of big fruit and tannin, very like French Burgundy.

Of the whites, Nobilo's Müller-Thurgau is the big selling wine produced entirely from Gisborne contract grapes; this is pleasant, flowery wine. The Riesling-Sylvaner is drier; the 1980 impressed for its big, fruity nose and deep flavour. There is also a Private Bin Dry White, an everyday quaffing wine blended from Palomino, hybrid and Müller-Thurgau grapes.

Gewürztraminer has not been a big success in my view; the 1983 and most earlier vintages are simply easy drinking wines without the typical firm spiciness of this variety.

Nobilo's best white wine is the Pinot Chardonnay. The wines have plenty of wood flavour, since the fermentation is finished off in oak hogsheads before further cask aging. Sometimes, especially in lesser years like 1979 and 1980, this strong oak flavour dominates the fruit.

Both the 1976 and 1978 wines, however, are soft, smoky Chardonnays with the fruit and oak in ideal combination. The 1977 was a bigger style, probably the best yet, with a deep, golden colour and a full, fat flavour. These wines have outstanding cellaring potential: the 1973, for example, was probably at its peak in 1980.

Wine maker and company head, Nick Nobilo Jnr, is convinced that Huapai is red wine country, a view strongly supported by his memorable 1976 Cabernet Sauvignon.

San Marino

San Marino, one of the first wineries to establish such classical grape varieties as Chardonnay and Pinotage, also enjoyed an early reputation for hybrid quaffing wines like its Kumeu Dry Red. Owned by the ebullient Mate Brajkovich, one of the most prominent personalities in the wine industry, the company has nonetheless struggled somewhat to keep up with the recent advances in New Zealand wine making.

The winery and vineyard are sited on the main highway, one kilometre south of Kumeu. Early Dalmatian settlers tended vines on the property for several decades before the nineteen-year-old Mate Brajkovich acquired a half-hectare vineyard and its surrounding land in 1944.

The vineyard now encompasses thirteen and a half hectares of Palomino, Müller-Thurgau, Cabernet Sauvignon, Pinotage, Gewürztraminer and Chardonnay vines. Contract growers in the Kumeu and Gisborne areas supply the remaining grape intake.

The strong impact of this winery on the Auckland wine scene of the 1950s and 1960s owed much to the generous hospitality still bestowed on visitors — a large proportion of sales are through the vineyard shop. The wines I have bought in recent years have not always been sound, and up to 1980 San Marino seemed destined to play only a backseat role in the wine industry.

However, the 1980s have brought evidence of a needed rejuvenation. Young Michael Brajkovich

San Marino adopts a low profile, but according to the formula for representation on the Wine Institute, ranks as a medium-size producer.

topped his oenology class at Roseworthy College in South Australia, and San Marino released in commercial quantities several white wines in clean condition.

The elegant, aromatic Riesling-Sylvaner 1981 scored a NWC gold medal in that year. White Sec is a light, semi-dry blend of Müller-Thurgau and Palomino. And San Marino Trinity is a pleasant, slightly spicy wine produced from an unusual combination of Gewürztraminer, Müller-Thurgau and Chardonnay grapes.

Selaks

Mate Selak with his beloved Champelle; after many years of experiments and a share of disappointments, the Champagne method looks to be mastered.

Selaks is an old-established family vineyard nestled on gently undulating land in Old North Road, Kumeu.

Marino Selak, another emigrant Dalmatian, arrived in Auckland in 1906. After many years on the northern gumfields, he planted vines, fruit trees and vegetables at Te Atatu. 1934 marked the first Selak vintage in New Zealand.

Mate Selak, then 17, made a similar trek from his homeland to join his uncle Marino in 1940. The vineyard gradually expanded, becoming one of the first to specialise in table wines. But in the early 1960s the north-west motorway sliced through the small vineyard.

In 1965 Mate Selak moved to re-establish the company at Kumeu, with the first vintage there in 1969. Recently Selaks — run by Mate (63) and his son Ivan (33) — has endeavoured to become established at the quality end of the market.

The company's ambitions were until recently hindered by a shortage of quality grape material, other than the Müller-Thurgau variety. Selaks were forced to rely heavily on Gisborne grapes. However, the company has recently replanted the ten hectare home vineyard with improved varieties and at Riverhead, on land sloping down to Brigham's Creek, a new sixteen hectare vineyard has been developed; the first plantings, of German C.D. varieties, followed by Rhine Riesling, came on stream in 1983.

A labour of love for Mate Selak has been his determination to produce a good 'méthode champenoise' sparkling wine. The wine, Champelle, caused many headaches in its development stages, including problems with oxidation and clarification and the perils of exploding bottles. A major drawback was the use of Chasselas as the base wine. However, Chardonnay and Pinot Noir are currently used and an all-Chardonnay, blanc de blancs version top-scored in the sparkling category at the 1983 National Wine Competition. An insulated tunnel has even been built in an effort to duplicate the unvarying cool temperatures of the chalk cellars of Champagne.

Since 1983 Selaks wines have been made by a young Australian winemaker, Kevin Judd. His arrival was soon followed by a marked lift in the quality of wine bearing the Selaks label. Selaks' Riesling-Sylvaner 1983, for instance, is about as good as any other dry New Zealand Riesling-Sylvaner. The Muscat Blanc 1983 and Müller-Thurgau 1983 are both impressive in their respective styles.

Over many years, Selaks have built up a loyal following for their White Burgundy. The grape material used has steadfastly been kept a secret. Pinotage fermented off the skins is one bet. The 1983 wine is dry and firm, but rather plain.

The Sauvignon Blanc/Sémillon is in a class apart; aged in German oak, this dry, full-flavoured wine is undoubtedly the best Selaks wine yet released. Other whites include a good wood-aged Chenin Blanc, Chardonnay, and a steely Rhine Riesling.

Selaks' reds, of vintages in the late 1970s and early 1980s, have been of somewhat erratic quality — both the 1980 Cabernet Sauvignon and 1980 Pinotage were undistinguished, yet the dark Pinot Noir 1981 won Selaks a gold medal at the 1982 Easter Show competition.

The company style has tended towards soft, easy-drinking red wines with light tannin, early maturing but a shade lacking in complexity.

HENDERSON

In the shadow of the Waitakere Ranges are grouped several of the oldest wineries in New Zealand.

Henderson, twenty kilometres west of Auckland city, has the largest cluster of wineries in the country. Strung out along Lincoln Road, Sturges Road and the floor of the Henderson Valley, all but two of the vineyards are small or medium-sized. The oldest — Corbans and Pleasant Valley — were founded in 1902.

Here a flourishing Dalmatian community has imprinted its energetic, vinous way of life on the entire district. Although wine making in New Zealand is no longer a Dalmatian preserve, here, numerically at least, they still prevail, and two-thirds of Auckland wine growers were of Dalmatian extraction in 1976.

Generally, these Dalmatian vineyards began life as small mixed holdings of fruit trees, vines and vegetables. Dalmatian settlers who had lived on peasant farms in Dalmatia, typically saved funds on the northern gumfields and then looked for self-sufficiency. Cheap parcels of land were available for purchase in the Henderson-Oratia area and the large Auckland market beckoned.

Since 1960 these holdings have shifted towards specialisation in market-gardening, orcharding or wine making. Also there has been a gradual shift of vine plantings away from Henderson itself. Back in 1960, eighty percent of Auckland's vineyards and orchards were in Henderson and Oratia. Later, the north-west motorway opened West Auckland up to the pressures of urban expansion and reduced the land available for viticulture. The surviving vineyards benefit from differential rating systems that significantly ease their rates burden, but some land values, especially those close to the Great North Road, soared too high to be kept in vines.

Between 1975 and 1982, vineyard areas in Henderson and Kumeu-Huapai combined slumped from 750 hectares — thirty-two percent of the national area — to only 455 hectares or 7.7 percent of entire plantings. Major companies like Montana and Corbans — which now prefers to expand into Gisborne and Marlborough — have severely reduced their dependence on Auckland as a source of grapes. And several smaller wineries — Western Vineyards, Spence's and Eastern Vineyards — have ceased production.

Henderson suffers from serious physical and climatic handicaps for viticulture. The rainfall, rising steeply from the city westwards to the Waitakeres, is far from ideal for wine making. The plentiful rains, in association with high humidity, create ideal conditions for fungous diseases, especially during the critical February-April ripening period. The soils, too, are heavy, requiring deep ploughing and tile draining.

Because of this wet climate, the hardy, weather and disease-resistant hybrid varieties were always more popular in Henderson than elsewhere. Two decades ago Auckland had twice as many hybrids as Hawkes Bay, and in 1980 the presence of hybrid varieties (twenty-eight percent) was still way ahead of the national average (ten percent).

The 1980 vineyard survey revealed that bulk white wine grapes, like Müller-Thurgau and Chasselas, are only lightly planted in Auckland. Here is another reason for Auckland's relative demise as a grape-growing area; most companies rely heavily on Müller-Thurgau as the basis for a wide variety of wine styles, and that variety crops poorly in Auckland. Gisborne and Hawkes Bay produce far heavier tonnages.

Henderson has proportionately heavy plantings of Cabernet Sauvignon, Pinotage, Seibel 5455 — all red varieties — Palomino and Baco 22A. Cabernet Sauvignon, Pinotage and Palomino flourish here — and produce some top wines.

Henderson may be in eclipse in terms of recent vineyard development, but in other respects the area remains vital to the wine industry. Although Auckland has only 7.7 percent of the national vineyard area,

fifty-six percent of the wine was made there in 1979. The headquarters and bottling plants of most of the large and medium-sized wine companies in New Zealand are in Auckland, close to the largest market. An enormous amount of the country's wine output is transported to Auckland as fruit, as partly processed wine, or as finished wine ready for bottling.

One intriguing aspect is the recent influx of non-Yugoslavs into the Auckland wine making scene. It was once the preserve of Dalmatian, Lebanese and English vintners, but now an Australian controls the wine making process at Penfolds, a German is chief wine maker at Corbans, and New Zealander Peter Hubscher directs much of the country's total production at Montana.

Despite the undoubted climatic difficulties, Henderson still produces wines of the calibre of Collard

Rhine Riesling and Babich Cabernet Sauvignon. Most recent viticultural research has been concentrated in the newer wine areas, so that considerable scope remains in Henderson for experimentation with new varieties, clones and rootstocks; who knows, this older wine district may yet provide further surprises.

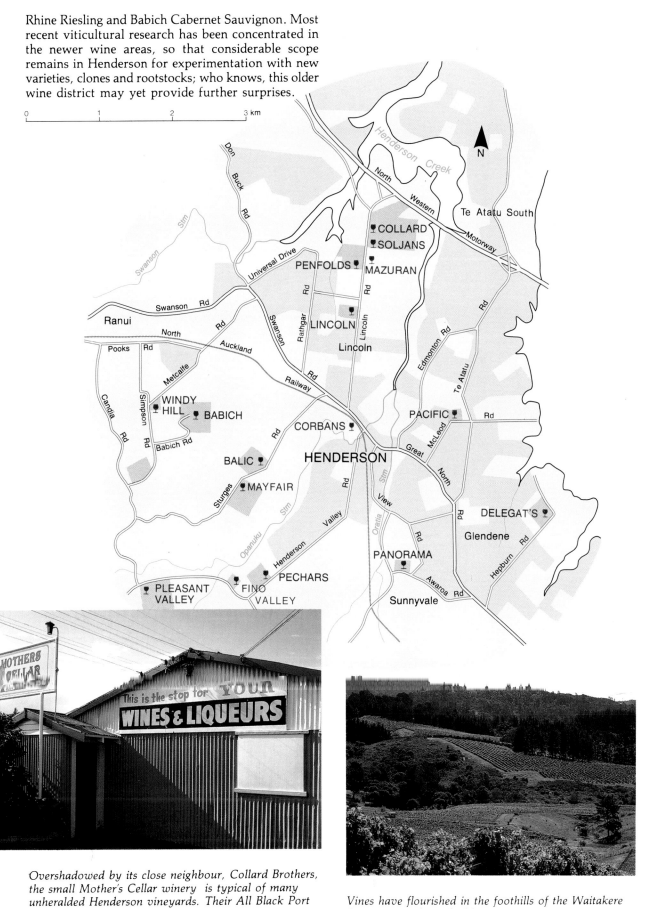

Overshadowed by its close neighbour, Collard Brothers, the small Mother's Cellar winery is typical of many unheralded Henderson vineyards. Their All Black Port has its followers.

Vines have flourished in the foothills of the Waitakere Ranges since the end of last century.

Babich

Founder Joe Babich Snr, flanked by sons Peter and Joe.

In the foothills of the Waitakere Ranges lies one of Auckland's best vineyards. After more than sixty years, the Babich winery is well established as the home of well priced wines ranging from sound vin ordinaire to several notable varietals.

This independent, family-owned vineyard is controlled by brothers Peter and Joe Babich Jnr. Peter (52) manages the company; Joe (44) makes the wine and serves as a national wine judge. Their father, Joe Babich Senior, until his death in 1983 was one of the Grand Old Men of the New Zealand wine industry.

Babich's ancestral home lies in the wine growing area of Imotski. In 1910, as a boy of 14, Joseph Babich left Dalmatia to join his three brothers toiling in the gumfields of the Far North. His first wine was produced in 1916. At Kaikino, on the last stretch of land leading to Cape Reinga, he grew grapes, trod them with his feet, and opened a wine-shop.

The shift to the Henderson Valley came in 1919. On a twenty-four hectare wilderness property, Joe milked cows, grew vegetables, established a small orchard — and planted classical Pinot Meunier vines. Ten years later Joe Babich wed another emigrant Dalmatian, Mara Grgic. Their lifetime of shared endeavour included the births of five children, and the steady expansion of the vineyard.

During the war wine making slowly became the family's major business activity. By the 1950s son Peter

was at the helm, and the 1960s saw the emergence of Joe Babich Jnr as wine maker.

About thirty hectares of grapevines now grow on Babich's loam clay soils. These are supplemented each year by grapes bought from growers in the Gisborne, Hawkes Bay and Auckland regions. The Babich vineyard is predominantly planted with Cabernet Sauvignon, Pinotage, Müller-Thurgau and Palomino vines, along with significant acreages of Gewürztraminer, Pinot Noir, Merlot and Chardonnay.

Very clean, crisp dry wines are the hallmark of the Babich style. Palomino Sherry (dry) and Dry White are two of the most widely seen lines. The Dry White, blended from Chenin Blanc, Chasselas and other unspecified varieties, is consistently a hard, flavoursome, dry wine with no holds barred.

The Dry Riesling-Sylvaner, one of the better dryish versions of this grape, is light, fragrant and delicately flavoured. Both the 1982 and 1983 releases have the typical Babich character. The Estate Riesling-Sylvaner is an interesting example of Henderson regional wine, of finer quality than the Dry Riesling-Sylvaner.

Müller-Thurgau, first produced in 1979, represented this firm's first significant entry into the medium white wine market. The 1980 early in its life showed plenty

The Babich winery viewed from the Sturges Road ridge.

of fruit, and developed after two years bottle-age a lovely honeyish character. The 1983 vintage also has depth of flavour and ideal sugar/acid balance.

Babich Gewürztraminer varies from year to year, reflecting this grape's erratic vineyard performance in Auckland. The 1979 vintage drew attention for its strong golden colour and intense—although not spicy—flavour. The 1983 gold medal wine has an appealing light style, flowery and delicate.

Other varietal white wines include Chardonnay, which shows restrained oak character, Sémillon, Grey Riesling, Chenin Blanc and a charming, very aromatic Muscat Blanc.

So far, however, the true distinction of the Babich winery lies in red wines—Pinotage/Cabernet, Cabernet Sauvignon, Pinot Noir and Merlot. The 1982 Pinotage/Cabernet, blended from seventy-five percent Pinotage, twenty-five percent Cabernet Sauvignon, is a soft fruity red wine, with less oak character than its predecessors. The 1970 vintage opened up well at a decade old, but most later vintages have reached top form at four to five years old.

The Cabernet Sauvignon is full flavoured and subtle. Produced from Henderson estate-grown fruit, held up to two years in French and American oak casks, this is a traditional red—tannic and austere when young, but maturing well for five to ten years. The 1976, 1977, 1979 and 1980 are all solid Cabernet Sauvignons but the best years, so far, are 1978 and 1981.

The Pinot Noir is highly promising. The first release, 1978, caught the elusive elegant suppleness of this variety. Later, the gold medal 1981 and the 1982 vintages have also displayed true Pinot Noir depth and roundness. Equally, the 1981 and 1982 Merlots are full, soft reds with good colour and bouquet.

Babich also produces two worthwhile ports—a small volume of seven year old Reserve Port, which has a mellow tawny style; and recently a Cabernet Sauvignon based Vintage Port which has the ingredients for a long cellar life.

Peter Babich—behind the warm friendly manner lies a fierce independence and considerable business acumen.

Part of the Babich vineyard with Mayfair vines in the distance. (overleaf)

Balic

One arresting feature about this low profile, medium-sized company in Sturges Road is the company head, Diana Balic (39); the Balic Estate (once called Golden Sunset) is the sole winery in New Zealand controlled by a woman.

A pioneer firm, the Balic Estate was founded in 1912 by Joseph Balic, a Dalmatian who had deserted from the Austrian army. Balic planted his vines at night, by candle-light, after a hard day's labour in the Corban vineyard. Today the Balic label still features the red Model T Ford in which Joseph Balic toured the area selling his invalid port — warmly recommended for medicinal purposes.

At present the Balic vineyard covers fifteen hectares of Henderson clay soils. Palomino, Pinotage and Baco 22A are the major varieties, with some Müller-Thurgau. Contract grapes are grown in Auckland and Gisborne.

Balic wine maker Vic Talyancich produces a surprising volume of sparkling wine. By far the most popular is Balic Asti Spumante, a sweet, fruity 'bubbly'

vinted from a blend of grape varieties with Muscat strongly and pleasantly in evidence. Another sparkling was for many years labelled 'Gold Medal Champagne', which, in view of the fact that no sparkling had then been awarded a gold medal in New Zealand for many years, was odd to say the least.

The table wines have generally fallen one or two steps behind the rest of the industry. Hybrids are sound: Vin Ché, for example, is a plain, dry white quaffer and, for a red blended from Seibel and Baco grapes, Bakaver has a notably robust flavour.

But the varietal table wines have not enhanced the firm's reputation. A Müller-Thurgau, non vintage, sampled in 1982 was somewhat thin. A 1976/77 Pinotage and 1981 Pinotage/Cabernet were both poor. The 1978 Chardonnay, a private-bin release, had no detectable varietal character at all.

Perhaps the Balic Riesendorf 1982 can be seen as a positive sign. A Müller-Thurgau and Chasselas blend made to a commercial medium style, this wine has greater body than its predecessors.

Of the Balic range of fortified wines, both the Flor Sherry and Tawny Port occasionally win medals. And the green Titoki Liqueur, produced from manuka honey, the leaves and berries of the titoki bush and (in the tradition of most liqueurs) other secret ingredients, is well worth trying.

Diana Balic is the only woman heading a New Zealand wine company. The 'h' was dropped from the family name, Balich, to avoid confusion with Babich.

Collard Bros

The company's meticulous approach to wine making is also reflected in its very tidy vineyard.

Collard Bros first burst into prominence by scoring five silver medals at the 1972 national wine show. At that stage, most members of the wine trade had not even heard of the vineyard before.

The founder, J.W. Collard, who bought the present property in Lincoln Road in 1910, called it Sutton Baron after the village in Kent where traditionally his family had grown hops and fruit. The first vines were planted in response to the urgings of Mrs Collard's brothers, the Averills. From 1946 until 1963, when Penfolds took over the Averill winery, Collard wines were made there.

Today this small, well-respected company is administered by Lionel Collard (62); the wine makers are Bruce Collard (34) and his brother Geoffrey (31). The home vineyard, just off the north-west motorway, is only ten hectares; on soils varying from deep peat to hard clay an extensive selection of varieties has been planted: Rhine Riesling, Müller-Thurgau, Gewürztraminer, Sylvaner, Palomino, a small plot of Hermitage, Cabernet Sauvignon and Merlot. Grapes bought in are exclusively from Auckland growers, to ensure the preservation of a regional wine style. And in response to intensifying urban pressures, and the possibility that the home vineyard may ultimately have to be uprooted, the company has bought a sixty-hectare property in the Waikoukou Valley, close to Matua Valley, for development as a new vineyard. Plantings here have centred on Müller-Thurgau, Rhine Riesling, Gewürztraminer, Cabernet Sauvignon, Cabernet Franc and Merlot.

The premium lines are scarce and released largely from the vineyard or by mail order. The white wine labels carry a useful indication of style; Dry Art for dry whites, Selected Vintage for off-dry and Late Harvest for those with plenty of residual sweetness. Three quaffing wines receive some commercial distribution — Country Red, a light fruity style; Dry White, a clean, flavoursome Sylvaner; and Rosé.

Although hybrids are being phased out of the Collard vineyard, the company handles these well. The Private Bin White Wine, vinted previously from Baco 22A but now Chenin Blanc grapes, had a full aroma and clean sharp taste; Len Evans, the renowned Australian wine man, was rapturous over the 1978: 'I'm impressed out of my mind by this wine. It is exceptionally clean, with lovely freshness, balance and harmony...' And the hybrid-based reds have lacked the sharpness typical of such wines. The Private Bin Claret, produced from selected Seibel 5455 and Pinotage grapes, is typically medium bodied, firm red wine with only a hint of coarseness to betray its hybrid origins.

The company's reputation has largely been built by three varietal white wines: Müller-Thurgau, Rhine Riesling and Gewürztraminer. These are often Germanic in style, for the Collards have deliberately set out to reproduce Down Under the harmony and elegance typical of the best German white wines. The Müller-Thurgau, fuller than most, derives flavour from a brief period of skin contact before the fermentation; the 1978 had a very ripe feel, sweet and slightly honied — perfectly balanced wine; the 1981, although a lesser wine still has more class than most.

Collard Rhine Riesling in its more successful years — 1978, 1980 — impresses as a wine of true Rhine Riesling character, perfectly balanced. But in other years — 1979, 1982 — a prominent acidity contributes to a rather austere style. These wines age well over three to five years.

Collard Gewürztraminer has often tended to a subdued style, lacking the characteristic pungency of this variety. However, such recent gold medal vintages as 1980 and 1983 have shown a more penetrating, spicy aroma and taste.

Lately the company has moved to develop a wider range of dry white wines. The Dry Chenin Blanc 1982 is a big, steely style that needs years to really unfold. The 1982 Dry Sémillon has finesse, the quality that has eluded most New Zealand wines of this grape variety. The 1983 vintage also yielded the first Collard Chardonnay and 1984 the first Sauvignon Blanc.

For many years the established top Collard red was the Pinotage/Cabernet — the 1974 and 1978 both won golds. This was consistently a soft, pleasant wine, but a shade too light to be really outstanding. A couple of vintages of unblended Merlot and straight Cabernet Sauvignon have been seen; however, the top Collard red since 1980 has clearly been the Cabernet Sauvignon/Merlot. The 1981 vintage is memorable for its lovely fragrance and elegant palate. A 3 : 1 blend of the two varieties, matured in French and American oak casks, this wine recalls the less tannic Bordeaux reds of St Emilion and Pomerol.

Two other Collard wines of interest are the Tawny Port made from blended, five to ten-year-old *vinifera* and hybrid material; and the Rosé of Pinotage, a pinkish-red, fresh and lively wine that at the 1981 National Wine Competition scored the first gold award in recent years for a rosé.

A hallmark of Collard's range is its immaculate presentation, including a special label designed by New York-domiciled, New Zealand artist Billy Apple for the 1981 Cabernet Sauvignon/Merlot.

Corbans

The winery entrance, about a stone's throw from Henderson shopping centre.

For forty years, the adroit management of the Corban family ensured their domination of the New Zealand wine industry. From its humble beginnings as a one-and-a-half hectare vineyard founded by the Lebanese immigrant, Assid Abraham Corban, at Henderson in 1902, the winery flourished through prohibition and depression and early established itself as a household name. But today the company is Corbans only in name, being a wholly owned subsidiary of Rothmans.

A.A. Corban, a stonemason from the village of Shweir on the flanks of Mt Lebanon, inland from Beirut, arrived in New Zealand in 1892. He travelled the gold fields and mining towns of the North Island, peddling ornaments and fancy goods, then set up as a dealer in Auckland's Queen Street. Two years later, he sent for his wife, Najibie, and sons Khaleel and Wadier to join him.

The beginning of Corban's 'Mt Lebanon Vineyards' lies in the 1902 purchase — for £320 — of four hectares of Henderson gumland, complete with a small cottage and a few Isabella vines. His strong ambition to produce wine — a family tradition back in Lebanon — led Assid Abraham Corban to establish a small vineyard: Black Hamburghs for the table and classic varieties like Chasselas, Hermitage and Cabernet Sauvignon for winemaking; no Albany Surprise — that, said A.A. Corban, was a vine suitable only for lazy wine growers. At the first Corban vintage in the

new country in 1908, the fruit was crushed by hand with a wooden club and an open hogshead used as the fermenting vat.

By 1916 son Wadier had assumed the duties of wine maker. At the New Zealand and South Seas Exhibition 1925-26, Wadier's Corbans port won first place. Khaleel took charge of sales, travelling the length of the country in an old Dodge van, building up a strong trade in tonic and restorative wines.

Although the arrival of a rotary hoe in 1934, and a caterpillar tractor soon after greatly eased the vineyard toil, by all accounts, until his death in 1941 of a stroke, Assid Abraham Corban remained a patriarch in the Old Testament mould, and a strong believer in the virtues of hard work. Najibie, too, until her death in 1957 remained in close touch with all aspects of management.

When the wine boom began in earnest in the 1960s, Corbans' plantings leap-frogged from the Henderson Valley north to Riverlea, Kumeu and Taupaki, and later contracts were negotiated with growers in Auckland and Gisborne. Alex Corban, as wine maker, demonstrated a flair for technical innovation: pioneering the use of refrigeration, installing the first pressure tanks, ushering in bulk fermentation of sparkling wines, and producing the first commercial releases of flor sherry, Riesling-Sylvaner and Chardonnay. To reinforce the company's economic

In Corbans' Henderson laboratory, the labels of competitors' wines being analysed are carefully hidden from the camera.

base, A.A. Corban and Sons admitted a nineteen percent shareholding by wine and spirits merchants.

But when the challenge from Montana emerged in the late 1960s, the Corban family's own financial resources proved insufficient to pay for the huge expansion necessary if the company was to retain its ascendancy. Rothmans became a shareholder and steadily increased its influence; although Joe Corban (vineyards manager) is still actively involved in the firm, today the Corban family has altogether lost its financial control.

Corbans planted new vineyards at Gisborne in 1968 and three years later sited a second winery there. Subsequently plantings spread up the East Coast to Tolaga Bay, and also to Te Kauwhata. At Marlborough, over 200 hectares of Gewürztraminer, Rhine Riesling, Sylvaner, Sauvignon Blanc, Chardonnay and Sémillon were established by 1982.

Through the mid-1970s Corbans struggled to match the quality advances of its rivals. The phasing out of hybrids, even from several top lines, seemed slow and top white wines such as Chardonnay and Chasselas were consistently plain. Until recently the company's prestige was in danger of erosion.

Since 1980, however, there has been a noticeable lift in quality, at least partly attributable to the arrival of German Norbert Seibel, a Geisenheim graduate with wine-making experience in Germany, France and South Africa. Corbans' haul of silver medals for table wines at the National Wine Competition tripled between 1978 and 1980.

Corbans market a wide range of wine in New Zealand under three different brands: Corbans, Riverlea (basic quaffing styles) and Robard and Butler.

The whites first. Over many years, the Riesling-Sylvaner has developed a sound reputation; the 1977 was — and remains — a dry, earthy style of pleasing depth; the 1981 vintage has a very good, elegant varietal aroma and crisp, sustained flavour.

Corbans Chenin Blanc is another respected line vinted from Tolaga Bay, East Cape fruit. The original version of this wine from the 1976 vintage created a big impression in the wine industry with its full body and distinctive taste. Here was an alternative to Müller-Thurgau, fruity, and bigger in the mouth. The good 1977 consolidated this early reputation but the more recent vintages have not been consistently as good.

Liebestraum is Corbans' major commercial white wine. For several years Liebestraum seemed to suffer from too much Palomino juice, which gives a dull, heavy character to white table wines. Recent vintages like 1983, however, show evidence of better grapes in the blend and this has become an appealing, perfectly acceptable commercial wine.

In the more exotic varietals, Corbans are demonstrating much ability with Gewürztraminer. The first straight Gewürztraminer, 1979, showed a full fruity

and spicy character in a style more akin to German than French equivalents. All subsequent vintages to 1983 have been similar: fragrant, medium wine with lots of spice.

The Chardonnay in its youth is a firm, acid style without wood influence. After two or three years' cellaring, Corbans Chardonnay usually shows much benefit, emerging — as the 1981 did in 1984 — impressively dry and flinty.

Other consistently good Corbans white wines include a surprisingly dry Müller-Thurgau vinted from Henderson fruit; a most elegant, medium-sweet Late Harvest Riesling-Sylvaner; and a rich and luscious Auslese.

Overall, Corbans' red wines in recent years have been relatively plain and undistinguished. For many years the winery adhered to a policy of marketing a claret rather than a Cabernet Sauvignon. Corbans Claret has its ups and downs — the 1975 silver medal vintage was probably the best; my bottle of 1980, showing predominantly Pinotage character, was more of an enjoyable everyday drinking standard.

The first release of Cabernet Sauvignon, 1976, was a big, ripe-tasting red that scored a gold medal. However, subsequent vintages like the 1980 and 1981, although showing some Cabernet Sauvignon character, have tended to lack any real intensity. One promising sign is the Cabernet Sauvignon/Merlot 1983, a deeply-coloured Easter Show 1984 gold medal winner in which the Merlot makes its presence well felt.

Both Corbans Pinot Noir — I have tasted the 1977, 1978 and 1980 vintages — and the Merlot — 1980, 1981 and 1982 — have never approached the standards normally associated with these outstanding red varieties. And several reds — Beaujolais Nouveau, Merlot, Cabernet/Pinotage and Velluto Rosso — display a degree of sweetness that confirmed red wine drinkers find perturbing.

The Cabernet Rosé, too, until recently had a sweet cloying character but the 1983 vintage is much improved — medium-dry, with an attractive, clear pink colour and a flavour that appeals as fresh, fruity and firm.

Alex Corban, pictured here in the old Corban family homestead, with his Cabernet Sauvignon 1961.

Delegat's

Delegat's has emerged from mediocrity in the past few years to earn recognition as a consistently fine producer of Chardonnay.

This family-owned, medium-sized winery tucked away in Hepburn Road, Henderson, was founded in 1947 by Nikola (Nick) Delegat. Delegat first arrived in New Zealand in 1923 but later retraced his steps to Yugoslavia, before finally establishing a two-hectare plot of vines at Henderson. Today his son Jim Delegat (35) is the company head.

The small vineyard at the winery and a larger block at Huapai are mainly planted in Cabernet Sauvignon, Palomino and Chardonnay vines. Contract growers in Gisborne and Auckland supply the majority of the grape intake.

Delegat's appeared to be content to produce sound, ordinary wines — until the 1979 arrival of a young Australian wine maker, John Hancock. Almost overnight, Hancock lifted the standard of Delegat's wines. The gold medal won by Delegat's 1979 Selected Vintage Riesling-Sylvaner was only the first of a string of subsequent successes.

The Riesling-Sylvaner, now called Müller-Thurgau, shows greater finesse than most others — typically this is very fragrant, crisp and delicate. The Muscat Blanc is perfumed, full bodied and sweet but tails away at the finish, like most Muscat table wines. The Pinot Gris 1982 is one of the best New Zealand versions of this variety: a full, basically dry wine. And the Gewürztraminer is fragrant and fresh, with a delicate, relatively restrained spicy character.

Outstanding among the Delegat's line-up of white wines are the Auslese Müller-Thurgau and the Chardonnay. The Auslese of the 1980-1982 vintages has been a very Germanic style with only eight to nine percent alcohol by volume, showing a lovely concentration of bouquet and flavour.

The Chardonnay ranks alongside Cooks' and McWilliam's as the best in the country. Truly fat on the palate, with strong French Nevers oak influence and deep Chardonnay fruit, these are superb wines. The memorable 1982 vintage scored highest among almost 800 entries in the 1983 National Wine Competition.

Only a single red wine is made, Cabernet Sauvignon. The first vintage, 1977, was only workmanlike, but the 1980, eventually awarded a gold medal at the 1983 National Wine Competition, made a strong impression even in its youth. Coloured deeply, with strong fruit and soft tannin, the wine matured rapidly and probably peaked after three years. The 1982 Delegat's Cabernet Sauvignon is similar, already drinking well at two years old and one to cellar probably only for a couple of years.

Pruned Gewürztraminer vines in mid-winter in Delegat's small Henderson vineyard.

Jim Delegat, drawing 1984 Sémillon from French Nevers oak barrels, hopes to position Delegat's at the premium end of the wine market.

Delegat's rank today as one of the largest family-controlled wineries.

Fino Valley

This small, basically undistinguished vineyard is run by Ivan Torduch (54) and his son Ivan (29).

Fino Valley has three hectares planted in a wide variety of vines and buys in an equal amount from Auckland growers. Back in the early 1970s, in roaring company at the winery on Saturday afternoons, Fino Valley Medium Dry Red served as my introduction to the world of wine. Today the big sellers are Moselle, White Moscato and Medium Sherry – but these wines no longer impress. A recent tasting of the red Alphonse Lavalee was sweet, high in alcohol.

These are basic wines, cheap to buy.

The vineyard is neatly and cleanly tended.

Lincoln

The undoubted strength of this medium-sized, family winery in Lincoln Road is dry sherry; of five silver medals awarded in this category at the 1981 Easter Show wine judging, three went to Lincoln.

Peter Fredatovich, the founder, worked in New Zealand as a stonemason for twelve years before acquiring the present property, then clothed in blackberry, in 1937. Today his son Peter Fredatovich Snr (58) and grandson Peter Fredatovich Jnr (33) run the company, with Peter Fredatovich Jnr as wine maker.

The home vineyard covers four hectares of heavy clay soil. At Riverlea, Lincoln has another eighteen hectares of hybrid and *vinifera* vine planted on better draining soils. The fruit from these holdings is augmented by contract grapes drawn from the Auckland and Gisborne regions.

Although Lincoln produces a large volume of table wines, including a well-known flagon Moselle, these tend to be only of a quaffing standard. All of my recent tastings – Grey Riesling 1980, Chenin Blanc 1981, Gamay Rosé 1982 and Müller-Thurgau 1983 – show these to be rather plain wines, lacking delicacy. These wines are sold at realistic prices.

The Lincoln Road winery viewed from the home vineyard.

Mayfair

The soft, sunlit entrance to the Mayfair winery.

A couple of decades ago Mayfair Vineyards enjoyed a strong reputation for its sherries, cocktails and liqueurs. But today the vogue for such products as Limbo Lime Gin, Rock 'n Roll and Blackberry Nip has vanished, leaving this small family winery in Sturges Road heavily reduced in output.

Mayfair Vineyards was founded by the late Mate Ivicevich, who planted one and a half hectares in vines in 1948. The company is now administered by his son, Victor (52) who is also the wine maker.

Mayfair once had a booming cellar trade, especially for Blackberry Nip, whose fame still lingers in many memories. Today most of the production is still in fortified wines, but only a few lines are sold at outlets other than the vineyard.

Vic Ivicevich's own fondness for Maraschino, a Dalmatian cherry liqueur, offers an insight into the style of his wines. Mayfair offers a phenomenal array of wines which, although down from the peak total of forty-eight, still includes nineteen cocktails and liqueurs. The table wines — Dry White, Moselle, Sauternes, Rosé, Dry Red, Claret and Burgundy — are of low quality, but also low-priced.

This vineyard has changed hardly at all in the last twenty years, preserving intact the styles and traditions of a departed era — like Eastern Vineyards, its now vanished neighbour.

Mazuran

This small vineyard has specialised in fortified wines with outstanding success. At the 1980 National Wine Competition Mazuran dominated the fortified classes, scoring ten medals including – for Old Mellow Sweet Sherry – the only gold award.

George Mazuran arrived in New Zealand in 1926, a seventeen-year-old intent on avoiding conscription into the Austrian army occupying Dalmatia. After labouring on dairy farms in the Waikato and running an Auckland fish-and-chip shop – losing his right arm meanwhile in a fishing accident – George Mazuran bought the present Lincoln Road property in 1938. The first vines were planted a year later; 1942 marked the first Mazuran vintage in New Zealand.

The manifold difficulty encountered in the post-war years in disposing of this wine led directly to Mazuran's long career as a political lobbyist. He set out in pursuit of more favourable selling opportunities for the small Dalmatian wine makers who lacked outlets through the established liquor distribution channels. To foster the sales of independent, family-owned wineries was the raison d'être of Mazuran's political involvement.

The payoff from his assiduous lobbying for the Dalmatian wine-growing community, according to a Parliamentary speech by the MP for Rodney, Peter Wilkinson, in October 1975, has been 'that it has been well recognised by the legislature for many years that if New Zealand is to have a healthy wine industry it is vital that the interests of the smaller growers should be constantly kept in mind.' In 1971, in his twenty-first year as president of the Viticultural Association, Mazuran was awarded the OBE for his services to the wine industry. He died in 1982, aged seventy-three and the company is now run by family members, Rado and Patricia Hladilo.

While his wife, Florence, made the vineyard's famous fortified wines, George Mazuran was free to concentrate on his unique lobbying career.

Ironically, the wine-growing bonanza that owed so much to his efforts largely passed his own company by. The Mazuran vineyard is small – only six hectares planted – with no other sources of supply. Hence the wines are hard to buy, and the range of products, concentrated on sherries and ports, has barely changed in the past twenty years.

The few table wines offered are not impressive; Mazuran in 1975 declared in *Accolade* magazine that 'any New Zealand grower who concentrates on table wines is digging his own grave'. The Pinot Chardonnay and hybrid Dry Red I sampled in 1983 were poor.

The true distinction of the Mazuran vineyard lies in sherries and ports. The Mazuran style is almost unmistakable: these are big dessert wines, richly flavoured, mellow, often sweet and syrupy.

Mazuran attributed his success with sherries to two factors: exclusive use of the classic Spanish sherry grape, Palomino, coupled with unusually long and patient wood aging. This vineyard is among the few still using the traditional solera system, based on rows, or tiers, of casks, graduated by age, to blend very old, fine sherries with younger ones. These dessert wines all spend at least five years in oak and some are matured for up to twenty years.

Some critics consider Mazuran's products slightly tired, not fresh or fruity enough; others have detected a rather obtrusive level of acetic acid. But for thirty years, at home and abroad, judges singled them out for praise.

111

Pechar's

Pechar's cellar shop in 1984 was selling table wine at only $2.60 a bottle.

This little winery caters to the bottom level of the wine market.

Yugoslav-born Steve Pechar came to New Zealand in 1962, at the age of sixteen. For two years he and his wife lived in a one-roomed bach, picking fruit, until they planted a small, half-hectare vineyard and began to make wine. The present cellar in Valley Road, Henderson was opened in 1971.

The four-hectare vineyard at the rear of the winery is all planted in hybrids apart from Palomino. Pechar's also draws grapes from a holding at Kumeu and from Auckland contract growers.

Mel Frey, previously of Corbans, Montana and Delegats is a partner of Steve Pechar. The wines are now marketed under the label 'Old Railway' — a name derived from the company's vineyard in Old Railway Road, Kumeu. According to Frey: 'What we are trying to do here is to make a reasonable wine at a reasonable price. Most of the others are getting too expensive.'

Although the sign outside read 'Export Quality Wines' those I tasted, including the big seller, Moselle, were mediocre.

Penfolds

Once the driving force behind Montana, Frank Yukich had a strong reputation in the wine industry as one who regularly achieved his goals. His original ambition after acquiring control of Penfolds (NZ) in 1977 was to become not the largest wine maker in the country but the best. Later he spoke of becoming both.

Penfolds (NZ) was established in 1963 on a small property in Lincoln Road bought from the old firm of Averill Brothers, who had planted vines there in 1922 and for many years supplied bulk sherry to Dominion Breweries. The new company was founded as a joint venture between Penfolds (Australia), with a sixty-two percent shareholding, and local brewers and merchants, operating mainly under the direction of the Australian parent. The home block was extended to sixteen hectares and at Waimauku a second, eighty hectare vineyard was planted, partly in hybrids. But little was spent on winery equipment. Although a sound reputation was built for sherry and port — Penfolds Medium Sherry remains a big seller — the table wines were plain. By the 1970s, Penfolds was sorely in need of a fresh impulse.

Then, in 1977 Penfolds (Australia) sold most of its shares to Frank Yukich. Yukich now controlled sixty-

Randy Weaver, left, and Frank Yukich parted company over Weaver's decision to establish his own Coopers Creek winery. Yukich controlled Penfolds from 1977 to 1982.

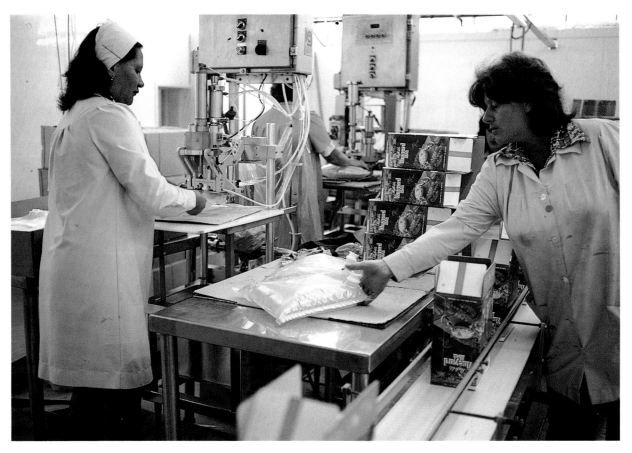

seven percent of shares, with the rest held by wine and spirit merchants, and two percent by Penfolds (Australia).

After his takeover, Yukich substantially revamped the Henderson winery, ripping out open fermenter vats and installing new storage tanks and bottling lines. Most Penfolds grapes have since been crushed at the company's new Gisborne winery while Henderson functions primarily as a storage, blending and bottling plant. The 'Hermitage' wine bar, restaurant, and vineyard planted in high-trellised Cabernet Sauvignon vines have since become a showplace for tourists.

A succession of winery managers — Keith Galvin, Randy Weaver and lately Australian John Baruzzi (36) — guided the company's switch to a new emphasis on table wines. By virtue of new products like soft packs and the sparkling Chardon, Penfolds began by 1980 to capture a rising share of the market. The Yukich flair for making wine and money was on display again; net profits soared from $17,212 in 1976 to $524,603 in 1979.

But the company suffered a severe setback in 1981 when the Health Department seized catering kegs of Penfolds Hock and Moselle on the suspicion that they contained illegal Rhine Riesling flavouring. Later the department altered its stance to say the wines contained a solvent, called propylene glycol, not permitted in table wines. Although no prosecution eventuated, Penfolds was forced by the controversy to withdraw a proposed $2.5 million share issue and face up to the difficult task of re-establishing credibility with consumers. Soon after, Lion Breweries bought a thirty-

The company has a strong presence in the 'bag-in-box' wine cask market.

five percent shareholding, which allowed the completion of the first stage of the new Gisborne winery. But when profits slumped from $1.12 million to $390,000 in the year ending June 1982, the brewery emerged as majority shareholder by buying out Frank Yukich.

Since the 1981 vintage, Penfolds has relied solely on contract growers to supply its grape needs. The Waimauku vineyard was sold, and Penfolds encouraged its growers to plant 1000 hectares of vines at Tikitiki, Gisborne, Hawkes Bay and Marlborough.

Penfolds wines have shown a steady improvement in the past two or three years. The wine casks have taken a significant slice of the market at the bottom end of the range. Two unabashedly sweet and popular members of the company's range are Chardon, a fruity, low-alcohol sparkling wine vinted predominently from Müller-Thurgau grapes, and the Rhinesdale Müller-Thurgau.

Of Penfolds' dry white wines, the Autumn Riesling-Sylvaner has traditionally been the flagship. The memorable 1976, awarded the THC Wine of the Year Trophy, was a magnificent wine, of intense bouquet, and deep dry flavour. The character this wine displayed in 1980 reflected the blending in of a proportion of Rhine Riesling as well as freeze-concentration. Such later vintages as 1979 and 1981, although good, have not reached this earlier standard.

Penfolds' range of top white varietals includes the Gewürztraminer, Chardonnay, Sauvignon Blanc, Chenin Blanc and Blenheim Riesling-Sylvaner. These are sound wines, generally showing some varietal character, but without real interest. The Gewürztraminer 1982 has overly subdued spiciness and the 1982 Chardonnay is light, plain wine. Probably the best of the line-up is the Blenheim Riesling-Sylvaner, fragrant and with the slightly fuller flavour of Marlborough fruit. These wines until recently were marketed under the Kastel brand, a source of some confusion to wine buyers.

Penfolds Verdernay and Cabernet Rosé are both worthwhile wines: one a dry, bottle-fermented sparkling based on Pinot Noir and Chardonnay, the other one of the best dry New Zealand rosés.

Penfolds' red wines are often under-rated. Some

Penfolds Henderson winery looking towards the Waitakere Ranges.

releases, like the Woodhill Cabernet Sauvignon 1980, have been unimpressive. Yet the Penfolds Cabernet Sauvignon 1978 lingers in the memory as a double gold medal winner, a ripe-tasting complex red with a long tannin finish. On a more humble level, Woodhill Claret shows a pleasant wood-aged Pinotage character.

Penfolds also produce several top fortified wines. Flor Fino sherry won the THC Trophy in 1977 as top wine of the year. The Director's Port, a leading tawny style, has recently been partnered by Penfolds Vintage Port, of which the 1980 and 1981 vintages won gold medals in 1983.

Pleasant Valley

Pleasant Valley, the oldest surviving Dalmatian vineyard in Henderson, has suffered a drastic decline in production since its heyday in the 1960s.

Stipan Jelich, the founder, arrived in Auckland in 1890 at the age of twenty-two. After five years' labour on the northern gumfields he bought, at five pounds an acre, thirty-two hectares of hill country in the Henderson Valley. His first crop of grapes, Black Hamburghs, fetched him less on the Auckland markets than the charges of the carrier and auctioneer. By 1902, wine making had emerged as a better source of income, and from then until Stipan Yelich (Stephan Yelas) retired in 1939, the vineyard served as a model of the fruits of peasant stubbornness: the land was turned over by spade; the vines, tied to manuka stakes, were hand-hoed, and sprayed from a knapsack mounted on the back. During Stipan's working life, not even a horse helped to ease the toil.

Yelas' son, Moscow, long ago introduced more modern vineyard techniques, replacing manuka stakes with wire trellises and knapsack sprayers with machine sprayers. Until his death in 1984, Moscow, although semi-retired, still made the wine while his son, Stephan, concentrated on viticulture.

Pleasant Valley has twenty-four hectares of vines planted on heavy clay soils: Palomino, Pinotage, Müller-Thurgau, Niagara, Seibel 5409, Baco 22A and Baco No. 1.

Today the cellars are quiet, even sleepy; much of the grape crop is sold to other companies and the wines are not widely seen beyond the winery. The range, bearing the inscription 'Chateau Yelas', occasionally wins bronze medals and some bottles sold at the

The rolling vineyard is too steep for mechanical harvesting.

vineyard are extraordinarily old: in 1981 a 'Royal Bin' Pinotage from 1973 was available.

Currently output consists predominantly of Amoroso Sherry, White Moscato — a fortified wine based on Niagara grapes — and Sauternes. No table wines, even reds, are wood aged: according to Moscow Yelas this process is too costly and instead to encourage a slight oxidation his reds were given an additional racking.

My tastings of Hock, Pinotage and Fino Dry Sherry revealed these to be sound, honest wines with reasonable fruit character, but lacking delicacy. However, these can be good value at very cheap prices.

Soljans

Soljans, traditionally one of the best small Henderson dessert wine makers, has recently developed a range of red and white varietal table wines.

The founder, the late Frank Soljan, arrived in New Zealand in 1927 at the age of fifteen. Today, the six-hectare block of fruit trees and vines he planted in Lincoln Road in 1937 is still a combined orchard and vineyard, run by his sons Tony (39) the wine maker, and Rex (40) who cultivates the impeccable vineyard. At Riverlea a second vineyard has been planted in Chenin Blanc, Cabernet Sauvignon, Müller-Thurgau and Sémillon vines.

This winery is largely respected as a sherry producer, and Soljans' top offering, the Private Bin Pergola Sherry, emerges after ten years in small oak, as a full bodied, mature dessert wine. The Reserve Sherry, aged for eight years in large barrels, is also a sweet, dark-brown dessert wine, a shade lighter than the Pergola Sherry; both are fine examples of this wine style.

Of the table wines, the sales success story so far is the Henderson Spumante, a clean sparkling wine with a full Muscat aroma and fruity flavour. The Dry White is a plain, crisp wine blended from hybrid and Müller-Thurgau grapes.

Of the premium table wines, Soljans' Chenin Blanc and Sémillon from the 1981 and 1982 vintages show hints of true varietal character but are dull, rather flat wines. By contrast, the Cabernet Sauvignon 1980 must be rated a success—a very pleasant, light style Cabernet with a brick red colour and soft delicate flavour.

A scene of rare beauty, Black Hamburgh table grapes trained along overhead trellises, greets visitors to Soljans during the summer months.

Windy Hill

Paul Erceg (37) the rangy, frankly-spoken son of the winery founder, ponders his glass of Windy Hill Pinotage/Beaujolais and declares: 'Let's face it, we're not making the world's greatest wine, but we are making sound, clean wine.'

Milan Erceg, a native of the village of Rascana in Dalmatia — and at sixty-six still heading his company — erected a tiny two-room bach on his Simpson Road market-garden property in 1934. Wind knifed through the cracks in the bare weatherboards and into the unlined bach, and so Windy Hill was chosen as an apt company name.

Over three decades later, when the only wine produced was Dry Red, a new cellar was erected. Today, the three-hectare vineyard established on rolling hill country sloping well to the sun, is closely planted with Pinotage, Gamay Beaujolais, Palomino, Cabernet Sauvignon and hybrid vines. Wire-netting cages two metres high protect the grapes from the ravages of birds and wasps.

Although the company has a good reputation for dry sherries, wine maker Paul Erceg is also determined to win recognition as a quality red wine producer. Rather than join the industry-wide rush into white table wines, Windy Hill has made a specialty of reds: the biggest seller is the flagon Dry Red.

These red wines can be quite long-lived — the last straight Pinotage, 1975, was still drinking well in 1980. The 1976 Pinotage/Beaujolais, first of this line, attracted attention by scoring a silver medal. My own tastings of several more recent vintages show this to be a consistently soft, light, easy-drinking red wine which, owing to the fairly unusual blend, has a slightly different taste well worth trying.

There is also a Riesling-Sylvaner, clean but rather plain, and the first Cabernet Sauvignon 1980, slightly green but a very traditional, firm style. These are reliable wines.

A heavy crop of overhead-trellised Palomino grapes used for Windy Hill sherry.

SOUTH AUCKLAND

Villa Maria

Under the single-minded guidance of George Fistonich (44), a half-hectare vineyard near the Manukau Harbour at Mangere, South Auckland, has grown to become the largest privately-owned wine company in New Zealand.

The origins of Villa Maria lie in a tiny operation called Mountain Vineyards, which was run as a hobby by Dalmatian immigrant, Andrew Fistonich. Fistonich worked on the gumfields, then later made a few bottles of wine for himself and friends before becoming a licensed wine maker in 1949. When illness slowed him down, his son George Fistonich abandoned his career plans in carpentry, leased his father's vineyard, formed a new company, and bought a press, barrels and pumps from Maungatapu Vineyards at Tauranga. In 1961, Villa Maria Hock nosed out into the market.

The winery initially made its presence felt at the bottom end of the market. The slogan 'Let Villa Maria introduce you to wine' associated with the sale of sherries and quaffing table wines, created an image the company has only recently overcome. But in recent years Villa Maria has established an excellent track record in wine competitions.

Villa Maria relies almost entirely on contract growers. The old vineyard near the winery in Kirkbride Road, Mangere, is still there, covering six hectares predominantly planted in Palomino, Chardonnay and Rhine Riesling. But ninety-eight percent of grapes are drawn on contract from several North Island regions — Hawkes Bay, Gisborne, Te Kauwhata and Auckland (town milk supply farmers at Ihumatao, beside Auckland International Airport, have planted thirty hectares of wine grapes, which are sold to Villa Maria).

To a greater extent than its sister company, Vidal — bought by George Fistonich in 1976 — Villa Maria has concentrated its strengths in white, not red wines. Wine makers Harry Wright (who has since left) and Mark Polglase have produced a good range of medium wines based on Müller-Thurgau grapes, especially the big-selling Brookvale Riesling-Sylvaner. The 1982 Brookvale was a sweetish, low-acid wine with markedly more fruit than previous years; the 1983 vintage is a repeat performance.

Late Harvest Müller-Thurgau is a cut above Brookvale, being perfumed and grapy. Hawkes Bay Riesling-Sylvaner is yet another medium white wine and the 1982 had full, elegant fruit. From 1983 an

Harry Wright, who recently left Villa Maria, produced the company's famous line of Private Bin Sauternes.

Storage tanks at Villa Maria with Mangere Mountain as the backdrop.

unusually assertive Müller-Thurgau has emerged, strengthened by the inclusion of 'pressings' which is the juice extracted from the grapes by mechanical pressing after the 'free-run' juice has been drawn off.

Villa Maria has also been the home of a trio of superb sweet wines – Spätlese, Auslese (these two are no longer produced) and Private Bin Sauternes. The prime here is the Sauternes, an intense liqueous wine made by the freeze concentration technique. The early 1976 and 1977 vintages established this as an outstanding New Zealand wine, and the 1980 is superb once again – oily, concentrated but not cloying and offering a long, succulent finish.

The Gewürztraminer forms the other pinnacle of the Villa Maria range. The 1982 and other vintages show strong perfume, coupled with a firm, spicy, not fully dry flavour. A big, fruity Riesling-Sylvaner/Gewürztraminer 1981, then available in carafes, scored a notable distinction at the 1982 Easter Show, as it received the first gold medal awarded for a wine available in other than bottles only.

The Villa Maria stable of white wines also has Chardonnay, Chenin Blanc, Sémillon, Sauvignon Blanc, Rhine Riesling and Grey Riesling. The

Chardonnay is usually sold early, with dominant oak and fruit too young to show its paces. The Chenin Blanc 1982 is good, oak-aged and strong in varietal character.

Both 1982 and 1983 Villa Maria Sémillons are typically New Zealand in character, grassy and slightly sweet. The Sauvignon Blanc is excellent, herbaceous yet not too aggressive. The Rhine Riesling, produced from Ihumatao and Te Kauwhata fruit, has tended towards a sharp, rather acid style.

The reds have tended to be sound but not exceptional. A light but astringent 'Melesconera' was rather a conversation piece for some years, but the standard ampelography – science of the grapevine – texts do not list such a variety and this line has been discontinued. The top Villa Maria red wine is the Cabernet Sauvignon, a fast-maturing style. The 1981 wine is a good, gutsy red, full in flavour yet rounded and clearly made to be consumed early.

WAIKATO/BAY OF PLENTY

Because of the Land Wars in the nineteenth century, the Waikato, bounded to the east by the Coromandel Ranges and to the west by the Tasman, was settled by Europeans comparatively late. From 1880, however, the forests were cleared, swamps drained and dairy farms established. The foundation of the Government viticultural research station at Te Kauwhata in 1897 gave an early boost to grape growing and by 1982, forty-one growers had 336 hectares, or 5.7 percent of the country's total plantings, under vines.

Viticultural activity is still centred at Te Kauwhata, with the Cooks winery and vineyards, the Government research station (see the Research section in Chapter Two), the small Aspen Ridge winery, and numerous contract growers. Further afield near Pokeno is the de Redcliffe vineyard and close to Thames lies the only Chinese winery in New Zealand, Totara SYC. Thus there are only a few wineries in the Waikato, and a significant proportion—higher than elsewhere—of the grape crop is not even processed into wine. In 1980 the number of growers producing fruit for grape juice outnumbered those who were producing it for making wine. Although the major vineyards belonging to the wine companies are utilised for wine production, one-fifth of the Waikato grape crop in 1980 was sold for table use or grape juice.

Despite the dominating presence of Cooks, between 1975 and 1980 the region's relative importance declined, as new plantings spread to the East Coast and the South Island. Yields are lower than in the fertile Gisborne soils, and Te Kauwhata shares most of Auckland's climatic disadvantages: although temperatures and sunshine hours are generally higher than in the top European table wine regions, the rainfall is higher too.

Cooks see Te Kauwhata as a potential premium red wine district, a claim suggested but not yet confirmed by their own Cabernet Sauvignon, typically an elegant light red. Yet recent plantings have emphasised white wine grapes, reflecting the heavier demand for these wines. In 1980, the major varieties in the Waikato were, in order: Palomino, Müller-Thurgau, Chenin Blanc, Albany Surprise and Cabernet Sauvignon.

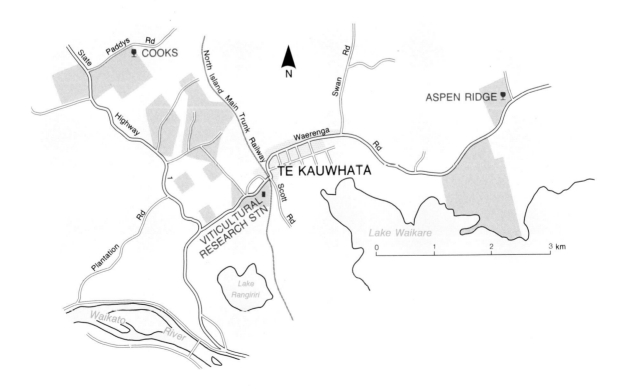

A corner of the de Redcliffe boutique vineyard in the Mangatawhiri Valley.

THAMES

N

0   1   2 km

State Highway 26

Frankton Thames Railway

Kauaeranga   Valley   Rd

Maramarahi   Rd

Waihou River

TOTARA SYC

*Vines displaying luxuriant vegetative growth at Cooks,
Te Kauwhata.*

Aspen Ridge

A very small winery near Lake Waikare, east of Te Kauwhata township, Aspen Ridge also markets a range of grape jellies and grape juices.

The company was established in 1963 by Alister McKissock—who also directed the Te Kauwhata research station from 1963 until his resignation in 1966—with the assistance of Nathan's liquor interests. The six-hectare vineyard on loam clay soils, badly run-down, includes such varieties as Gewürztraminer, Cabernet Sauvignon and Chardonnay.

Since Nathans severed their distribution link with Aspen Ridge, the wines have not been widely seen. A Chardonnay sampled at the winery was poor. Three reds, Spanish Red, Reserve Dry Red, and Cabernet Chambourcin were all fruity, purplish, and sweet. The prices asked for these wines are low.

The vineyard in mid-summer at Aspen Ridge.

Cooks

Following a 1967 proposal for the formation of a new wine company, Cooks burgeoned in the 1970s into a major force in the industry. Of late, however, the company has been engaged in a grim struggle to survive.

David Lucas—entrepreneur, retailer and the original driving force behind Cooks—noted the prosperity even of hybrid-producing wineries in the 1960s, and concluded that the planting out of *vinifera* vines should allow wines of superior quality to be made. Wrote Lucas in a widely circulated prospectus: 'The demand for wine of domestic production cannot be satisfied by present and known projected grape plantings. Additionally, about one-third of the present plantings are of poor quality grapes or are used by wine makers unable to produce either a consistent or a quality wine. There is thus an inviting and profitable opportunity to establish a major new vineyard in New Zealand.'

Cooks, whose name was chosen for its power to evoke thoughts of age and respectability, was sited at Te Kauwhata, as advised by Californian viticultural expert Professor Petrucci, who was impressed by the close parallel between the heat summation readings of Bordeaux and Te Kauwhata. The closeness of the Government research station and the Auckland market also swayed Cooks' decision. Eighty hectares of easily

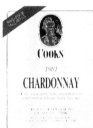

Cooks winery graces the Te Kauwhata skyline.

absence from the range and a disappointing 1979 release.

The Pinot Noir 1981, made from Hawkes Bay fruit, lacks body and seems to reflect use of unripe fruit – a pity, after the very promising, deep, 1978 private bin wine. And the pale, light Pinot Meunier is the only varietal red I have encountered from this once extensively planted variety in New Zealand.

Cooks Chasseur, one of the country's top selling wines, used until recently to be mediocre, sugary sweet and reflected the use of hybrid material. But since the 1981 release, bearing a new label, this blend of Müller-Thurgau, Chasselas and Chenin Blanc has sharply improved, to emerge clean, not too sweet and well-balanced.

Te Kauwhata Riesling-Sylvaner is probably the best known of Cooks' wide range of varietal white wines. As a group, Cooks' varietals – Chenin Blanc, Müller-Thurgau, Sylvaner, Chauché Gris, Sauvignon Blanc, Pinot Gris, Gewürztraminer, and Chardonnay – have more often than not been of a high standard, although high-priced. The Te Kauwhata Riesling-Sylvaner 1978, top commercially available wine in its category at the National Wine Competition, later impressed the French and won first prize in the Alsace Riesling class of a contest organised by Gault-Millau magazine. The 1983 vintage, only 9.5 percent alcohol, is a medium-dry, fruity wine in an easy-drinking style.

Cooks Chauché Gris – Grey Riesling – shows slightly stronger flavour than Müller-Thurgau, and the ability to develop well over several years – the 1979 vintage opened in 1983 had a full, earthy bouquet and a palate that had built up well with age. Pinot Gris has displayed varying form – the 1981 vintage very light and restrained; the 1982, produced for the first time from Hawkes Bay fruit, full of slightly smoky varietal character.

Sauvignon Blanc entered the Cooks range in 1982 in two versions, one made from fruit from Gisborne, the other from Hawkes Bay. Only the Hawkes Bay, Michael Hewitt Estate wine was successful – a pale green tinged, full-flavoured Sauvignon Blanc, muted slightly in its cut-grass taste by the rather pronounced sweetness. Chenin Blanc has not been consistently impressive, but Cooks Chenin Blanc 1982 and Fernhill Chenin Blanc 1982 are both slightly sweet, high acid, full bodied and clean wines.

Cooks Gewürztraminer rates alongside the country's best. The wines from the 1979, 1980 and 1982 vintages have captured pronounced varietal character, although the 1981 in this sense missed the boat. The gold medal Dry Gewürztraminer 1983 is a brute 13.2 percent alcohol, but the wine is not imbued with the very finest Gewürztraminer quality.

Chardonnay from Cooks is a champion wine, vying with McWilliam's and Delegat's for top New Zealand honours with this variety. Cooks 1980 Chardonnay has classic style, distinctly smoky with a beautiful complex balance of ripe fruit and oak. The 1981 was comparatively ordinary but in 1982 Cooks again produced a top Chardonnay – superbly perfumed, with a ripe, rather buttery taste. Cooks' Chardonnays

drink well when young and so far have peaked at around three years of age.

Also worth pursuing is the delicate Late Pick Müller-Thurgau, a gold medal winner from the 1983 vintage – a sweet dessert wine, nectareous and not at all cloying.

The winery has an imposing array of advanced technical equipment.

Natural light penetrates the winery interior.

de Redcliffe

De Redcliffe wines are crushed and fermented elsewhere, but blended and matured at the vineyard.

An attractive vineyard encircled by hills. Roses add a touch of real beauty at the end of the rows.

Only two blended wines, the Cabernet/Merlot and Chardonnay/Sémillon, have carried the de Redcliffe label, yet this isolated vineyard in the Mangatawhiri Valley has a reputation for producing wines that are out of the ordinary.

Wellington-born Chris Canning (45) returned to New Zealand in 1975 after many years in Europe, having tended vines in France and been part-owner of a vineyard in Italy. In a natural basin among bush-clad hills at the end of Lyons Road, off the Thames Highway, Canning began in 1976 to plant his own vineyard. On river silt soils with a gravel base, nine hectares are now established in Cabernet Sauvignon, Merlot, Pinot Noir, Chardonnay and Sémillon varieties.

De Redcliffe wines are crushed and fermented elsewhere, at a larger winery, to reduce capital outlay on equipment. Blending, wood treatment, maturation and sales however are handled at the estate. The vineyard shop is open only on Saturdays, or by appointment, and the wines are also available from some merchants and wine shops or by mail-order.

The Chardonnay/Sémillon is a dry, flavoursome wine, barrel-aged, with the typically assertive Sémillon character nicely reined in by the Chardonnay. The 1982 and 1983 vintages both drink well.

The silky Cabernet/Merlot 1980 was a lovely red, with a fragrant bouquet and firm Cabernet fruit softened by the Merlot. Home vineyard fruit was matured twenty-two months in new American oak casks, producing a medium-bodied red wine of unusual delicacy and finesse. As the result of heavy flooding around the vines during vintage, the 1981 Cabernet/Merlot was less successful. The 1982, an elegant light red needing more weight across the palate, at a cost around ten dollars looks over-priced.

The first de Redcliffe Pinot Noir will emerge from the 1984 vintage.

Morton Estate

The winery creates a strong impact on the highway near Katikati.

Traditionally the Bay of Plenty region has been of minor wine-making importance, with only two vineyards having been known to have existed, at Maungatapu and Maketu. Wide interest has consequently been aroused by the foundation of the new Morton Estate winery.

Morton Brown, a former Wellington car dealer who later invested in kiwifruit, erected his winery near Katikati on the main highway on the Auckland side of Tauranga. At present the company draws its grapes from Gisborne and from the home vineyard of ten and a half hectares, established on sloping volcanic soils in 1979.

John Hancock, the man partly responsible for putting Delegat's on a sound footing, is the wine maker. From the first vintage, 1983, a broad range of wines emerged, uniformly well made. Similar in style to the Delegat's, the Morton Estate Müller-Thurgau 1983 is crisp and flowery, with a delicate flavour. The dry Riesling-Sylvaner 1983 also extracts an unusually full aroma and flavour from the variety.

John Hancock does not like very pungent Gewürz-traminers, and his preference is reflected in the 1983 Morton Estate Gewürztraminer, a light and restrained style. There is also an elegant Müller-Thurgau/Gewürztraminer, showing an excellent balance of Müller-Thurgau fruitiness and spicy Gewürztraminer character.

The Sauvignon Blanc 1983, not aged in wood, has a ton of varietal character but rather too obtrusive sweetness. The success of the 1983 Chardonnay — awarded a gold medal at the NZ Easter Show 1984 — was a shot in the arm for the young company; this is a very elegant Chardonnay, full-bodied at thirteen percent alcohol and enhanced by the restrained wood treatment. One to drink from 1985 onwards.

The premium varietal range also includes Chenin Blanc, a dry wood-aged Sémillon, an Auslese Müller-Thurgau and a silver medal 1983 Cabernet Sauvignon.

John Hancock has built up something of a cult following, born during his successful years at Delegats.

Totara SYC

Ah Chan of Canton – 'Kumara Joe' to most people –
planted in 1925 a small plot of Albany Surprise table
grapes, together with kumara, to supply the Thames
market. Stanley Chan, no relation of Ah Chan
although from the same village in Canton, bought the
tiny vineyard in 1950, and started wine making. So
began Totara SYC Vineyards, the country's only
Chinese-owned wine company.

The name Totara SYC was derived from the Totara
Valley – near the winery site just outside Thames –
and Stanley Young Chan's initials. Stanley Chan's
mother's family brewed and sold rice wine in their
Canton shop; his father was a distiller before
emigrating to Dargaville at the turn of the century.
Today, this small, low-profile vineyard is run by two
sons of Stanley Chan, Ken (53) the managing director
and Gilbert (44) the wine maker.

The winery itself surprisingly presents to the visitor
a Spanish facade with a curved archway. Grapes are
drawn from all over the North Island, from the home
vineyard of seven hectares, another company vineyard
of six hectares at Kumeu planted in Müller-Thurgau,
Cabernet Sauvignon and Muscats, and from contract
growers at Te Kauwhata and Gisborne.

Up to a few years ago, Totara's reputation hinged
on its fortified wines and sweet white table wines. A
puzzlingly wide array of labels, too often claiming

Totara Vineyards – a Chenin Blanc worth trying.

Ken Chan heads a company with a strong export orientation, but in New Zealand the image is not as high as it could be.

'private-bin' status, won limited respect. Yet although the company is not generally considered a producer of quality wine, recent performances at competitions have been impressive — four gold medals at the 1982 National Wine Competition, including three for sherry, Golden, Brown and Cream.

Totara's strength in table wines is confined to white wines — the Cabernet Sauvignons are only of a quaffing standard. The wine that lingers most in the memory is the Riesling-Sylvaner 1979 — from a poor vintage, this displayed plenty of fruit and matured superbly. Totara produces bigger wines from this variety than do most other wineries.

Chenin Blanc is well handled here; the 1982 Chenin Blanc is typical, one of New Zealand's best, showing a good green-gold colour, strong Chenin flavour and crisp, but not sharp finish.

Totara Fu Gai is listed at most Chinese licensed restaurants; made to accompany Chinese cuisine, this blend of Chenin Blanc, Müller-Thurgau, Chasselas and Muscat makes fruity, slightly sweet, easy drinking. Another feature of this winery is its liqueurs, including Kiwifruit and the coffee based Totara Café, similar to the Mexican product Kahlua and sold at about half the price.

POVERTY BAY/EAST CAPE

From a paltry acreage of vines supplying the old Waihirere winery, since 1965 viticulture has swept the Gisborne plains. Corbans, Montana and Penfolds have large wineries in the area and by 1982 almost 200 grape growers had between them one-third of New Zealand's total area in vines. Although some have called Gisborne 'carafe country' — a reference to its fertile soils and heavy cropping ability — the region has emerged in the last decade as a mainstay of the whole industry; McWilliam's apart, all wine companies of any size draw at least some Gisborne fruit.

The East Cape, dominated by the Raukumara Ranges, has only very limited lowland areas ideal for viticulture. Grape growing is confined to the Poverty Bay flats around Gisborne, which form the largest of the coastal alluvial plains, and to smaller ones further north at Tolaga Bay and Tikitiki. Sheep and dairyfarming traditionally were the bread-and-butter activities of the plains, then maize and later process vegetables succeeded. The area devoted to viticulture stayed insignificant until late in the 1960s, when a decline in the profitability of small-holding pastoral farming encouraged farmers to look at grape growing. When Corbans and Montana began offering lucrative contracts, vineyards spread rapidly, reaching a total of 1922 hectares by 1982, more than any other region.

There remain some doubts over grape quality. Although the vines get ample sunshine, the soils are deep and highly fertile. With plentiful autumn rains, over-vigorous growth poses a real problem. The vines tend often to yield bumper crops of low acid, low sugar grapes suitable only for everyday wines. Even Bragato recognised in his handbook, Viticulture in New Zealand with Special Reference to American Vines, *published in 1906, that 'a vine planted in a rich loamy soil with an abundance of moisture ... will grow vigorously ... and yield a heavy crop of large berries. This condition, however, does not result in the production of a good wine: it can be made only with great difficulty...'*

To determine the effect heavy cropping has on the quality of finished wines, Corbans performed experiments on Müller-Thurgau vines planted in the Matawhero district; not surprisingly, subsequent tastings showed that the wines made from lighter cropping vines had superior bouquet and body.

Overall, Gisborne is best suited to the production of grapes for white wines. Here, Müller-Thurgau vines yield heavy crops of 20-25 tonnes per hectare, processed into the light fruity styles of the popular commercial wines. Gewürztraminer and Chardonnay have also both proven their potential, by producing several gold medal winning wines.

But red varieties appear to be ill-suited — ripening later, the berries tend to become swollen, at the cost of flavour and colour intensity. Cabernet Sauvignon has not performed well here.

The Poverty Bay region forms the bread basket of the New Zealand wine industry.

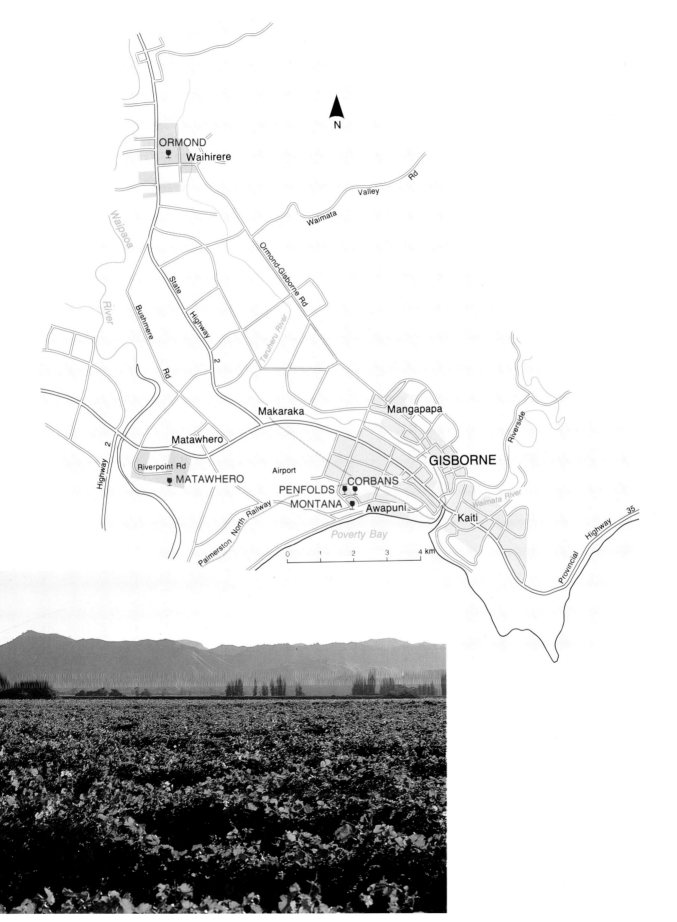

Corbans at Tolaga Bay, Penfolds at Tikitiki...

At Tikitiki, near Ruatoria, Maori landowners and Penfolds' expertise have combined, with the aid of Government finance, to establish vineyards. Having previously seen dairy farming, maize, peas and wheat fail the locals were originally wary of the idea. Multiple land ownership raised obstacles, as some blocks had from three to four hundred owners. Yet by 1980, twenty-eight hectares of Cabernet Sauvignon, Pinot Noir and Gewürztraminer were planted here, with further expansion planned. The gravelly soil, which drains more freely than Gisborne soil, has to contend with a marginally higher rainfall. The vineyards,

terraced down to the river, derive good drainage from a thick bed of river slate about a metre below the surface.

Penfolds' involvement in the venture included a forty-year contract for purchase of the grapes.

Bay of Islands Maoris last century uprooted vines in search of a root crop. The Maori-owned vineyards at Tikitiki, however, are a major commercial venture in an isolated region suffering from severe economic problems. On the left, Manu Mauheri; centre, Moon Koia; right, Fraser Taiapa.

Corbans' growers dominate plantings at Tolaga Bay.

The tiny rural settlement of Tolaga Bay, fifty-five kilometres north of Gisborne, and its surrounding vineyards, first attracted attention as the source of Corbans' fine 1976 and 1977 Chenin Blancs.

This was dairying country, until the closure of the local dairy factories and soaring transport costs forced the dairy farmers out. After Corbans invested in vineyards in the area and entered into partnership with Marshall Savidge — who provided the fruit for the early Chenin Blancs — interest in grape growing soared. Two

Maori corporation blocks, Paroa and Hauiti, have large vineyards established and several other local land-owners have contracts to supply Corbans. The area, a natural basin of flat river silts along the Uawa River, enjoys higher temperatures than the coast a few kilometres distant.

Matawhero

In a country earning increasing international praise for the standard of its Gewürztraminers, the small Matawhero winery has built a reputation second to none for its handling of this grape.

Wine maker Denis Irwin (38) heads the Irwin family's twenty-six-hectare vineyard in Riverpoint Road at Matawhero, near Gisborne City, established in 1969. Much of the crop from the vineyard is sold to larger wine companies, but Irwin has first choice of the available fruit, principally Gewürztraminer, Müller-Thurgau, Chenin Blanc, Chardonnay and Sauvignon Blanc.

So far, Matawhero's success has hinged primarily on Gewürztraminer and blends of Müller-Thurgau with Gewürztraminer. The Gewürztraminer is everything that wine of this variety should be: pungent, very aromatic, unmistakably spicy in taste. The first vintage, 1976, was made in a converted chicken shed and scored a silver medal at that year's National Wine Competition. The 1978 scored a gold medal and remains a magnificent wine. Over the years the style has fluctuated from dry to medium-dry but consistently the wines have captured intense Gewürztraminer flavour. The Gewürztraminer 1983 is a powerful wine, deep in colour, and needs a couple of years to realize its potential. The wine is deliberately made to last.

The Traminer/Riesling-Sylvaner is crisp and flavoursome — the 1982 vintage is outstanding. The Riverpoint Riesling-Sylvaner once used to be back-blended with Gewürztraminer juice, but now is entirely made from Müller-Thurgau; the 1983 version is perfumed and deep flavoured, carrying the dry style well.

Chardonnay is rarely seen but shows promise. Awarded a gold medal at the 1982 Easter Show competition, Matawhero's 1980 Chardonnay is an elegant, oaky style with ripe fruit, needing lengthy bottle-aging to round out. The vineyard also has a very good Chenin Blanc, with strong fruit flavour and a proven ability to mature well.

Matawhero's efforts are mainly devoted to white wine production — but the reds are also enjoyable. One recalls the Beaujolais/Pinotage 1976, Pinot Noir 1977 and Cabernet Sauvignon 1978 all showing the slender body typical of Gisborne red wines. The 1980 Pinot Noir displays true varietal fruit and ample tannin. The 1981 Estate Red is a light blend that includes Gamay

Beaujolais, Merlot and Cabernet Sauvignon. And from 1983 appeared the first straight Gamay Beaujolais, aged in French oak for seven months and capturing plenty of typical Beaujolais character.

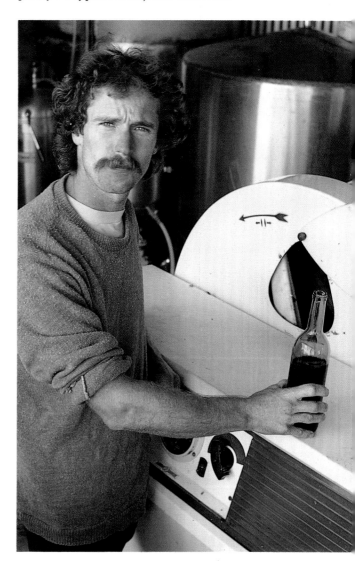

Denis Irwin shares a bottle of Cabernet Sauvignon at the press during vintage.

The reputation of Matawhero has spread far from this true 'boutique'-scale winery and its encircling vineyards.

Montana

Montana early in its expansion announced an ambition which was extraordinary for the wine industry: to produce not only the most but the best wine in the country. Over a decade ago, in a dramatic burst it overhauled the traditional market leaders, McWilliam's and Corbans, and at present commands a hefty thirty-seven percent share of the market. The range of products is sound throughout and several, notably the Marlborough Sauvignon Blanc and Marlborough Rhine Riesling, must be rated among New Zealand's top wines.

With vineyards at Mangatangi, Gisborne and Marlborough, wineries at Gisborne and Marlborough and a bottling and warehousing facility at Auckland, Montana's is a vastly fragmented operation. Here, the focus is on the firm's North Island operations, especially in Gisborne, where wine maker Rosemary Butler oversees production. Montana's presence in Blenheim — the vineyards, winery and Marlborough regional wines — are treated later in the Marlborough section.

Ivan Yukich, founder of this giant company, arrived in New Zealand from Dalmatia as a youth of 15. After returning to his homeland, he came back to New

Montana's winery at Gisborne is controlled by Rosemary Butler, a wine maker who qualified at Roseworthy College in South Australia.

Ormond

Ormond is the label Montana uses to market its second-string range. Called Waihirere for fifty years, the old winery now renamed Ormond lies in the Waihirere Valley, fifteen kilometres north of Gisborne. Until the 1970s the winery was owned by descendants of the founder, Friedrich Wohnsiedler.

Wohnsiedler pioneered wine making in Gisborne after the false start by Marist missionaries, who landed by mistake at Turanganui (Gisborne) in 1850 and there planted vines before departing for their original destination, Hawkes Bay. Wohnsiedler, born on a tributary of the Rhine, arrived in New Zealand around the turn of the century. When patriots laid waste his Gisborne small-goods business during the 1914-1918 War, Wohnsiedler moved out and onto the land. He planted vines at Ormond in 1921. The first vintage, a sweet red, was labelled simply as 'Wine'. By the 1930s Waihirere was also producing sherry, port and madeira.

When Friedrich Wohnsiedler died in 1956 his vineyard only covered four hectares. In 1961 a rapid expansion programme began using new capital invested by wine and spirit merchants, a large forty-hectare vineyard was planted and production soared. But in 1970, liquidity problems forced the family business to accept further injections of capital and, after a series of financial restructurings, the Wohnsiedler family eventually lost control altogether. By 1973 Montana had completely absorbed Waihirere.

For several years the Waihirere label was retained for Montana's more humble wines, then the Waihirere brand was dropped and replaced by Ormond. The Ormond label is aimed at the young, price-conscious buyer: Ormond sells a lifestyle while Montana's Marlborough wines instead more seriously emphasise grape varieties. The Ormond brand was used to open up the wine cask market in New Zealand—a move soon copied by other firms.

Showing signs of advanced age, the old Waihirere winery is today used mainly for maturing fortified wines. The vineyard of forty hectares is mainly planted in Müller-Thurgau, Dr Hogg Muscat and Chardonnay.

Ormond wines are clean but plain. To promote the Gisborne regional image, the wines are all named after local features. Chandos and Hassendean are light everyday whites, without any real fruit interest, the first being fairly sweet, the other medium dry. Of the reds, Oakleigh Burgundy is also fractionally sweet. Woodland Claret is a more traditional red, light and dry. These non-vintage wines in bottles, carafes and casks sell at reasonable prices.

The Ormond vineyard is one of the first to see—and lose—the sun each day, owing to its easterly site.

HAWKES BAY

Hawkes Bay, one of New Zealand's pioneer wine-making districts which today still retains its traditional importance, may also have the potential to become one of the world's great wine regions.

Here is located the oldest wine-making concern in New Zealand still under the same management — Mission Vineyards, established by the Catholic Society of Mary in 1851. The oldest winery still operating, erected in stages from the 1860s can be found at the Te Mata Estate. In 1982, with 1891 hectares (or thirty-two percent of the national total), Hawkes Bay ranked a close second to Poverty Bay in the extent of its vineyards. Yet the region's proven ability to produce outstanding table wines, red and white, is still largely untapped.

The terrain of Hawkes Bay varies from the rugged inland ranges, the Ruahines and Kawekas, climbing to over 1600 metres, to the coastal Heretaunga Plains. In this sheltered environment, protected by the high country from the prevailing westerly winds, agriculture thrives: pastoralism, process cropping, orcharding and market gardening. And on the margins of the plains, at Taradale, Te Mata, Haumoana and in the Esk Valley, the favourably dry and sunny climate supports an easy growth of the vine.

Hawkes Bay is one of the sunniest areas of the country; the city of Napier, for instance, enjoys slightly longer sunshine hours and warmer temperatures than Bordeaux. In summer, anticyclonic conditions sometimes lead to droughts; such weather can produce grapes with high sugar contents and forms a key advantage of Hawkes Bay for viticulture.

One drawback is that the easterly facing aspect renders Hawkes Bay vulnerable to easterly cyclonic depressions and their accompanying rainfall. Some of the heaviest rains ever recorded in New Zealand have descended on the region. In bad years such as 1979, the vineyards of Hawkes Bay can be deluged with autumn rains. Nevertheless, in most years the autumn rainfall is markedly less than at Gisborne.

One of Hawkes Bay's prime viticultural assets is its wide range of soil types: the Heretaunga Plains consist mainly of fertile alluvial soils over gravelly sub-soils deposited by the rivers and creeks draining the surrounding uplands.

The pioneer wine makers headed close to the lower hills of Hawkes Bay as the best sites. At the 1896 Conference of Australasian Fruitgrowers held in Wellington, Whangarei vine grower L. Hanlon enthused: '... on the gently sloping limestone hills that are so characteristic of the (Hawkes Bay) district ... may be found hundreds of ideal sites for vineyards. In some places the hills present the peculiar truncated appearance of the vine-clothed hills of the celebrated Côte d'Or district in France...' But recently most vineyards have been planted on the plains to secure higher grape yields.

Vines have been grown in Hawkes Bay since the early years of European habitation. The first vineyard was established in 1851 and by the early 1890s the first commercial enterprises had appeared. When Romeo Bragato visited in 1895 he was greatly impressed by the achievements of Henry Tiffen, the Mission and others. 'The Hawkes Bay province is, in my opinion, the most suitable for vine-growing I have visited in New Zealand.'

But only in the past fifteen years has viticulture reached significant proportions in Hawkes Bay: in the late 1930s, for instance, only twenty-five hectares of vines were grown in the province. Then in 1967 contract growing extended to Hawkes Bay. Where previously the established wineries had concentrated their plantings in the Esk Valley, Taradale and Haumoana areas, the arrival of contract grape growing opened up new sub-regions, notably the Fernhill-Korokipo district. By 1980 the vineyards of 120 grape growers stretched over a forty-kilometre belt running

from the Esk Valley, at the north end of the plains, to Te Mata in the south. With the 1975 plantings of 537 hectares soaring to 1891 hectares by 1982, viticulture in Hawkes Bay has undergone a phenomenal period of growth.

Yet although McWilliam's, with a famous series of Cabernet Sauvignons dating back to 1965 and several extraordinarily fine Chardonnays, has proven the province's ability to produce some superb table wines, vine plantings to 1980 almost eschewed these varieties. The 1980 vineyard survey revealed that Müller-Thurgau constituted half of Hawkes Bay's vines — yet only McWilliam's, with their Late Pick Riesling-Sylvaners, had made wines of interest from this grape. The only other varieties to top 100 hectares planted were Chenin Blanc and Palomino: the first still largely unproven in the area, the second suitable only for sherry.

However, in the last few years more widespread plantings have occurred of premium classical varieties like Cabernet Sauvignon, Sauvignon Blanc, Chardonnay and Chardonnay and Gamay Beaujolais. As the wines from these vines come on stream, it will become even clearer how much better Hawkes Bay can do than wines such as Cresta Doré and Bakano.

There are nine wineries here, ranging in size from Eskdale Winegrowers with only seven hectares in vines, to McWilliam's with company vineyards covering 360 hectares.

In the Esk Valley, Eskdale Winegrowers has its winery and vineyard, and larger companies like McWilliam's and Glenvale cultivate extensive vineyards.

Brookfields

Peter Robertson of Brookfields Vineyards at Meeanee typifies the recent influx of dedicated table wine enthusiasts into several of the small Hawkes Bay wineries.

Brookfields, traditionally a producer of sherry, was founded in 1937 by Richard Ellis, born in Hawkes Bay. The Ellis family retained ownership for 40 years. Robertson (33) is a BSc graduate whose interest in wine making was aroused when he was employed as a student at Barker's fruit winery at Geraldine in the South Island. After spending two years at McWilliam's, working his way up from labourer to laboratory chemist, Robertson, with his wife Ngaire, took over the old winery and three-hectare vineyard in 1977.

Up to and including the 1981 vintage, Brookfields had to rely heavily on Müller-Thurgau and Chasselas grape varieties. But recently Gewürztraminer, Pinot Gris, Rhine Riesling and Cabernet Sauvignon have come on stream, with Chardonnay soon to follow. The home vineyard remains small, and about three-fourths of the grape intake is bought from Hawkes Bay growers.

The wines I have tasted have been sound although not memorable: a dry, light Riesling-Sylvaner; an easy-drinking, pale Müller-Thurgau; a crisp, dry Pinot Meunier rosé. Of late a fruity, medium Autumn Muscat, a dry Gewürztraminer and medium-dry Chenin Blanc have filled out the range, with the first Cabernet Sauvignon due for release in 1984.

Peter and Ngaire Robertson — scored one silver and seven bronze medals at the 1983 National Wine Competition.

Eskdale

On the Napier-Taupo road in the Esk Valley lies one of Hawkes Bay's smallest and most individual vineyards.

Kim Salonius (41) came to Auckland from his native Canada in 1964 to read for a degree in history. Later, while advancing his medieval studies in Europe, his interest switched to wine making. By 1973 his first vines were planted.

Eskdale's only source of grapes is the seven-hectare home vineyard, established in Chardonnay, Gewürztraminer, Cabernet Sauvignon and Pinot Noir. Three wines are regularly made, while Eskdale Pinot Noir appears occasionally. The award of silver medals to two early releases, Cabernet Sauvignon 1977 and Chardonnay 1978, amounted to an auspicious beginning; the Chardonnay, particularly for a wine made from fruit off young vines, showed good flavour. From the adverse 1979 vintage, no wine was made apart from a small amount of Chardonnay.

Probably uniquely among the country's table wine makers, Kim Salonius ages all his wines in oak. The Chardonnay spends up to five months in wood — Yugoslav oak for the 1981 wine, French Limousin oak in 1982. The 1982 Chardonnay shows firm and true Chardonnay character, and more restrained oak handling than the rather woody 1981 wine.

Three vintages of Gewürztraminer I have tasted have been very different in style. 1978 lacked typical varietal character; in 1980, the wine was filled out well by the use of oak; but the Gewürztraminer 1982, is

Kim and Trish Salonius — Kim is the only medievalist among New Zealand's wine-making fraternity.

a real style departure, full bodied and sweet with light yet definable spice.

Of the red wines, the Cabernet Sauvignon has not so far been entirely successful. The pleasant, light 1977 soon faded, and my tastings of the 1978 and 1981 have not confirmed these as sound cellaring material. The 1980 Pinot Noir showed rich colour, but was dominated by oak.

Eskdale Winegrowers may not currently rank among the country's top boutique producers, yet the white wines particularly show an individuality that can be quite absorbing. The range is sold largely from the gate and through a few wine shops and merchants.

Glenvale

The approach to the rambling complex of buildings.

Hillsides closely covered with timber ring the Glenvale winery.

For several decades, Glenvale captured a large slice of the market for sherry. Under the Esk Valley label, in recent years the winery has also emerged as a producer of table wines, usually rather plain but showing a dramatic rise in quality from the 1983 vintage.

Two young brothers, Robbie Bird (30), who studied at Davis University of California, and Don (28), who spent time at Roseworthy College in Australia, run this large, family-owned company. In 1933 their grandfather, Englishman Robert Bird, bought five hectares of land at Bay View, north of Napier, planning to establish a market garden and orchard. But during the Depression returns for grapes of under twopence per pound soon encouraged Bird to enter the wine industry. In the original cellar, a tunnel scooped out of the hillside, Glenvale wines were vinted using the humble Albany Surprise variety.

Today the firm draws one-third of its grape intake from local contract growers and the rest from its seventy-five hectares of company vineyards — fifty-five hectares in the Esk Valley and twenty hectares at Bay View. Formerly the predominant vines were Müller-Thurgau, Seibels, Baco 22A and Chasselas but recently Gewürztraminer, Cabernet Sauvignon and Muscat have also been planted.

Glenvale's production is still around half fortified wine and its Extra Strength Sherry, at twenty-six percent alcohol by volume, has its loyal enthusiasts. But in 1976 the release of two varietal table wines — Müller-Thurgau and Sonnengold (Chasselas) — marked the company's serious move into the table wine market. Earlier Glenvale table wines had had a deservedly low image.

Esk Valley white wines from vintages early in the 1980s tended to be rather plain. My tastings included the 1980 Chablis and Moselle, both light, clean, low-priced hybrid wines; Müller-Thurgau 1981, pleasant but rather bland; a white Pinot Noir 1981, lacking any real depth; and a Riesling-Sylvaner/Gewürztraminer 1982 also short of fruit intensity.

The far superior Esk Valley releases from 1983 are led by two silver medal wines, Chenin Blanc and Chardonnay. The Chenin Blanc 1983 is a big, ripe-tasting medium style that was already drinking well at less than one year old. The Chardonnay 1983 is also full bodied, dry, with restrained wood character derived from several months aging in French Limousin oak puncheons. Together, these enjoyable wines undoubtedly represent a decisive forward step for Glenvale.

The red wines have usually not been impressive. Claret 1979 was a rough, obviously hybrid red and the 1980 Cabernet Sauvignon, although reasonably robust, lacked flavour complexity. But the rise in the quality of Glenvale wines from 1983 was confirmed by the winning of the trophy for top blended red wine, at that year's National Wine Competition, by Esk Valley Claret 1983, a Cabernet Sauvignon and Merlot blend.

Glenvale fortified wines in wood storage. The company has a heavy share of the market for dessert wines.

Lombardi

Italian traditions in wine making are followed at this small, family-owned winery near Havelock North. In 1948 an Englishman, W.H. Green, and his wife, planted a 1.2-hectare vineyard on a soldier's rehabilitation block in Te Mata Road. Mrs Tina Green, born in the Bay of Naples, turned to her grandparents in Italy for wine-making advice, and 1959 brought the first Lombardi vintage.

Today the founders' son Tony (32), a Massey University chemistry graduate, runs the company. The three-hectare vineyard is planted in Muscat, Seibel, Black Hamburgh, Pinotage, Müller-Thurgau, Chasselas, Baco 22A and Palomino vines.

Production is still centred on fortified wines; golden sherry is a strong seller. But the vineyard specialties are Italian-style liqueurs and vermouths. Vermouths range from Dry (white) to Vermouth di Torino (medium red) and Vermouth Bianco (sweet white). The liqueurs are based on essences imported from Italy.

Table wines sampled at the winery — Riesling-Sylvaner, Pinotage and Baco Bianco — were all clean quaffing wines. Most of the output is sold at the gate and the Lombardi range is only rarely seen beyond Hawkes Bay.

Mrs Tina Green, born in Italy and determined to reproduce in Hawkes Bay the wine styles of her native country.

McWilliam's

Bob Knappstein, McWilliam's production manager since the retirement of Tom McDonald, has several outstanding Chardonnays to his credit.

Once the dominant force of the New Zealand wine industry — with Cresta Doré, Marque Vue and Bakano virtually household names — McWilliam's, although no longer nationally number one, still rules in the Bay.

The company was wholly Australian-owned until 1962. A branch for the distribution of McWilliam's Australian wines had opened in Auckland in 1928 and later, in the conviction that their interests would be best advanced by establishing a winery locally, several members of the McWilliams family toured the country inspecting potential wine-making regions. The result was the founding of McWilliam's Wines (NZ) Ltd in 1944. After the first plantings of vines at Te Awanga in 1947, the first vintage followed in 1952.

The company grew rapidly until 1961, when it merged with McDonald's Wines to become the largest winery in New Zealand. McDonald's, once a familiar dessert wine label, dated back to 1897. Bartholomew Steinmetz, a native of Luxembourg, had left his position as a lay brother at the Society of Mary's Mission Vineyards to run his own two-hectare vineyard, on land formerly part of Henry Tiffen's Greenmeadows estate. A fourteen-year-old labourer called Tom McDonald began work there in 1921 — and by 1926 had taken over the business.

Keen to increase production, Tom McDonald passed control to the Christchurch-based brewers and merchants Ballins in 1944 but stayed on as manager. McDonald, who retired from the post of McWilliam's production manager in 1976, and later chaired the Wine Institute from 1980 to 1982, for decades dominated the Hawkes Bay wine scene.

In a deal to secure the involvement of New Zealand brewery interests, in 1962 the shareholding of the Australian parent company was reduced. Today, Lion Breweries with forty-five percent has the largest shareholding, together with McWilliam's Australia, still holding twenty one percent, and Dominion Breweries has thirteen percent. The participation in McWilliam's of these liquor distribution heavyweights has traditionally ensured McWilliam's wines of a place on most of the country's merchant shelves and hotel wine lists. Despite this, in the face of aggressive competition, McWilliam's former market share supremacy has faded to about eleven to twelve percent.

McWilliam's production manager Bob Knappstein oversees three winery sites — the old McDonald's winery at Taradale; a new multi-million dollar winery development in the Pandora industrial area of Napier, with three crushers connected to silo juice-drainers fifteen metres high; and the main Faraday Street winery on the site of an old quarry, where the fermentations and bottling are still carried out.

155

McWilliam's grapes are drawn entirely from the Hawkes Bay region. The company's own 360 hectares of vineyards are widely scattered around the Bay, with Müller-Thurgau the most widely established variety (150 hectares), plus Palomino (53 hectares), Cabernet Sauvignon (50 hectares), red hybrids (21 hectares) and Gamay Beaujolais (18 hectares). Contract growers nonetheless supply over half of the annual McWilliam's grape intake.

Fortified sales remain strong. At the top of the range, old wood-aged material is marketed under the Saccone and Speed label – Pale Dry Fino Sherry, Fine Old Ambrosia Sherry and the Finest Rich Tawny Port.

Only two table wines have over the years shown real class – McWilliam's Chardonnay and McWilliam's Cabernet Sauvignon. Of the reds, Bakano, Gamay Beaujolais and Cabernet Sauvignon are all well-known to wine enthusiasts. Bakano up to and including the 1978 vintage was a sharp, light hybrid red – often ten or fifteen-year-old bottles show up at tastings in drinkable condition yet barely improved. In 1979, a poor year when McWilliam's varietal Cabernet Sauvignon was not produced, the Bakano label had a detectable, light Cabernet character. The 1981 vintage is ruby red, light in body and short on aroma, but clean and pleasant.

Gamay Beaujolais is a relative late comer to the commercial range. The early experimental 1977 wine had a degree of Beaujolais' supple charm; unfortunately, the widely available 1979 to 1982 releases have lacked this variety's usual fruity appeal.

The famous Cabernet Sauvignon is altogether a different story. McWilliam's Cabernets form a suc-

Tom McDonald, well into his seventies, among thirty-five-year-old Cabernet Sauvignon vines at Greenmeadows; the McWilliam's Cabernet Sauvignon 1967 he opened mid-morning, although fading, was mellow and deeply scented.

cession – broken by the poor 1972 – of classic reds which, since the superb 1965, have proved beyond doubt New Zealand's ability to produce red wines of top class. Tom McDonald, who made the wine up to 1975 and realised early the crucial importance of maturing red wine in quality oak cooperage, says his Cabernets were deliberately made to keep – the 1966, opened in 1983, had a mellow, deep flavour and a lovely bouquet of violets and all the other delights that fine old Cabernet smells of.

Since the 1976 vintage, when Bob Knappstein assumed responsibility for production of the wine, the trend has been away from the firm, tannic reds of McDonald's heyday to a lighter, softer, faster-maturing style. The inclusion of material from young vines in McWilliam's newer vineyards has also been a factor. Among recent vintages the 1978 was a fragrant, light red, at five years old nearing its peak. The 1980 – no 1979 was made – once again is a pleasant, sound wine but not one for cellaring. Five years rather than the former ten to fifteen appears to be the average time necessary to mature these reds.

Of McWilliam's white wines, the Chardonnay clearly is the pick of the bunch. In the best years – 1974, 1978, 1980 and 1981 – it is the equal of most French white Burgundies. Although the mouth-filling, deeply-scented 1974 Chardonnay was for many observers a revelation of how outstanding New Zealand white wines can be, McWilliam's have been slow to work the wine into commercial quantity – in 1984, however, phylloxera-infected vines at Taradale were replaced, and new Chardonnay vines were established at Bay View.

The famous 1978 Chardonnay, aged for eight months in American oak, was the first one treated in wood. The 1980 and 1981 wines are again full-bodied, austere Chardonnays, showing strong oak influence but with powerful fruit to match. In average years like 1977, although leaner, the wine remains stylish; in poor years, like 1975 and 1979, no Chardonnay is released.

McWilliam's have not yet marketed a wide range of varietal white wines. A heavy reliance on the Müller-Thurgau grape was seen in the late 1970s, when six different wines were based on that variety, including a stop-fermented, full-flavoured Late Pick Riesling-Sylvaner, unfortunately no longer in the range.

Cresta Doré over the years has been a sound, very plain dry white. The best version yet is the silver medal 1983, a good, solid, not especially dry wine showing more depth on the palate than usual. Both the dry Riesling-Sylvaner and medium Müller-Thurgau are pleasant, uncomplicated white wines.

White Burgundy, introduced to the McWilliam's range in 1982, proved no substitute for the Chardonnay. Made from unspecified varieties, this dry medium-bodied white has a disappointingly dull flavour. Another first release, Chenin Blanc 1983, is a good flavoursome wine, medium-dry, with typical acidity balanced by reasonable body and a slight sweetness.

Gewürztraminer is now coming to the fore, after many years of producing experimental wines from low-grade vines. Opened in 1983, McWilliam's Roter Traminer 1975 was still firm, with a full and honeyish bouquet – but hardly any varietal spice.

In the tasting room at the old McDonald's winery in Church Road, Taradale, scarce wines like the Chardonnay can be bought. Also look for the Riesling Ice Wine, a fine, scented dessert wine, intensely flavoured.

McWilliam's Taradale winery, snug against the Taradale hills, is the old McDonald's winery and now caters for cellar sales.

Müller-Thurgau vines at McWilliam's vineyard at Haumoana in mid-March.

Mission

The Society of Mary, housed in a cluster of wooden buildings in the midst of lawns, trees and vines at the base of the Taradale hills, is New Zealand's only nineteenth-century producer of wines still under the same management.

The present site is the last of several occupied by the Marist mission during its long history in Hawkes Bay. Father Lampila and two lay brothers, Florentin and Basil, after mistaking the Poverty Bay coast for their real destination, Hawkes Bay, planted vines near Gisborne in 1850. A year later they moved south and planted more vines at Pakowhai, near Napier. The story goes that in 1852, on a return visit to Poverty Bay, Father Lampila found the abandoned vineyard bearing a small crop of grapes, made a barrel of sacramental wine and shipped it to Napier. But the seamen broached the cargo, drank the wine — and the cask completed its journey full of sea water.

A Maori chief, Puhara, took the French missionaries under his protection at Pakowhai. The brothers taught and nursed the local Maoris, and gardens and vineyards were laid out. After Puhara was killed, however, in an inter-tribal clash in 1857, the brothers were forced to move again, this time to Meeanee.

For several decades wine production at Meeanee was very limited, sufficient only to supply the brothers' needs for sacramental and table wines. A son of a French peasant wine maker, Brother Cyprian, arrived in 1871 to take charge of wine making — but not until 1895 were the first recorded sales made, mainly of red wine.

The Society of Mary is commercially involved in wine production in order to fund the Marist Seminary.

Two years later, local rivers burst their banks, flooding the Meeanee plains and inundating the Mission cellars. After deciding to shift to higher ground, the Society of Mary bought 240 hectares of the dead Henry Tiffen's land at Greenmeadows and established a four-hectare vineyard there. But not until 1910, after further disastrous floods, was the seminary itself moved to Greenmeadows; the wooden building was cut into sections and hauled there by steam engine. Fire almost destroyed the wine vaults in 1929, and thousands of gallons of wine were lost in the Napier earthquake of 1931, but of late nature appears to have made its peace with the Mission.

Until the end of the 1970s Mission wines, often mediocre and lacking depth, were hindered by a lack both of finance and of advanced wine making equipment. To many consumers, a halo appeared to encircle bottles of Mission wine, yet medal successes were few. The improved industry-wide standards left the church authorities with a basic decision: to be left further behind, or to compete.

The result was a programme of major expansion, designed to lift both the production level and the standards of Mission table wines. $250,000 was allocated for winery equipment and vineyard improvements. New plantings at Meeanee, plus an upgrading of the Taradale vineyards, have concentrated on Müller-Thurgau, Cabernet Sauvignon, Pinot Gris, Sauvignon Blanc, Chasselas, Sémillon, Gewürztraminer and Merlot vines. At present the Mission-owned vineyards cover forty-three hectares,

Monastic routines survive in the late twentieth century at the Mission's Catholic Seminary. Wine was produced from the beginning to supply the priests' sacramental and table needs.

with about twenty percent of grapes bought from contract growers.

The 1979 vintage marked a turning-point in the standard of the Mission's wines. New labelling helped, but behind the more sophisticated marketing lay a leap forward in the flavour intensity. The Mission Sylvaner/Riesling-Sylvaner 1979, for instance (previously called Riesling Hock) was full-bodied and flavoursome; that year's Chasselas was a well-handled version of the variety, dry and surprisingly robust.

The range of white table wines now covers Tokay d'Alsace, Gewürztraminer, St Mary Riesling-Sylvaner, Chardonnay, White Burgundy, Sauvignon Blanc and Sémillon/Sauvignon Blanc. In 1983 the Mission produced a fine Tokay d'Alsace (Pinot Gris) with powerful bouquet and taste, and strong acidity, making this a good cellaring prospect. A consistent style of Tokay d'Alsace has run through the 1981 to 1983 vintages; the wine is uniformly full-bodied, medium-dry, and more forceful than other New Zealand wines of this grape.

Of equal interest is the Sémillon/Sauvignon Blanc 1982, one of the first blends produced here from the two Bordeaux grapes. Strong and stalky in bouquet, this clean, sharp, rather aggressive dry wine partners seafood well. The Sauvignon Blanc 1983 is also firm, fresh and full of varietal character.

The White Burgundy 1982 has definite hints of herbaceous, Sémillon or Sauvignon Blanc aroma, and a broad flavour. The 1980 and 1982 Chardonnays are slow maturing styles, rather dominated by oak for the first couple of years but with the depth of fruit to repay cellaring.

St Mary Riesling-Sylvaner is this vineyard's medium, commercial white wine. Pleasantly fruity, with a touch of spice, St Mary is made largely from Müller-Thurgau, with some Chasselas, and back-blended with Gewürztraminer. The 1981 was generous in fruit, the 1983 rather lighter.

The Mission red wines were once distinctively light and pale, verging on rosés. Mission Pinot, made from old Pinot Meunier vines, was soft and fruity and made an ideal chilled luncheon wine. The Reserve Claret, formerly called Cabernet Pinot and a blend of

Cabernet Sauvignon and Pinot Noir, even from the 1981 vintage is red/orange to the eye and deficient in body.

Mission Cabernet Sauvignon, partly due to a shortage of new oak casks, has never approached McWilliam's standard. The 1980 Cabernet has deeper fruit than usual for this wine, but is lacking in complexity. Pinot Noir looks more promising. The 1982 has a true Pinot bouquet, light body and plenty of flavour – a step forward for Mission reds.

The brothers' bottle-fermented sparkling wine, Fontanella, blended from Pinot Gris and Pinot Meunier, has not been made for several years.

Brother Osika, a Tongan who has spent twelve years as a lay brother, heads the Mission's viticultural activity.

Ngatarawa

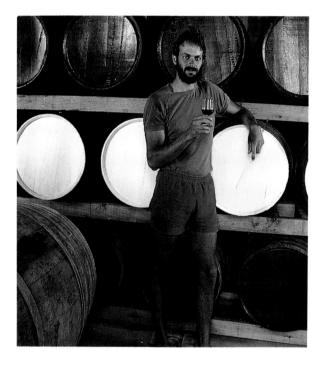

His impressive academic record and family background mean Alwyn Corban's performance at Ngatarawa will be closely watched.

The sole new wine company to emerge in Hawkes Bay in the last decade, Ngatarawa Wines lies a ten minutes' drive south of Hastings, at Bridge Pa.

Ngatarawa is a partnership formed in 1981 between the Glazebrook family, of the 2400-hectare Washpool sheep station, and Alwyn Corban — son of Alex Corban, the Wine Institute's first chairman — who qualified with a master's degree in oenology and viticulture at the University of Davis, California. The winery is based on a converted stables, built of rimu and totara almost a century old, and the labels carry a stylised horse's head.

The vineyard, which yielded its first crop in 1984, covers 10.5 hectares of Sauvignon Blanc, Rhine Riesling, Chardonnay, Cabernet Sauvignon and Merlot. But 1982 was the winery's first vintage, based on contract-grown Te Kauwhata grapes.

Ngatarawa looks to have a sound future — the few wines so far released show signs of skilled wine making. Of the two Müller-Thurgaus, one dry and the other medium, the Müller-Thurgau Dry 1982 impresses one as a clean, crisp wine, handling the dry style well. Sauvignon Blanc appears promising — made from Hawkes Bay fruit, briefly aged in oak, the 1983 vintage scored silver at that year's national competition.

A pair of Cabernet Sauvignons came from the 1982 vintage. One, labelled Ngatarawa Cabernet Sauvignon, spent twelve months in new French oak, and looks set for a steady improvement over several years. The Stables Red is an earlier drinking style, not aged in oak, already smooth at a couple of years old. Each red has pleasing body and colour.

At Ngatarawa the winery is based in converted stables, with a vineyard bar licence planned.

Te Mata

This historic, recently rejuvenated winery has in recent years built up a strong following for its magnificent red wines.

Bernard Chambers, a member of the wealthy landowning family that ran Te Mata Station, as a hobby in 1892 planted a hectare of vines supplied by the Mission brothers. The vines flourished, leading Chambers to convert a stable erected in 1872 into his cellar, to employ an Australian wine maker and, in 1896, to plunge into commercial wine production.

By 1909 the Chambers vineyard was the largest in the country, annually producing 54,000 litres of wine from the fourteen hectares of Pinot Meunier, Shiraz, Cabernet Sauvignon, Rhine Riesling and Verdelho vines. Commented the NZ Journal of Agriculture in May 1914: 'Mr Chambers' wines are principally hocks, claret and sweet, and are commanding a large sale.'

But from this peak, production declined and eventually during the Depression the vineyard went into receivership. A series of new owners failed to restore the vineyard's fortunes.

The revival of Te Mata's reputation began in 1974. Michael Morris and John Buck, both established wine judges, acquired the run-down company. The cellars, built of brick and native timbers, were restored to their original condition and equipped with stainless steel tanks and new oak casks. Local growers with shares in the company planted around thirty hectares of new vines, predominantly Cabernet Sauvignon, Sauvignon Blanc and Chardonnay. Buck, convinced of Hawkes Bay's potential to produce red wines of world class — given the correct combination of site, soils and grape varieties — planted his own two-hectare vineyard, called Coleraine, with a mix of varieties modelled on Château Lafite-Rothschild: Cabernet Sauvignon seventy-five percent, Merlot twenty-two percent and Cabernet Franc three percent.

Labouring under a temporary shortage of good fruit material, wine maker Michael Bennett produced in 1979 a range of basic quaffing wines from Chasselas, Palomino, Baco 22A and Müller-Thurgau. 1980, however, although not without some disappointing releases — notably a rather thin Chalino — saw a marked lift in wine quality overall.

Te Mata's range of white wines includes Sauvignon Blanc, Furmint, a rarely-seen Chardonnay, Müller-Thurgau, Chalino and White Burgundy. The Müller-Thurgau is a fragrant, crisp stop-fermented wine, drier than most. The White Burgundy, a blend of classic varieties aged in oak, has lacked the fullness of body normally associated with this style. Chalino, a medium wine made by back-blending Muscat juice into a blend of Chasselas and Palomino, has lately improved and the 1983, although slightly coarse, is full-bodied and the best yet.

One has no reservations about Te Mata Furmint. In Hungary this variety contributes to the sweet white Tokay wines; Te Mata's, made from fruit off old

rehabilitated vines, is medium-dry but full of interest — robust and, by any standards, strongly-flavoured.

The winery intends to market its top wines whenever possible with a vineyard site designation, e.g. Coleraine Cabernet Sauvignon/Merlot. 'Castle Hill' on the label indicates blending of more than one vineyard, as for the Castle Hill Sauvignon Blanc. The 1982 Sauvignon Blanc was a woody, rather subdued wine and has been overshadowed by the excellent 1983, a big sweetish wine with a lovely, sustained aftertaste.

The reds are big, richly coloured wines, showing all the hallmarks of fully ripened Cabernet Sauvignon grapes. Not a great deal is made, only 165 cases in 1980, rising to 1000 cases by 1983. The Cabernet Sauvignon 1980 stood out at the 1981 National Wine Competition, carrying off the trophy reserved for the best red wine. Soft and ripe flavoured, with noble deep colour and fragrant aroma, the style of the 1980 was repeated in 1981, which scooped the THC Trophy as the top wine of the 1982 National Wine Competition.

The Cabernet Sauvignon 1981 was made from Havelock fruit harvested in late April at twenty-three degrees brix (a measure of the sugar-level in the must) and matured for eighteen months in French and American oak casks. Avoiding all the traditional weaknesses of New Zealand reds, this wine is reminiscent of the Bordeaux clarets of 1976 — full of intense fruit, but not austere. Now called Awatea Cabernet Sauvignon, from 1985 it will be a Cabernet Sauvignon/Merlot blend.

The most expensive New Zealand red wine yet is the Coleraine Cabernet Sauvignon/Merlot 1982, released at $14.95 at the winery. This lovely, deep red has all the elements needed to age superbly — undoubtedly Bernard Chambers would have approved of it.

Since 1980 the Te Mata winery has been the source of the finest red wines in the country.

Vidal

An intense and complex personality, Warwick Orchiston in ten years at Vidals has emerged as one of the most accomplished wine makers in Hawkes Bay.

Vidal, a long-established Hastings winery, has in recent years released several wines of strong interest to wine enthusiasts. Anthony Vidal, the founder, came to New Zealand from Spain at the age of 22 in 1888. After eleven years working with his uncle, Wanganui wine maker Joseph Soler, Vidal experimented with viti-culture at Palmerston North before shifting to Hawkes Bay. In 1905 he bought a half-hectare property at Hastings, converted the existing stables into a cellar and planted grape vines.

The winery flourished; a new, three-hectare vineyard was established at Te Awanga in 1916 and, a few years later, another three hectares was acquired from Chambers' Te Mata vineyard. After Anthony Vidal's death, control of the company passed to his three sons: Frank, the wine maker; Cecil, who concentrated on sales; and Leslie, who supervised the vines. For decades the winery enjoyed a solid reputation. John Buck, now of Te Mata Estate, in 1969 stated in his book *Take a Little Wine*, that Vidal's Claret and Burgundy were 'the two finest, freely available dry reds on the New Zealand market.' Using Cabernet Sauvignon, Pinot Meunier and hybrid fruit, the brothers produced a Burgundy of 'style, good colour, body and balance' and a Claret 'lighter in body and more austere to taste.'

But after 1972, when Seppelt's of Australia acquired a sixty percent share of Vidal, standard lines were dropped, labels changed and the quality of the wine began to fall away. The slide continued under another owner, Ross MacLennan, from 1974 to 1976.

The steady restoration of Vidal's reputation began in 1976, after George Fistonich of Villa Maria bought the company. Vidal has retained its separate identity under management policy and the grapes, all contract grown, are drawn entirely from the Hawkes Bay region. Warwick Orchiston, the intense, talented wine maker has worked for the company since 1974.

The dryish Te Moana Riesling-Sylvaner and fruity Mt Erin Müller-Thurgau are sound commercial wines. The Te Moana Riesling-Sylvaner in 1976 won widespread praise as the best dry Riesling-Sylvaner of that vintage, although subsequently the line has shown a varying degree of sweetness. Mt Erin Müller-Thurgau is the more popular style, with more back-blended juice. The 1983, with its delicate flavour and lower acidity, is probably the best yet.

Vidal's Chardonnays a few years ago lacked the customary full body of this variety, but the excellent 1981 vintage made amends. Advanced in its youth, this Chardonnay was firm, full-bodied by New Zealand standards. The 1983 Vidal Chardonnay seems to vary, some bottles opening up ripe-tasting, round and complex and others less impressively.

Chenin Blanc can be recommended, after such good wines as the fine, rather delicate 1981 and the assertive, steely, deep-flavoured 1982. Vidal's Gewürztraminer

varies from year to year and occasionally reaches excellence — the gold medal 1981 was memorable for its slightly sweet, yet penetrating flavour and firm finish.

Fumé Blanc 1983 impresses as capturing typical Sauvignon Blanc/Sémillon herbaceousness in a restrained manner, less aggressive than some rival wines. Oak aging has produced a dry, not acid wine, full-bodied and flavoursome. A lot milder, but also interesting, is the Sylvaner 1983, showing a pleasantly luscious taste and rather lingering finish. 1983 also produced a low-alcohol, sweet and charming Muscat Blanc.

Vidal's red wines have stood out of late as being more robust than most New Zealand reds. They appear on the market early, at only one year old, full of potential and a long way from being ready to consume.

Vidal's Cabernet Sauvignons 1982 and 1983 are both powerful wines, dark, with plenty of fruit and strong oak and tannin. Extraordinarily rich colour is a feature of the Cabernet Sauvignon/Merlot 1983 as well; markedly softened by the Merlot presence, this blended red will mature more rapidly, but still needs several years in the bottle to really unfold.

Alone among the Hawkes Bay wineries, Vidal has a solid reputation for Pinot Noir. Undoubtedly the best release is the 1980, soft and supple and stamped with unmistakable Pinot characteristics. The Pinot Noir 1983 also shows promise — a tannic, sturdy red that demands to be left alone until four years old.

The St Aubyn's Claret can be consumed younger. Although made mainly from Cabernet Sauvignon, this typically fruity and full-flavoured red is less tannic than the wine labelled as Cabernet Sauvignon.

In 1979, Vidal opened New Zealand's first vineyard bar and restaurant and in rooms lined with casks of maturing sherry, visitors purchase and sip wines by the carafe, bottle and glass. Finish your meal with Vidal S.V. 56 Port, a fine old tawny made by the Vidal brothers in 1956.

Vidal's popular cellar restaurant and wine bar.

WELLINGTON

The southern part of the North Island, one of New Zealand's minor wine regions, has nevertheless inherited its own wine-making legacy. In 1883 William Beetham, a wealthy Wairarapa landowner, had a tiny vineyard at Masterton from which he produced wine. Later, Beetham planted a larger vineyard in various Pinot varieties and Hermitage. Bragato visited in 1895 and was given a Hermitage wine of 'prime quality'.

Today, a handful of growers own seven hectares of vines at Waikanae, on the coast north of Wellington, and in the Wairarapa.

Pierre

Only this one winery operates in the region, and it was established at Waikanae in the 1960s. Owner Peter Heginbotham, a Wellington optometrist, has a small three-hectare vineyard, growing Pinot Noir, Cabernet Sauvignon, Merlot, Müller-Thurgau, Chenin Blanc and Chardonnay.

I have tasted a light, promising Pinot Noir 1976; two overly-sulphured 1979 wines, Chenin Blanc and Riesling-Sylvaner; and an acceptable bronze medal 1981 Müller-Thurgau. The range, not on sale at the winery, can be obtained by mail-order from 48 Willis Street, Wellington, or from selected outlets in Waikanae and Wellington.

NELSON

Overshadowed by fruit, tobacco and hop growing, viticulture has only a modest foothold in Nelson province. Early German wine makers who landed at Nelson in 1843 and 1844 looked askance at the steep, bush-clothed hills and departed for South Australia. Today the region is equally recognised for its cider and fruit wine makers—Robinson's, Rochdale, Noslen and Semaine's. But in the past few years the efforts of a small knot of enthusiasts—Hermann Seifried, Rod Neill, Craig Gass, Tim Finn and Trevor Lewis—have put Nelson on the New Zealand wine map.

The Austrian-born Seifried, who established his vineyard in the hills at Upper Moutere in 1974, has so far produced the most wines. But Viggo du Fresne preceded him. Du Fresne, of French Huguenot descent, from 1967 to 1976 made dry red wine at a tiny, half-hectare vineyard planted in deep gravel on the coast at Ruby Bay. The vineyard, dating back to 1918, was originally established with Black Hamburgh table grapes; du Fresne took over in 1948 and waged a long, unsuccessful struggle to establish classical vines. After his Chardonnay, Sémillon and Pinot Meunier vines all failed—probably due to viruses—he produced hybrid red wines from the Seibel 5437 and 5455 varieties. Opened in 1980, the Ruby Bay Seibouchet 1976 stood up dark and gutsy, with plenty of life remaining.

Nelson is unlikely to emerge as a major district for wine. In 1982 only thirty-nine hectares were planted in vines, 0.6 percent of the national vineyard area. The climatic advantages of warm summers and high sunshine hours are counterbalanced by a strong risk of damaging autumn rainfall during the harvest. Other problems include a shortage of large holdings suitable for viticulture and the region's distance from principal transport routes.

Yet tourists respond with enthusiasm to promotion of the Nelson Wine Trail featuring the vineyard bars at Neudorf and Korepo, which sell wine by the glass and wholesome food in lovely surroundings. And new labels are emerging. Ranzau, founded by Trevor and Rose Lewis at Hope, south of Richmond, in 1980, made its first vintage in 1983.

On stony, free-draining soils, one and a half hectares of vines are planted—Gewürztraminer, Müller-Thurgau, Rhine Riesling, Cabernet Sauvignon and Gamay Beaujolais. The Gamay Beaujolais 1983 is pale, with a slightly fiery thirteen percent alcohol; the 1983 Rhine Riesling is a crisp, high acid medium-dry style, unmemorable but sound.

A section of Transport Nelson Limited's plantings in the Redwood Valley.

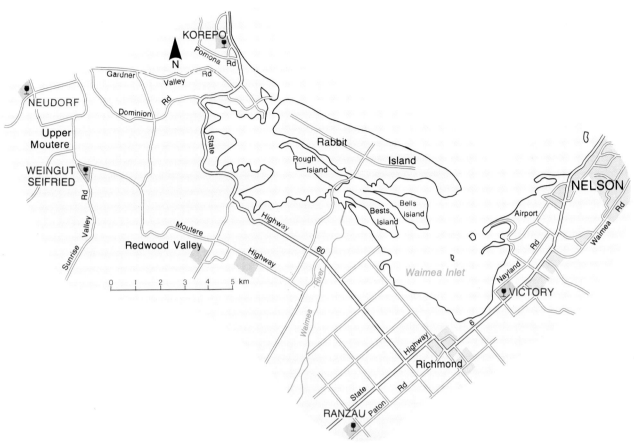

Viggo du Fresne, a pioneer Nelson wine maker, prefers today to devote his hours to chamber music, Haydn and Mozart above all others.

Korepo

The wine making tradition at Ruby Bay remains alive—in the same year that pioneering Viggo du Fresne completed his last vintage, Craig Gass planted the first vines at Korepo Wines.

Gass (36), who has a Massey University degree in food technology, worked at Villa Maria before establishing his own winery on a north-facing slope overlooking Ruby Bay. The vineyard, planted in 1976, produced a small initial crop in 1979. Today the production level remains low, at only 2500 cases annually. Visitors to the vineyard wine bar, serving salads and barbecued meat, consume much of the output.

Korepo rose to industry attention when the Sauvignon Blanc 1980 won a silver award at that year's National Wine Competition. Sauvignon Blanc, although vulnerable to botrytis rot, crops well in the Korepo vineyard. The 1980 wine opened in 1983, was still in fine condition with a mature, developed bouquet and excellent varietal 'gooseberry' flavour.

Two red wines I have sampled, Gamay Beaujolais 1980 and Pinot Noir 1980, were soft pale wines—ideal served with lunch. The range includes a medium-dry Gewürztraminer, Rhine Riesling, Chardonnay and Cabernet Sauvignon. Craig Gass also produces a Palomino Flor Dry Sherry and, to satisfy local demand, a sweet sherry.

On the coast at Ruby Bay, Korepo produces pleasant light red wines and a Sauvignon Blanc worth trying.

Neudorf

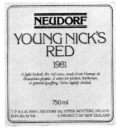

Judy and Tim Finn — producing under the Neudorf label a Cabernet Sauvignon that has attracted international praise.

Superb Nelson food and promising wines, half an hour's drive from Nelson city.

A fresh label on the national wine scene, Neudorf derives its name from the surrounding district, settled by Germans last century. The winery lies off the Nelson-Motueka inland highway, on a back road between the settlements of Upper Moutere and Dovedale.

Owner Tim Finn is an MSc graduate, formerly a dairying advisory officer with the Ministry of Agriculture and Fisheries. For his first vintage in 1981 — output 300 cases — Finn used an eighty-year-old barn on his property as a temporary winery. For 1982, he built his own winery from trees milled on the site. On a terrace overlooking the vineyard and the Tasman Ranges beyond, visitors come today to enjoy wine by the glass and some memorable Nelson food — scallops, mussels and fruit.

The four-hectare vineyard on clay soils sloping north has many varieties planted — Rhine Riesling, Gewürztraminer, Chardonnay, Cabernet Sauvignon, Müller-Thurgau and Gamay Beaujolais among others. According to Tim Finn, rain before harvest can adversely affect Rhine Riesling but early varieties like

Müller-Thurgau do well here. Soon the vineyard will be rationalised to concentrate on a few varieties only.

The wines I have sampled show promise. The Traminer/Riesling 1982, blended from Gewürztraminer and Rhine Riesling, was light and dryish but rather overly sulphured. Young Nick's Red 1982 won a silver medal — this is a fresh fruity, light red produced from Gamay Beaujolais grapes.

The 1982 Cabernet Sauvignon is rather extraordinary — a big, forceful red, strong in tannin and densely coloured. Awarded the Easter Show Cup in 1983 as the best South Island wine, this undoubtedly is Neudorf's success story so far.

Striking architecture in a tranquil back-country setting.

Victory

A pocket size vineyard, Victory Grape Wines rose fleetingly to prominence at the 1980 National Wine Competition, scoring a silver medal for its Gamay Beaujolais 1978.

Irish-born Rod Neill (54) started producing wine as a hobby in 1972, calling his vineyard Victory in remembrance of Admiral Nelson's ship. On the main road south at Stoke, near Nelson, one hectare of loam clay land bears Chasselas, Müller-Thurgau, Seibel 5455 and Gamay Beaujolais vines.

Victory Gamay Beaujolais is a light red, pale and fruity. The wine does not receive any wood aging and — to match local preferences — is not dry. With production amounting only to a few hundred cases per year, Victory wines are rarely seen beyond Nelson.

173

Weingut Seifried

Looking across the Seifried vineyard to the quiet village of Upper Moutere.

Weingut Seifried, by far the largest Nelson winery, lies in undulating country near the village of Upper Moutere. The label, proudly adorned with the Austrian eagle, early won respect when, from the first vintage, the Sylvaner 1976 won a silver medal — but of late the standard of Seifried wines has been uneven.

Hermann Seifried (38) graduated in wine technology in Germany, and made wine in Europe and South Africa before arriving in New Zealand in 1971, as wine maker for the ill-fated venture by the Apple and Pear Board into apple wine production. In spring 1974 Seifried planted his own vineyard in the clay soils of the Upper Moutere.

Today the twelve-hectare home vineyard, plus further fruit drawn from the Redwood Valley, is concentrated upon Gewürztraminer and Rhine Riesling; both varieties flourish in the district, says wine maker Seifried. Smaller areas are devoted to Sylvaner, Müller-Thurgau, Pinot Noir, Chardonnay, Sauvignon Blanc, Chenin Blanc and Cabernet Sauvignon.

So far, red wines have not been a company strength. Seifried does not employ traditional production methods, but prefers to use heat treatment of the must for colour extraction, followed by removal of the skins before fermentation. No time is allocated for wood aging.

Seifried Refosca, a north-eastern Italian variety, is a plain, purplish red, not altogether dry. The Cabernet Sauvignons I tasted, from the 1979 and 1980 vintages, were both light and, once again, plain. Pinot Noir has fluctuated in style, from the light and fresh wines made in 1982 and 1979, to the dark, robust and tannin-laden 1983 and 1980 vintages.

Seifried Gewürztraminer has its ups and downs — but at its best this is an excellent wine. The silver medal 1980 vintage was an elegant, strongly spicy wine; 1983 has produced a well-balanced, dryish Gewürztraminer, firm and assertive. To my palate, the medium-dry wine, labelled simply as Gewürztraminer, shows more depth, and better balance, than the Gewürztraminer Dry.

The Rhine Riesling is a hard, steely wine, strong flavoured and with prominent acidity. I prefer the Sylvaner, pale and flowery and charming in the best years.

Neither the Chenin Blanc nor the Chardonnay has been outstanding, and the Chardonnay has often displayed an unexpected degree of sweetness. For a medium white wine based on an unusual blend of Chenin Blanc, Chardonnay, Rhine Riesling and Gewürztraminer, try the Moutere Reserve.

Agnes Seifried, wife of Hermann, picking Pinot Noir grapes in late March.

Hunter's

Hunter's Wines startled observers of their first vintage in 1982 by scoring six medals, including three silvers, with their six entries in the 1982 National Wine Competition. The promise in that performance, however, was not fulfilled in the 1983 vintage wines.

Ernie Hunter, born 36 years ago in Ireland, came to New Zealand in 1973 and in 1982 produced several wines under primitive conditions in an old Christchurch cider factory. Later, unable to secure the premises he wanted in Christchurch, Hunter erected a new winery and restaurant in Rapaura Road, off the Blenheim-Picton highway. Almuth Lorenz (26) makes the wine: she comes from a Rhine wine-making family, and has studied at the famous Geisenheim Institute.

The twenty-five hectares of Marlborough vineyard, not yet fully bearing, include Rhine Riesling, Gewürztraminer, Müller-Thurgau, Sauvignon Blanc, Chardonnay, Chenin Blanc and Cabernet Sauvignon vines. Hunter's also retains an outlet in Belfast, Christchurch, and another four-hectare vineyard there planted in Pinot Gris, Grey Riesling, Pinot Noir, Rhine Riesling and Gewürztraminer.

Helped by enterprising marketing, including a public own-a-vine scheme, production swiftly reached a substantial volume. The wines are sold through some licensed outlets, at the winery and by mail-order.

The 1983 vintage wines I tasted include Hunter's Marlborough Gewürztraminer, Late Pick Gewürztraminer, Rhine Riesling and Müller-Thurgau Dry. Disappointingly, in view of the generally favourable vintage, the wines lack both pronounced varietal character and intensity of flavour.

Almuth Lorenz, wine maker at Hunter's, has so far concentrated on white wines.

Young Müller-Thurgau plants in Hunter's vineyard near Blenheim.

Montana

A pair of Californian wine authorities, Dr L.R. Lider and Professor A.R. Berg, investigated Marlborough's viticultural potential for Montana in 1973. They disagreed on the region's probable strengths — Lider plumped for white wines, Berg for red — but, overall, both were impressed.

Acting on their recommendation, the company soon acquired over 1600 hectares and in the winter of 1973 the first vines were planted. A severe drought in 1974 killed many of the young vine cuttings, forcing a rapid replanting, but by 1983 Montana was drawing fruit from 480 hectares of vines. The principal vineyards, with names now appearing on labels, are at Brancott (the largest single vineyard in New Zealand) Renwick Fairhall and Woodbourne.

Wine maker John Simes heads the Riverlands winery, a strictly functional looking operation a few kilometres on the seaward side of Blenheim. From the mezzanine floor, visitors can view the barrel hall and rows of stainless steel fermenting tanks. The winery in the 1983 vintage processed 6000 tonnes of grapes, compared with 9000 tonnes at Montana's Gisborne winery.

So far, Montana's range of Marlborough white wines has featured four varietal wines — Rhine Riesling, Sauvignon Blanc, Riesling-Sylvaner and Gewürztraminer — plus the recent Renwick Traminer/Riesling-Sylvaner blend and, still in the wings, Chardonnay. Overall, the quality of this line-up has fully justified the company's faith in the district.

Interior view of Montana's winery at Riverlands. Overseas visitors are often struck by the pervasive use of stainless steel in New Zealand wine making. Its popularity stems from the fact that, unlike copper or iron, stainless steel does not react chemically with wine.

The first Marlborough Riesling-Sylvaner, from the 1976 vintage, scored a silver medal. Since then, the wine has established itself among the country's top Müller-Thurgaus. The style is light, elegant and drier than most wines of this variety, with an abundance of fruit flavour. Crisp and delicate, Montana Marlborough Riesling-Sylvaners age well up to five years.

The stronger Rhine Riesling is probably even more successful. Since the first, 1979 vintage Marlborough Rhine Riesling has stood out — a fragrant, flowery, polished wine with steely fruit flavour and crisp acidity. On aging, the aristocratic steely character remains, yet interestingly the honey character typical of German Rhine Rieslings does not emerge. The 1982 vintage, which scored top in its class at the 1983 Australian National Competition in Canberra is the best yet.

Gewürztraminer is more subdued, a light, floral wine lacking the impressive varietal spice frequently exhibited in Gisborne Gewürztraminers. The first Renwick Traminer/Riesling-Sylvaner, 1982, showed only hints of Gewürztraminer in the blend, although the 1983 possesses a more satisfactory balance of spicy Gewürztraminer taste and Müller-Thurgau fruitiness.

Montana Marlborough Sauvignon Blanc is full of distinctive herbal varietal character. Unmistakably Sauvignon Blanc in its youth, with its assertive grassy/capsicum aroma and flavour, this medium-dry wine needs bottle aging for the inherent complexity of the grape variety to emerge. The 1980 vintage, for instance, by 1983 had developed a mature gooseberry-like character, mellow, subtle, and more interesting than the powerful stalky condition of its youth.

Montana Marlborough Cabernet Sauvignon stands out among the company's range of Marlborough reds, which also includes Woodbourne Cabernet Sauvignon, Fairhall River Claret and Pinot Noir. Pinot Noir, to judge from the 1979 and 1980 vintages, has not the promise of Cabernet Sauvignon in the region, as both years lack colour and flavour intensity.

Fairhall River Claret in style and name probably reminds many of Australia's famous Jacob's Creek Claret. Blended from Pinotage, Cabernet Sauvignon and Pinot Noir, this is a smooth, easy-drinking red but rather bland.

The Woodbourne Cabernet Sauvignon, sold in a glass crock, in both 1980 and 1982 was light and rather sharp upon release. But the Cabernet Sauvignon labelled Marlborough has much more appeal. After the promising 1976 and rather indifferent 1977 vintages, since 1978 a uniform style has been created, to give a wine with medium body, strong colour, plenty of Cabernet Sauvignon fruit and firm tannin. Distinctly cool-climate in style, Marlborough Cabernet Sauvignon needs medium term cellaring (a minimum of five years) for its potential to really unfold.

Of recent vintages, 1978 and 1981 have been the highlights.

Müller-Thurgau vines late in the afternoon at Montana's Renwick vineyard.

CANTERBURY

French peasants last century used to make wine at Akaroa on Banks Peninsula, but in 1982 Canterbury had only a scant forty-nine hectares planted in vines.

The climatic hazards for large scale viticulture in this region are severe. Canterbury, although nearer the equator than many European wine districts, often fails to accumulate the heat readings necessary to fully ripen grapes. In this respect it parallels parts of Germany. October spring frosts are a risk and April frosts can retard ripening.

Canterbury, however, like Marlborough, enjoys one significant advantage over the North Island wine-growing regions — low rainfall. Dry weather reduces the problems with disease and can encourage the development of 'noble rot'.

The current resurgence of interest in Canterbury wine stems from research conducted at Lincoln College. Since the first grape vines were planted in 1968, research has focused on testing the proposition that the cool, dry Canterbury climate favours the production of German-style wines, and on identifying the most suitable varieties. Trial plantings of over sixty varieties have shown, according to the College, that Canterbury produces grapes of high sugar levels and high acidity. Lincoln College uses its commercial wine maker's licence to produce a range of experimental wines. Although the College claims to have 'consistently good' wines from Pinot Gris, Müller-Thurgau, Grey Riesling, Pinot Noir and Pinot Blanc, those I have tasted were sharply acid, with the exception of a very promising Pinot Noir.

St Helena is Canterbury's first commercial winery but other moves are afoot. A group of farmer partners, including former National Party MP Derek Quigley, have substantial plantings in the Waipara district, with plans to build a winery. And the Geisen brothers, from Germany, have begun to make wine from their vineyard at Burnham.

St Helena

In Austrian-born Danny Schuster, Canterbury wine has its most passionate advocate. Intrigued by the province's hazardous wine climate — in such climates not only the risks, but also the potential rewards are great — Schuster, formerly wine maker at Lincoln College, now guides Canterbury's first commercial vineyard.

Schuster is wine maker for a company, St Helena Wine Estates, owned by the Mundy brothers at Coutts Island, north of Christchurch. On sandy, silty soils a twenty-five-hectare vineyard has been planted in an area with a relatively low frost risk and good drainage. Four hectares each of Rhine Riesling, Gewürztraminer, Pinot Gris and Müller-Thurgau vines are supplemented by lesser areas of Pinot Noir, Cabernet Sauvignon, Merlot, Chardonnay and Pinot Blanc.

Because of the marginal climate for viticulture, Schuster is reconciled to a possible alternation of good and bad vintages. One year, he suggests, perhaps a fine Pinot Noir can be made, while a light Beaujolais-style red could be created the next.

1981, the first year of production, yielded a small volume of blended wines, a Müller-Thurgau/ Gewürztraminer and an Estate White. The 1982 Estate White, blended from Müller-Thurgau, Pinot Blanc,

Danny Schuster is totally absorbed in the exploration of Canterbury's table wine potential. Those who stated that the region is too cold for wine production must now grapple with the contrary evidence afforded by his gold medal 1982 Pinot Noir.

Rhine Riesling vines at St Helena and, in the background, the winery.

Rhine Riesling and Pinot Gris was light and crispy the Riesling-Sylvaner/Gewürztraminer 1982 only reached a quaffing standard. Both the 1982 and 1983 Gewürztraminers, although commendably dry, lack positive varietal character.

Pinot Blanc looks to have more promise. The Pinot Blanc/Müller-Thurgau 1982, a 2 : 1 blend, was dry and flavoursome and the 1983 Pinot Blanc, aged in oak, shows the same quality.

But St Helena Pinot Noir is the real success story so far. In a breakthrough for Canterbury wine, Pinot Noir 1982 was awarded a gold medal at the 1983 National Wine Competition. Produced from ultra-ripe bunches, slow-fermented for eleven days then aged in new French oak, the wine has intense colour and very soft, ripe-fruit flavour. Already the Pinot Noir 1983 has won a silver award.

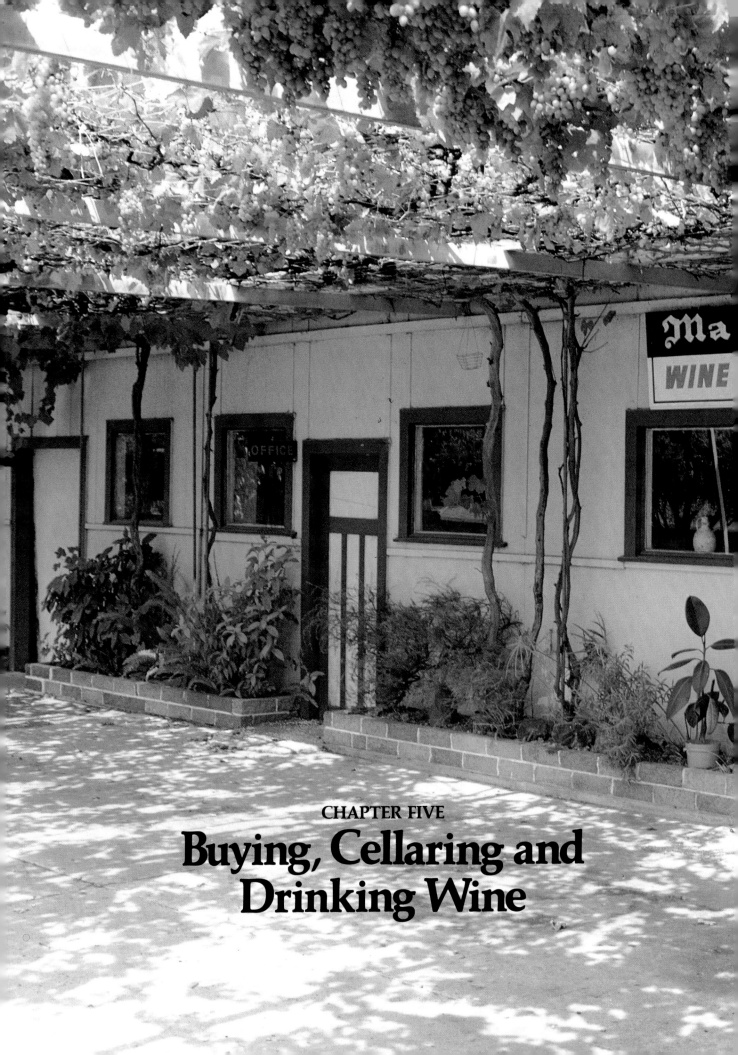

CHAPTER FIVE
Buying, Cellaring and Drinking Wine

BUYING NEW ZEALAND WINE

To sell wine in New Zealand is a privilege restricted to approved licence-holders — notably restaurants, hotels, wine resellers, 'wholesale' wine and spirit merchants and, of course, vineyards. For the wine buyer, each point of sale has its advantages and disadvantages.

Vineyards

If you want value for money, the chance to obtain wines which are hard to obtain elsewhere, plus enjoyment, visit the vineyards. You can sample the wines, although not always the very best ones, and some vineyards, perhaps a little short on sales, will ply you on the spot with as much as you may have intended to buy. The opportunity to try before you buy is a big advantage, and on top of that, many swear that the wine always tastes best at the winery.

Overall, vineyard prices tend to be a shade lower than wholesale. The fact is that vineyard sales afford wine makers a handsome profit, since there are no merchant discounts and profit margins included in the price. Thus, apart from the 'specials' offered by other outlets, this is the most economical way to buy wine. Often the medium-sized and small producers with their relatively low overheads provide the best value.

As the best wines are frequently sold only at the winery, an annual pilgrimage around the Auckland or Hawkes Bay vineyards can uncover a hoard of treasures. The rules of the National Wine Competition prescribe that wines eligible for trophies must be on sale once the judging is finished — thus early November is the best period for pursuing special releases. Regardless of competition fortunes, many vineyards traditionally release their premium lines once the November judging is over.

Only about five percent of New Zealand wine is sold direct to the public over the vineyard counter. But some small companies rely heavily on vineyard and mail-order sales. For the wine enthusiast eager to explore the full array of local wines, vineyard visits are essential.

Wholesalers

Large volumes of wine are sold by so-called 'wholesalers', in reality wine and spirit merchants who also sell direct to the public. Most wine companies sell in large volumes to merchants, who warehouse the wine and then distribute to resellers (hotels, wine reseller shops and restaurants), who in turn sell directly to the public. But these merchant 'wholesalers' also operate their own sales outlets.

Through a very complex, rather incestuous set of company associations, many wholesalers are now in the hands of the two major brewery groups, who themselves are shareholders in some leading wine companies. As a result, the consumer's freedom of choice may suffer — the merchants tend to heavily promote the products of their affiliated wine companies, making it more difficult for the smaller, independent wineries to achieve adequate exposure.

Wine merchants are only occasionally competent to give professional advice. Also, the merchant's traditional role of selecting, holding and aging wine has been conspicuously ignored. However, although the law insists that at a wholesaler you must buy a minimum of eight litres, prices are normally cheaper here than anywhere other than the vineyards, and often a wide range is stocked.

Hotels

Corner hotel bottle-stores typically offer only a very narrow selection of wines, so that being able to buy a single bottle is the only real advantage they offer. So lacking has been the management's understanding of wine on occasion that real finds have been made. Francis Colchester-Wemyss, in his *Souvenirs Gastronomiques*, recalls discovering thirty-five bottles of the great Bordeaux, Chateau Latour 1899 in 'a New Zealand hotel'; the publican was happy to be rid of his old 'French Burgundy' at a price lower than his cheapest Australian imports.

Often hotels operate their own 'wholesale' departments which, in reality, are bottle-stores operating off reduced margins.

Wine Resellers

The local wine reseller shops usually carry a wide selection and offer the convenience of single bottle purchases. But the wine shops, set up in 1948 to provide the New Zealand wine industry with an independent channel of distribution to the public, more often than not are unable to match the prices offered by the merchant 'wholesalers'.

Although discounting has spread recently, the average shelf price still does not encourage a bulk purchase. However, these shops are convenient and well-stocked outlets.

It must be said that the level of wine expertise generally encountered in these shops is low. For specialised outlets, a more professional approach to staff education is sorely needed.

Corbans' early bottles, for example this port, relied on neck labels to specify the wine type.

Restaurants

One of the dearest places to buy wine is in a licensed restaurant. Hotel dining-rooms which once opened fleetingly from 6 to 7 pm, gave no encouragement to linger over a bottle of wine. But since 1961 when the Gourmet in Auckland became the first restaurant legally allowed to serve wine, hundreds of licensed restaurants around the country have aroused interest in New Zealand wine.

Mark-ups are commonly in the order of 100-200 percent — to cover the costs of tying up capital, storage, glasses, stewards' wages and so on.

Unless something outstanding is featured on the wine-list, order the meal first and then select the wines to suit. As an aperitif while pondering the menu, a bone-dry sherry or a dry white stimulates the appetite wonderfully. Should you want only a single bottle to be consumed throughout the meal, choose it to match the main course. A pleasant and common procedure is to consume a dry white wine with the initial courses, followed by a red wine or another white wine to accompany the main dish.

Care should be taken to ensure that the food and wines chosen complement each other, avoiding the danger that the flavour of one may swamp that of the other. Light wines should therefore be chosen to partner the more delicate dishes, and robust, full-bodied wines to partner strongly flavoured foods.

Delicate seafood dishes combine well with mild white wines like Müller-Thurgau, Pinot Gris and Grey Riesling. For heavier, flavoursome seafoods like oysters, try the more assertive grape varieties — Chardonnay, Sauvignon Blanc or Gewürztraminer.

With steak and beef dishes, robust reds like Cabernet Sauvignon come into their own, the strong flavours of both the food and the wine affording an ideal match. Chicken, lamb and pork suit flavoursome white wines, such as Chardonnay and Gewürztraminer, or medium-bodied reds like Pinot Noir and Pinotage.

If ordering a wine especially to accompany dessert, choose something unabashedly sweet like an Auslese or Sauternes — anything drier simply will not match the sweet food. At the very end of the meal, port, sweet sherry and red wine all combine admirably with cheeses.

Order the house wine if you want only a glass or two. Only recently, unfortunately, have some licensed restaurants realised that the house wine should not be the cheapest vin ordinaire they can lay hands on.

Be careful to order the precise style of wine you want. After the wine steward has opened the bottle is no time to decide that you would rather have a medium than a dry white. When the steward pours a little wine in your glass, you are merely checking that your chosen wine is in sound condition.

If you want to save money and enjoy your own wine, eat at a BYO restaurant. Bring-your-own restaurants have permits that authorise liquor consumption with a meal, and are entitled to charge for opening your bottle, providing glasses and so on. You pour your own wine.

Labelling

New Zealand up to 1980 had very incomplete labelling laws. Only the name of the wine producer, the volume of wine, and its percentage by volume of alcohol were mandatory. Such labelling laws — or the lack of them — allowed open season on the use of varietal names: a Cabernet Sauvignon, for example, was not required by law to contain any Cabernet Sauvignon juice at all.

Even today some bottles carry labels and names of doubtful validity. Are we entitled to assume that a New Zealand 'burgundy', for instance, in some respect resembles the original French Burgundies? If so, what does 'burgundy' mean on the label of a sweet hybrid red? New Zealand, along with other New World wine nations, still arbitrarily apes the most famous European wine names.

The position of wines labelled with the name of a particular grape variety is more clear-cut. Amendments to the wine-labelling regulations introduced in 1980 provided an important element of consumer protection. In essence, any wine named after any grape variety must contain at least seventy-five percent of the stated variety. A Pinot Noir, for example, should have no less than seventy-five percent Pinot Noir content.

Hybrid and *Vitis labrusca* wines cannot be labelled as varietals. Blends of two or more varieties must be named in order of the proportions used, with the predominant grape first; once again the named varieties must constitute no less than seventy-five percent of the overall blend.

In Europe, most consumers pay little heed to individual grape varieties and relatively few wines are labelled by grape variety. The practice in New Zealand, however, is for the majority of the best wines to be sent into the world under the name of the principal grape used. A prestige Chardonnay will normally be sold as such; 'a 'Chablis', by contrast, probably has more humble grape origins.

Sparkling wines have their own nomenclature. The 1980 regulations allow the term 'Champagne' to be used only for 'bottle-fermented' sparkling wine, which may only contain CO_2 gas generated by its own natural fermentation. That last requirement also applies to 'Charmat process' or 'naturally fermented' wine, but the crucial difference is that any wine labelled 'Champagne' or 'bottle-fermented' must have had its secondary fermentation in a container of a capacity of five litres or less. The others may be produced in tanks of any size.

A carbonated 'bubbly' is entitled to no other term than 'sparkling wine'.

Reading a New Zealand Wine Label

Wine labels vary around the world from the sterling prose efforts of many Australian wineries to the sparse, uncluttered labels of the top châteaux of Bordeaux. New Zealand labels, which by law are required to carry the producer's name and address, the country of origin, contents by volume and the alcohol content, fall into three broad categories according to the name of the wine: varietal, branded and generic.

Varietal wines, which tend to be the best and most highly priced, are labelled after the grape variety which constitutes at least 75 percent by volume of the wine — for example St Helena Pinot Noir — or the blend of varieties which also conforms to the same rule, for example Villa Maria Riesling — Sylvaner/Gewürztraminer. That percentage, of course, may well be 100 percent. Branded wines may or may not specify the grapes used, but seek to achieve a consistent style, for example McWilliam's Cresta Doré, Babich Vintara Red, Selak's Champelle. Generic wines, like Te Mata White Burgundy or Esk Valley Claret, aim to conform to an internationally recognised wine style.

THE VARIETAL LABEL

Grape Variety, Wine Style and Wine making Technique

Alcohol and Volume of Contents

1981
CHENIN BLANC
This variety is the principal grape grown in the Loire Valley district of France.
This wine displays typical varietal characteristics with a natural acidity balanced by residual sugar. The delicate flavour of this variety has been enhanced by a period of oak maturation. Further bottle ageing will result in a wine of increased complexity. Serve slightly chilled. 10% alcohol by volume 750ml.

DELEGAT'S

CHENIN BLANC 1981

SELECTED VINTAGE

Produced and bottled by Delegat's Vineyards Ltd.
Hepburn Road, Henderson, New Zealand.

Producer

Grape Variety

Vintage

Winery Name and Address and Country of Origin

THE BRANDED LABEL

Producer

Category of Wine
(required by law for
branded wines)

Brand

Wine Style and
Grape Varieties

Winery Name and
Address

Alcohol Percentage
by Volume

Contents by Volume

Country of Origin

THE GENERIC LABEL

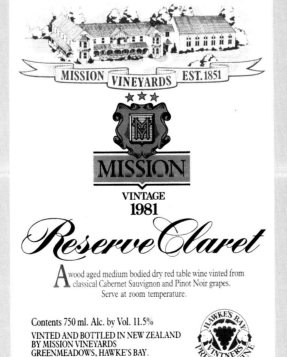

Producer

Vintage

Generic Wine
Name

Contents by Volume
and Alcohol Percentage
by Volume

Wine Style and
Grape Varieties

Country of Origin

Seal of Hawkes Bay
Regional Origins

Winery Name and
Address

Vintages

Does New Zealand experience good and bad vintages as do the European wine districts? Are vintage dates on wine labels of importance to the consumer?

The answer is yes. In Europe, the traditional emphasis placed on vintages as a guide to wine quality stems from the weather which can acutely affect ripening patterns in such northerly areas as Germany and Champagne.

New Zealand growing seasons also vary, from fine dry summers like 1983 to near-disasters like 1979. Flavour development in the berries and their sugar/acid ratios are closely related to the caprices of the weather. In fact, our climate is so variable that the concept of good and bad years for wine is rather clumsy: poor conditions for early-ripening varieties like Müller-Thurgau and Chasselas, for instance, may be followed by an Indian summer that brings late grapes like Cabernet Sauvignon into the winery in peak condition.

Here is a summary of recent vintages.

Long, hot summers and very light autumn rains yield the best New Zealand vintages. Here grapes ripen in late summer at the Sapich brothers' property in Forest Hill Road, Henderson.

1976

Described by Nick Nobilo as 'the year of the decade' for the 1970s. Following very unpredictable weather in early summer, with heavy rain in December and January, later the weather improved. In Hawkes Bay the vintage was two to three weeks late and the fruit was high in sugar. Auckland enjoyed warm, sunny weather through February and March and the season, one to two weeks late, produced grapes with excellent sugar/acid levels. A few reds have proved outstanding.

1977

After a poor spring in which wet weather affected the crop at flowering, by late December most vines were several weeks behind. Following more settled weather in February and March, picking began towards the end of March, a month later than normal.

Hawkes Bay and Gisborne escaped the worst of the heavy rains which then descended on Auckland at the height of the vintage. But the sun was absent everywhere. Despite the late vintage, the grapes stayed high in acid, and sugar levels were below those of 1976. Overall 1977 was a year that produced ordinary wines.

1978

A wet spell before Christmas made this the third late vintage in a row. However, fine sunny conditions late summer and early autumn yielded a heavy crop, clean and ripe. Some memorable Chardonnays and Cabernet Sauvignons emerged.

1979

After a dry, settled spring and warm summer, by February this promised to be the best vintage for several years, but abnormally heavy March rains ruined it: Hawkes Bay suffered its wettest March since 1923, and botrytis in Gisborne, and low sugars, meant this region was the worst hit of all. Only Marlborough produced grapes in reasonable condition — elsewhere the grapes came in rain-damaged, low in sugars and in the worst overall condition for many years.

The wines emerged with little depth and many proved short-lived.

As a rule the reds lacked body.

1980

A mediocre year. After another favourable spring the summer proved wetter and more cloudy than usual. Again it rained during the vintage period, although not so badly as in 1979. Gisborne encountered a spell of warm wet weather which led to a swift gathering of the grapes to minimise losses. Unseasonal winds gave the Marlborough vineyards one of their wettest years. Overall crops were heavy, clean, but not entirely ripe. Some good white wines emerged but the reds again proved disappointing.

1981

A low-volume, sound white and good red wine vintage. A difficult period at flowering in November produced small crops of white grapes throughout the country. The season was the best for whites since 1976, with clean grapes showing higher sugar levels than 1980. Yet, with February unseasonally cloudy, the vintage was not absolutely ideal, needing more sunshine to ensure maximum flavour development in the grapes.

The later-flowering reds escaped most of the adverse early weather and the fruit responded well to a sunny April. The 1981 reds show good colour and flavour development, a needed lift after 1979 and 1980.

1982

A good yet not perfect vintage. Fine summer weather in January and early February was later marred by heavy rains late in February. Gisborne and Auckland were the regions most affected, while Hawkes Bay and Marlborough suffered to a lesser degree.

Yet 1982 overall produced grapes with higher sugars than usual. The wines emerged with reasonable character but subsequently were overshadowed by those of 1983. The reds maintain the improvement in quality noticeable from 1981.

1983

A much vaunted vintage that set new records both for quantity and quality levels.

The season was exceptionally dry, especially on the East Coast where the lack of rain led to drought. In Gisborne and Hawkes Bay the fruit quality was excellent, with sugar levels, for most varieties, being the highest ever recorded.

The grapes came in free from disease and with good acid levels. Although Marlborough growers were troubled by wind problems, overall the 1983 vintage yielded the best fruit in memory.

The well-ripened grapes produced wines of higher alcohol than usual, showing plenty of body and aging potential. The higher sugars allowed wine makers to ferment varieties like Sauvignon Blanc and Sémillon to dryness, rather than Germanising them with a touch of sweetness. From the beginning, the reds displayed deep colour and real intensity of flavour.

1984

After the intensely favourable publicity that surrounded the vintage of 1983, inevitably the 1984 harvest suffered a little by comparison.

The grape crop, down by one-third on the record 1983 level, was reduced by adverse weather at flowering, which affected the berry 'set'. Rain and humidity in February and March brought the fruit into the wineries at average sugar levels, and the 1984 wines, correspondingly, are lighter in body than those of 1983.

Yet in 1984 white wines showed in their infancy an abundance of flavour that often is associated with low-yield vintages. Overall, an average to good year in terms of quality.

Wine Competitions

Judging standards are usually high at New Zealand's two annual wine competitions, making the results worth careful scrutiny.

The National Wine Competition, organised by the Wine Institute since 1976, carries the most weight. On a panel not always entirely appointed on the basis of judging ability — people with a high public profile have been frequent panellists — the influence of wine makers is not heavy. The entries are judged early in November, when current vintage wines are still very young.

The New Zealand Easter Show competition, held under the auspices of the Auckland Agricultural and Pastoral Association, dates back to 1952 as the country's first regular wine show. Wine makers are by tradition quite strongly represented on the Easter Show panels. Another difference between the two competitions is that the Easter Show judging is held in February, when the current season's wines are almost a year old. Also, at the Easter Show all entries in a class under review are presented simultaneously to the judges, whereas at the National Wine Competition entries are evaluated one at a time.

Yet the two shows have a lot in common. Both award medals in accordance with absolute quality standards, rather than by a first-past-the-post system; for example, it has not been unusual for several gold medals to be awarded in the Cabernet Sauvignon class and for the highest marked sparkling to score only a silver medal. Also, both shows score entries out of 20 points; three for colour and clarity, seven for bouquet and ten for the taste and general impression. The judges' marks are averaged to reach the final score. 13 to 14.9 points is the bronze medal standard, 15 to 16.9 silver, and 17 points and above earns a gold medal.

As many as eighty percent of the total entries receive an award. At the 1983 National Wine Competition, for instance, of 798 entries 32 won gold medals (4 percent), 248 won silver medals (31 percent) and a huge total of 359 won bronze medals (45 percent).

Since about one-third of entries receive a silver or gold medal, the temptation may exist to reduce one's interest only to these top award winners. However, bronze medal winners, which must be sound and free from obvious fault, are in fact frequently wines of real merit.

A silver or gold medal awarded in New Zealand today gives a more realistic guide to quality than those given a decade ago. Des Lagan, who judged at the 1971 national competition, later recalled that one particular wine was overlooked for a medal, '... a fact for which some of my brother judges must accept responsibility. It was a classic from a classic grape and it was this that probably had some judges puzzled'.

Our present judging standards are certainly higher than those at many overseas wine competitions. The majority of New Zealand wines that have won gold medals overseas in recent years, have scored silver or bronze medals at home. Often cited are the results of the annual Viticulture and Wine Growing Fair at

Ljubljana, Yugoslavia — where in 1965, more than ninety percent of 1103 entries scored gold or silver medals — and the International Wine and Spirits Competition in London, which in 1978 mustered 105 golds for only 428 entries.

1983 NATIONAL WINE COMPETITION GOLD MEDALS

MÜLLER-THURGAU, DRY (RIESLING-SYLVANER)
Robard and Butler 80

MÜLLER-THURGAU, MEDIUM (RIESLING-SYLVANER)
Montana Marlborough 80

MÜLLER-THURGAU, SWEET (RIESLING-SYLVANER)
Cooks Late Pick 83
Corbans Late Harvest 80
Nobilo Late Harvest 81

CHARDONNAY
Cooks 83
Cooks 82
Delegat's 82
Delegat's 81

GEWÜRZTRAMINER
Cooks 83
Cooks Medium 83
Matawhero 82
Villa Maria Reserve 82
Collard Dry 83
Penfolds 81
Robard and Butler 81

SAUVIGNON BLANC
Montana Marlborough 82
Montana Marlborough 80

RHINE RIESLING
Montana Marlborough 83
Montana Marlborough 82
Montana Marlborough 80

CABERNET SAUVIGNON
Cooks 83
Delegat's 80
Penfolds Woodhill 78

PINOT NOIR
St Helena 82

FINO DRY SHERRY
Montana Pale

TAWNY PORT
Babich Reserve
Robard and Butler Artillery

VINTAGE PORT
Cooks 82
Corbans 83
Penfolds 81
Penfolds 80

CELLARING

What happens to wine as it ages is still largely a mystery. To some extent a maturing wine undergoes a slow, controlled oxidation, not so much from the tiny amount of air that enters the bottle through the cork, but rather from the presence of air in the wine when it was bottled. With age the acidity declines and the alcohol, acids and other components are transformed into complex compounds such as esters and aldehydes. The bouquet and flavour develop complexity, one of the hallmarks of a mature wine.

The old belief that New Zealand whites do not keep well is incorrect. Even Müller-Thurgau, the most common variety, has the ability to age well over many years. Most of this wine is consumed long before it has even approached its potential. I recently found Corbans 1965 Riverlea Riesling was very alive; over another lunch, Babich 1975 Riesling-Sylvaner opened up crisp and elegant.

Such varieties as Rhine Riesling, Chardonnay, Sauvignon Blanc, Gewürztraminer, Sémillon and Chenin Blanc all need two to five years to mature. It is difficult to be precise about the long-term aging prospects of these varieties, as only recently have they been widely established in New Zealand. A few wines, for example Nobilo's Pinot Chardonnay, have already demonstrated an ability to age well up to ten years.

Our best reds are able to develop gracefully over a decade and beyond. The early McWilliam's Cabernet Sauvignons from the mid and late 1960s are mostly still intact. One reason for the supremacy of Cabernet Sauvignon among red grapes is that its high levels of alcohol, acid and tannin allow it to develop over a long period. J. R. Roger's book on Bordeaux has a memorable and amusing description of the 1945 vintage: 'exceptionally great ... full and round ... wines to lay down with.'

Choose reds with plenty of body, acidity and tannin. Only Pinot Noir, Pinotage and Cabernet Sauvignon in New Zealand have proven themselves to respond well to medium-term aging. At four to five years old, most Pinotages and Pinot Noirs are nearing their best — soft and fruity — and thereafter sometimes lack staying power. Among fortified wines, the flush-corked vintage ports are the only ones that improve markedly after bottling.

As wine is a natural, living substance it is vulnerable to external influences. Be sure to position your cellar in a cool area with even temperatures. Cool conditions foster a long, slow development in wine; higher temperatures hasten the maturing process but prevent wines from reaching their full potential. Rapid fluctuations in temperature must also be avoided; so must vibrations and direct sunlight.

For storage materials, the commercial wine racks are useful for a small cellar. Beyond that, beer crates or wine cartons stacked on their sides are hard to beat — cheap but functional. Place your bottles in a horizontal position to ensure contact between the wine and corks, and so far as possible avoid repeated handling.

Building a personal cellar couples the pleasures of anticipation with the rich rewards of patience.

TASTING AND DRINKING WINE

Serving and tasting wine need not be an elaborate process: you can simply pull the cork, fetch a glass and drink the wine. All over the world wine is most often consumed casually, as a thirst quencher, with no ceremony at all. The following suggestions are for those other occasions, when you are in the mood to treat wine appreciation seriously.

The opening of the bottle is simple enough. Cut the capsule off sufficiently below its top to prevent contact with the poured wine. If necessary, wipe the lip of the bottle clean. To extract the cork, use a wine-waiter's knife or any of the several other devices available — the advantage of the knife is that it houses both a blade and a corkscrew. When opening sparkling wine, hold your thumb firmly over the cork, then twist the bottle sideways and downwards.

Pour your wine into glass rather than pottery or silver, if you want to study its appearance. Select a glass with a large bowl and a stem that allows the glass to be handled without touching the bowl. Half fill the glass, leaving room for the wine to be swirled around. As you finish pouring, give the bottle a quick sideways twist to prevent any drips falling.

White wines should be tasted cool, not cold: an overly chilled wine loses its bouquet and nuances of flavour. In winter whites can be served at room temperature; summer calls for an hour in the refrigerator or a short plunge in an ice-bucket. Light, dry styles are at their best when served less chilled than sweet wines and sparklings.

Red wines taste best at room temperature. In the cooler seasons, avoid warming a red hurriedly in front of a fire or heater — instead, leave it in the hot-water cupboard, well away from the pipes, for a half-day or so. If you are forced to open a too cool bottle of red, try warming the wine by nursing the bowl of the glass in your hands.

Breathing red wine by pulling the cork achieves almost nothing, since only the wine in the neck of the bottle has any contact with the air. Rather pour the wine back and forth between the bottle and a decanter several times, or allow it to breathe in a decanter for a couple of hours. An old wine that has thrown a sediment will need decanting too. Stand the bottle upright, preferably for a couple of days, then carefully pour out the wine into the decanter, stopping when the sediment reaches the shoulder of the bottle.

Now on to the tasting. Hold the glass before a sheet of white paper — to eliminate background colours — and then tilt the glass and look closely at the wine near the lip. Grape varieties, wine styles, and wines of different ages can often be identified by their characteristic shades of colour.

A white wine should be distinguishable by its appearance from a glass of water; pale green or straw are the usual colours for a youthful wine. The colour deepens as the wine matures, turning gold in maturity and yellow-brown in old age. Advanced browning is a sign that the wine has oxidised.

Youthful reds have a purplish hue that turns red with age and eventually starts to brown when full maturity is reached. Deep colour in a red also indicates the probable presence of plenty of tannin, acid and extracts.

Apart from the precise colour, wine clarity is also important. Is the wine clear and free of suspended material? Any cloudiness or haze is undesirable.

Now, gently swirl the wine before raising the glass to your nose. The bouquet should be appealing, free of unpleasant odours, and should communicate something about the grapes from which the wine was made, its vinification, perhaps its age and country of origin. A young Müller-Thurgau, for example, has an immediately recognisable, fruity and fresh smell.

The sense of smell can be extraordinarily accurate in pinpointing the nature of an individual wine. Pay heed especially to your initial impression — the sense of smell is rapidly fatigued — and often this first impression will be confirmed on the palate.

Now, tasting the wine, hold it in your mouth while drawing air in over the tongue; you will notice that the flavour is accentuated. This technique helps to bring out some of the myriad taste elements that are the very essence of pleasure in wine.

Sweetness is measured on the front of the tongue, acidity on the sides and bitterness or astringency at the back. Are there any foreign or unpleasant flavours present? 'Body' is the relative fullness of the wine in the mouth; a Gamay Beaujolais will feel relatively light-bodied and this is part of that grape's appeal; a Cabernet Sauvignon should be more weighty. Look for overall balance. A mature red should taste of fruit foremost, with the oak and tannin flavours secondary. A fine balance between sweetness and acidity is very important for a medium white wine. In a well made wine the component flavours will all be in harmony.

After the wine has been swallowed comes the 'finish'. Ordinary wines slip down with little remaining trace, but a long, trailing finish is one of the identifying marks of a wine of true quality. The taste of a superb red wine can stay with you long after the wine itself leaves your mouth.

Wine Glasses

Wine glasses are sold in a confusing array of sizes and shapes. One glass, however, will suffice for all occasions and all wine styles, provided it is clear, stemmed, and has a generously proportioned bowl that narrows at the top.

Clear glass, or crystal, is necessary to allow a clear view of the wine; the stem prevents unnecessary touching of the bowl, which can warm a chilled white wine; a bowl of decent proportions allows the drinker to swirl the wine to savour its bouquet; and the taper at the top of the bowl concentrates the bouquet.

A. *This common glass is too small to allow a decent serving to be comfortably swirled.*

B. *An ideal all-purpose wine glass.*

C. *A standard sherry glass, also useful for port.*

D. *Two champagne glasses—the thin tulip style concentrates the bouquet, and disperses the bubbles less rapidly than the popular saucer-shaped style.*

E. *This tulip-shaped glass has a long stem suitable for serving lightly chilled white wines.*

F. *A classic design for serving red wines.*

A Vocabulary of Wine Tasting

A knowledge of the following terms is useful when reading other people's descriptions of wine, or trying to formulate one's own tasting notes.

Acetic	wine soured by contact with air, vinegary.
Acidity	tart, sharp taste in wine, normally from natural grape acids.
Aftertaste	the last impression lingering in the mouth after swallowing.
Aroma	that part of the 'nose' derived from the grape itself. See Nose.
Astringent	having a mouth-puckering character, caused by tannin from grape skins, seeds and wood storage.
Balance	the harmony of flavour constituents.
Blackcurrants	the smell and taste of some red wines is likened to these fruit, particularly Cabernet Sauvignon.
Body	fullness or weight of wine in the mouth, largely related to alcohol level.
Bouquet	that part of the 'nose,' or smell, which develops as a wine matures in casks and bottles. See Nose.
Bright	clear, with no suspended matter.
Clean	free from obvious defects.
Coarse	rough, of poor quality material or poorly made.
Cloudy	with suspended matter present in the wine.
Complex	showing subtle integration of various taste and smell factors.
Condition	clarity and soundness.
Corked	tainted by a mouldy cork.
Dry	where all or nearly all sugar has been fermented into alcohol—where sweetness is absent.
Earthy	having the smell and taste of the soil.
Elegant	showing finesse.
Firm	showing tannic/acid backbone, not flabby or soft.
Finish	same meaning as Aftertaste.
Flowery	appealingly aromatic.
Fruity	with pronounced flavour and fragrance of the grape, the term being commonly used of slightly sweet wines.
Hard	having the hardness of flavour which tannin imparts to young red wines.
Honey	this is sometimes referred to in describing the bouquet of good sweet white wines.
Medium	level of residual sugar between dry and sweet.
Mellow	having a softness derived from maturity.
Nose	Aroma and Bouquet combined.
Oak	character imparted to wine by wood maturation.
Oxidised	having a browning of colour and taste deterioration caused by exposure to air or excessive aging.
Ripe	tasting of well-ripened fruit—not green or sour.
Rough	low grade, poorly made wine.
Round	smooth and well balanced.
Ruby	full red colour of young wine, especially port.
Soft	gentle finish.
Spicy	having a taste as though some spice were present, a character most pronounced in Gewürztraminer.
Sulphury	having an unpleasant excess of the preservative sulphur dioxide.
Supple	not hard, having an agreeable soft character.
Sweet	with residual sugar; in New Zealand this usually means sweeter than medium.
Tannic	a wine showing strongly the presence of tannin from the grape skins, pips and oak storage. Especially in young reds.
Tawny	faded amber of old wine, especially port.
Thin	deficient in body, almost watery.
Volatile	bacterial spoilage causes an excess of volatile acids (acetic acid or ethyl acetate).

Bibliography

This bibliography is based on the most valuable published material used by the author during research for a 1977 M.A. Thesis, *The Wine Lobby*, and subsequently for this book.

All listings have been organised into one of several categories: Books, University Theses, Government Publications, Articles, Pamphlets etc., Magazines and Newsletters, and Wine Columns.

An alternative starting-point is S.M. Bradbury's *Wines and Winemaking in New Zealand: A Bibliography*, Wellington Library School, 1970.

Books
Beaven, D.W., *Wines for Dining*, 1977.
Bollinger, C., *Grog's Own Country*, 2nd ed., 1967.
Buck, J., *Take a Little Wine*, 1969.
Evans, L. (ed.), *Australia and New Zealand Complete Book of Wine*, 1973.
Graham, J.C., *New Zealand Wine Guide*, 1971.
Graham, J.C., *Know Your New Zealand Wines*, 1980.
Graham, J.C., *Jock Graham's Wine Book*, 1983.
Johnson, H., *Hugh Johnson's Wine Companion*, London, 1983.
New Zealand Wine and Food Annual, 1984.
Reid, J.G.S., *The Cool Seller*, 1969.
Saunders, P., *A Guide to New Zealand Wine*, published yearly since 1976.
Scott, D., *Winemakers of New Zealand*, 1964.
Scott, D., *A Stake in the Country*, 1977.
Southern, E., *New Zealand Wine and Cheese Guide*, 1969.
Thorpy, F., *Wine in New Zealand*, 1971, revised ed. 1983.
Thorpy, F., *New Zealand Wine Guide*, 1976.
Trlin, A.D., *Now Respected, Once Despised: Yugoslavs in New Zealand*, 1979 (see Chapter 4, 'The Winemakers', pp.81-98).

University Theses
Cooper, M.G., 'The Wine Lobby: Pressure Group Politics and the New Zealand Wine Industry', University of Auckland M.A. Thesis, 1977.
Corban, A., 'The History, Growth and Present Disposition of the New Zealand Wine Industry', Dissertation for a Diploma in Biotechnology, Massey University, 1974.
Corban, A.C., 'An Investigation of the Grape Growing and Winemaking Industries of NZ', University of New Zealand, M.D. Thesis, 1925.
Forder, P.G., 'The Te Kauwhata Viticultural Research Station', University of Auckland M.A. research essay, 1977.
Marshall, B.W., 'Kauri-Gum Digging 1885-1920', University of Auckland M.A. Thesis, 1968.
Moran, W., 'Viticulture and Winemaking in New Zealand', University of Auckland M.A. Thesis, 1958.
Townsend, P., 'Location of Viticulture in New Zealand', University of Auckland M.A. Thesis, 1976.
Trlin, A.D., 'From Dalmatia to New Zealand', Victoria University M.A. Thesis, 1967.

Government Publications
Bragato, R., 'Report on the Prospects of Viticulture in New Zealand', 1895.
'Viticulture in NZ with Special Reference to American Vines', 1906.
Berrysmith, F., *Viticulture*, rev. ed., 1973.
The Chemical Composition of some Experimental NZ Table Wines, DSIR Report No. CD 2290, Sept 1979.
The Chemical Composition of some Musts and White Wines from the Henderson Valley and Kumeu Areas, DSIR Chemistry Division Report No. CD 2222, Jun 1976.
The Chemical Composition of some NZ Red and Rose Wines, DSIR Chemistry Division Report No. CD 2247, Dec 1976.
Conference of NZ Fruitgrowers and Horticulturists, Dunedin, Jun 1901, NZ Department of Agriculture.
'Control of Vine Diseases and Pests Occurring in NZ', NZ Department of Agriculture, Bulletin No.134.
The Customs Tariff (Wine) Amendment Order, 1975.
'Grape Varieties for New Zealand', Department of Horticulture Lincoln College, Bulletin No. 21, 1977.
New Zealand Department of Trade and Industry, Public Tariff Inquiry, Report No. 199 to the Tariff and Development Board, August 1973.
New Zealand Department of Agriculture and Fisheries, Annual Reports.
The New Zealand Official Year Book.
Oenological and Viticultural Bulletins, Ruakura Agricultural Research Centre.
Papers in Viticulture, Lincoln College Bulletin No. 22A, 1978.
Papers in Winemaking and Wine Evaluation, Lincoln College, Bulletin 22B, 1978.
'Phylloxera-resistant vines', NZ Department of Agriculture, Bulletin No. 276, 1947.
Report of the Winemaking Industry Committee, AJHR, I-18, 1957.

Report of the Industries Development Commission: The Wine Industry Development Plan to 1986, 1980.
Report of the Flax and Other Industries Committee on the Wine and Fruit Industry, AJHR, I-6B, 1890.
Report of the Licensing Committee, AJHR, I-17, 1960.
Report of the New Zealand Commission to Inspect and Classify the Kauri Gum Reserves in the Auckland Land District, AJHR, C-12, 1914.
Report and Evidence of the Royal Commission on the Kauri Gum Industry in New Zealand, AJHR, A-12, 1898.
Report of the Royal Commission on Licensing, 1946.
Report of the Royal Commission on the Sale of Liquor in New Zealand, 1974.
Report of the Industries Committee, AJHR, I-12, 1919.
Report No. 76c to the Tariff and Development Board, Certain Wines and Spirits, New Zealand Department of Industries and Commerce, 9 June 1970.
Report of the Licensing Control Commission 31 March 1955, AJHR, A-3.
The Wine Duty (South Africa) Order 1938, Statutory Regulations, 1938.
Wine in New Zealand, published annually in the 1960s by the New Zealand Department of Industries and Commerce.
Wines and Certain Other Fermented and Spiritous Beverages, Tariff and Development Board, Public Hearing, 6-8 August 1973, Transcript of Proceedings.

Articles, Pamphlets and Miscellaneous

Anderson, S.F., 'Grape Culture', *NZ Journal of Agriculture* Vol. 8, 1914, pp.496-508.
    'Outdoor Culture of the Grape Vine in NZ', *NZ Journal of Agriculture*, Feb 1917.
    'The Viticultural Industry', *NZ Journal of Agriculture*, 20 Oct and 21 Dec, 1914. pp.272-3 and 488-90.
Atkinson, J.D., 'Injury to grapes from hormone weed killer', *NZ Journal of Agriculture* 83, Nov 1951, pp.389-90.
Beaven, D.W., 'Wine Through the Ages', *NZ Medical Journal* 79, 23 Jan 1974, pp.611-15.
Berrysmith, F., 'Double-Curtain Grape Trellising System', *NZ Journal of Agriculture* 133, No. 6, Dec 1976, pp.29-30.
    Five-yearly surveys of New Zealand Vineyards. *NZ Journal of Agriculture*, October 1961, Aug 1966, Jul 1971, Jun 1976.
    'Grape Saboteurs', *NZ Journal of Agriculture* 131, No. 5, Nov 1975, pp.39-41.
    'Grapegrowing Prospects Throughout NZ', *NZ Journal of Agriculture* 117, No. 1, Jul 1968, pp.91-5.
    'Grapes for Export Quality Dry Red Table Wine', *NZ Journal of Agriculture* 131, No. 2, Aug 1975, pp.14-15.
    'The Grape-wine Industry', *NZ Journal of Agriculture* May 1974, pp.33-37.
    'Highlights of the 1975 Vineyard Survey', *NZ Journal of Agriculture* 132, No. 6, Jun 1976, pp.12-13.
    'New Zealand's Wine Industry is Flourishing', *NZ Journal of Agriculture*, Mar 1968.
    'Prospects for Brandy Production in NZ', *NZ Journal of Agriculture* 118 (5), May 1969, pp.60-3.
    'Soil Management in Vineyards', *NZ Journal of Agriculture* 93, Aug 1956, pp.139-46.
    'Viticultural Growing Pains', *NZ Journal of Agriculture* Jan 1972.
    'Viticulture in NZ 1817-1975', *Royal NZ Institute Horticulture Annual Journal* No. 4, 1976, pp.9-12.
    'Wines and Winemaking', *NZ Journal of Agriculture* Vol. 86, 1953, pp.262-72.
Black, C., 'Perfectionism may make NZ wine a luxury', *Better Business* Vol. 42, No.437, May 1978, p.40.
Blackburn, A., 'Wine — fruit of the Vine?' *Thursday* 6 and 20, Feb 1975.
Blakey, J., 'Viticulture on the Gisborne Plains', *Auckland Student Geographer* No. 6, 1969, pp.37-39.
Bolster, T.N., 'Lucky Break for New Zealand Winemakers', *Weekly News*, 24 Sept, 1958, p.3.
Bridges, J., 'Mechanical Grape Harvester solves Labour Problems', *NZ Journal of Agriculture* 130, No. 2, Feb 1975, pp.33-35.
Burney, B., 'Weed Control in Vineyards', *NZ Journal of Agriculture* 128, No. 3, Mar 1974, pp.63-4.
'Buying Cheaper Wine', *Consumer* No.201, Dec 1982, pp.334-37.
Cartwright, R.W., 'Marketing Challenge for New Zealand Wine Manufacturers', Proceedings of the Biotechnology Conference on Wine Technology, Massey University, May 1976, pp.69-75.
'Central Otago Grapes', *Otago Daily Times*, 14 Jul 1973, p.4.
Chamberlain, E.E., Over de Linden, A. and Berrysmith, F. 'Grapevine Virus Diseases' *NZ Journal of Agriculture* 122, No. 3, Mar 1971, pp.62-73.
    with Over de Linden, A. and Berrysmith, F., 'Virus Diseases of Grapevines in NZ', *NZ Journal of Agricultural Research*, 3 May 1970, pp.338-58.
Clarke, A.D. and Honare, E.N., 'Weeds in Auckland Vineyards', NZ Weed and Pest Control Conference Proceedings, 26: 1973, pp.112-116.
'Classical Wine Grapes of Earnscleugh', *Otago Daily Times*, 11 May 1977, p.17.
Clifton, E., 'Table Grapes: the Albany Surprise', *NZ Journal of Agriculture* 3, No. 2, 1911, pp.131-132.
'Cooks Wines: Success from an unusual partnership', *Management*, Vol. 27, No. 11, Feb 1981, pp.16-19.
Cooper, M.G., 'A Little Wine Goes a Long Way', *NZ Listener*, 8 Mar 1980, pp.14-15.
Crane, K., 'Production and Planning in a NZ Wine Company', *NZ Valuer*, 25 Sept 1982, pp.161-62.
Creswell, K.J., Eschenbruch, R., and Winn, G.W., 'Extract: its determination and significance in some NZ experimental wines', *Food Technology in NZ* 16, No. 8, Aug 1981, pp.7-9.
    'The Variation in Magnesium Levels of some Experimental Grapes, Grape Juices and Wines', *Food Technology in New Zealand*, Vol. 16, No. 1, Jan 1981, pp.37-41.
Dasler, Y., 'Laying Waste the Wine Business', *NZ Listener* 101, 22 May 1982, pp.24-5.
Dunleavy, T., 'NZ Wine Earns its Place', *NZ Gardener*, p.15, Apr 1978.
    'The Progress of NZ Wine', *NZ Gardener*, 11-12 Dec. 1978.
'Dutch Learn about NZ Wine', *Food Industry*, Mar 1984, p.2.
Dye, M.H. and Hammett, K., 'Corban Pioneers More Efficient Winemaking', *Food Technology in NZ* 6, No. 3, Mar 1971, pp.22-5.
    'Effects on Fruit Yield and on Powdery Mildew Infection of Fungicide and Bactericide Sprays Applied to Grapes during Flowering', *NZ Journal of Experimental Agriculture*, 5 Mar 1977, pp.63-5.
    'Fostering the Grape: Research Projects' (at Ruakura and Te Kauwhata), *NZ Journal of Agriculture* 124, No. 3, Mar 1972, pp.40-5.
'Early Settlers Keen on Wine and Winemaking,' *Otago Daily Times*, 12 Jun 1976, p.8.
Epicurean, Feb-Mar 1979, p.46. (Review of NZ Cabernet Sauvignons).
Eschenbruch, R. and Sage, N.F., 'Small scale winemaking at Te Kauwhata Viticultural Research Station', *Food Technology in NZ* 11, No. 3, Mar 1976, pp.15-19.
Evatt, L., 'Penfolds Rhinesdale Winery: Fingertip Control of Winemaking', *Food Technology in NZ* 18, No. 4, Apr 1983, pp.11-13.

Ewart, A., 'Grape Varieties in Poverty Bay', *NZ Journal of Agriculture* 129, No. 4, Oct 1974, pp.58-9.

Fairburn, A.R.D., 'Crisis in the Wine Industry', 1948 (pamphlet).

'Father to Son Tradition in Wine Making, A.A. Corban & Sons', 1st ed. 1961, 2nd ed. 1965, pamphlet.

'A Flattering for New Zealand Wines', *NZ Journal of Agriculture*, Apr 1984, p.32.

'Food and Wine', *NZ Listener*, special feature, 6 Jun 1981, pp.72-79.

Franklin, S., 'Growing Grapes in C. Otago', *NZ Journal of Agriculture* 118, No.6, Jun 1969, pp.71-5.

'Fruitgrowers Union: Visit to Wairangi', *The New Zealand Herald*, 12 Dec 1902, p.7.

'Government Investment in Wine Industry', *Horticulture*, Mar 1984, p.16.

Graham, J.C., 'The Wine Boom Needs Money', *NZ Economist*, 1 Aug, 1967.

'The Grape Crisis — how and why', *Horticulture*, Feb 1984, p.15.

'Grape Growing in NZ', *Southern Horticulture* No. 5, Winter 1982, pp.6-19.

'Grapes can be grown in C. Otago but at a great cost', *Orchardist of NZ* Vol. 42, 1969, p.124.

'Grapes in Gisborne — a chance for change?' *Southern Horticulture*, No. 11, Spring 1983, pp.33-5.

Hampton, P., 'Protection and the New Zealand Wine Industry', *New Zealand Economic Papers* 7, 1973, pp.128-34.

Harvey, B., 'Cruising Down the Valley — Rough Reds of Henderson', *Auckland Metro*, No. 8, Feb 1982, p.63.

Hewitson, D., 'Wine', *Salient*, Vol. 33, No. 3, 1970, p.10.

Hewlett, F.E., 'Historical Background to the Establishment of the Maungatapu Vineyard'. *Tauranga Historical Society Journal*, No. 8, 1957, pp.10-15.

'History of Mission Vineyards 1838-1979', produced by Mission Vineyards (pamphlet), 1980.

'How One Industry Learnt Cost-Plus is not Forever', *National Business Review*, Dec 1983, p.31.

Hubscher, P., 'Developments in the Wine Industry', *Food Technology in NZ*, Sept 1981, p.45.

Jackman, W.H., 'Vine Culture for Winemaking in NZ', *NZ Illustrated Magazine*, Apr 1902, pp.22-32.

Jackson, D.I., 'Planting and Training Grape Vines', *NZ Journal of Agriculture* 138, No. 1, Jan 1979, pp.25-8.

  'Mechanical Grape Harvesting', *NZ Journal of Agriculture* 140, No. 6, July 1980, pp.53-5.

  'Grape Growing Trials in Canterbury', *NZ Journal of Agriculture* Vol. 134 (3) pp.23-26.

Jenkins, C., 'Cooks: Weathervane of the Wine Industry', *New Zealand Company Director*, Oct 1973.

Jones, M., 'The Dominion Vines and Wines', *Weekly News*, 27 Aug 1952, p.3.

Kasza, D.S., 'Research Work on Maturation of Grapes', *NZ Journal of Agriculture* 90, Feb 1955, pp.159-60.

  'Selection of Grape Vine Varieties', *NZ Journal of Agriculture* 94, No. 3, 1957, pp.251-6.

'Keeping the Whine out of Wine', *NZ Gardener*, 10-13, Apr 1978.

Kelly, G.L., 'Judging the Sparkling Class in NZ', *Food Technology in NZ* 18, No. 10, Oct 1983, pp.39-41.

Kelly, M., 'Wine's done a lot to cheer up Tolaga Bay', *NZ Farmer* 99, No. 23, pp.26-31, 14 Dec 1978.

King, J.M., 'Viticulture Viability', *NZ Valuer*, 25 September 1982, pp.163-7.

King, P.D., Meekings, J.S. and Smith S.M., 'Biology and Control of Grape Phylloxera in North Island Vineyards', Proceedings of the NZ Weed and Pest Control Conference, 34, 1981, pp.86-91.

'Kumeu-Huapai Vintage Wine Country', 1979 (pamphlet).

Lindeman, B.W., 'Downy mildew of the vine', *NZ Journal of Agriculture* 61, No. 2, 1940, pp.137-38.

  'Grape Anthracnose or black spot of the vine', *NZ Journal of Agriculture* 61, No. 4, 1940, pp.296-97.

  'Tannin and its uses in NZ Wines', *NZ Journal of Agriculture* 61, No. 1, 1940, pp.60-1.

'Living in the Shadow of the Grapevine', (Northland Wines), *Northern Advocate*, 20 Oct 1976, pp.12-13.

McCissock, A., 'Two Important Virus Diseases of Grapevines in NZ', *NZ Journal of Agriculture* 108, Apr 1964, p.332.

McDonald, T., 'A Display of the NZ Wine Industry', *Royal NZ Institute of Horticulture Annual Journal*, No. 4, 1976, pp.52-7.

McDonald, T.B., 'The New Zealand Wine Industry', News Media forum of the NZ Liquor Industry Council, 1973.

McIndoe, D., *Chapman's NZ Grapevine Manual*, 1862.

McKinnon, D., 'Potato Pest Drives Brothers to Drink', *NZ Farmer* 104, No. 15, 11 Aug 1983, pp.14-17.

'The Maturing of Cooks Wine Co.', *Management* 21, No. 4, Jul 1974, pp.6-9.

Mazuran, G., 'NZ Wines: Bright Future is Predicted', *Orchard* 34, Jul 1961, p.34.

Money, S.P., 'Grapegrowers hold field day at Auckland', *NZ Journal of Agriculture*, Sept 1968.

'Mt Lebanon Vineyards, Henderson', in *Farms and Stations of NZ*, Vol. II, 1958.

NAC's New Zealand, Dec 1977. Feature on NZ Wine.

'New Zealand Wine', *The New Zealand Herald*, 11 Mar 1958, special feature.

'New Zealand Wine — An Industry in Ferment', *ANZ Bank Quarterly*, Oct 1973.

'The New Zealand Wine Industry', *ANZ Bank Quarterly*, Jul 1968.

'New Zealand Wines', *Auckland Star*, 10 Apr 1959, special feature.

'New Zealand Wines', *Consumer*, Dec 1969.

'New Zealand's Vintage: A Promising Industry', *Auckland Weekly News*, 31 May 1906, p.47.

'The Northern New Zealand Wine Industry: Glen Var Wine Company', *NZ Graphic*, 8 Jul 1899, p.45.

'Not from the Rhine Valley but from the Manuherikia', *Otago Daily Times*, 29 Oct 1977, p.23. See also: 7 Jul 1973, p.11; 13 Jan 1962, p.8; 7 Jul 1965 p.4.

'NZ Wine Exporters Need Finer Perception of Diverse Australian Market', *Food Industry*, Dec 1983, p.5.

'NZ Wines in the US — an update', *Export News*, Dec 1983-Jan 1984, p.19.

'Observations at the Shrine of Bacchus', *Here and Now* 2, No. 4, Jan 1952, p.2.

O'Hagan, J.J., 'How Much Wine is Enough for NZ?', *NZ Medical Journal* 96, 27 Apr 1973, pp.295-98.

'The Old Days are Gone Forever', *NZ Financial Review*, No. 9 Oct 1982, pp.25-31.

Over de Linden and Chamberlain, E.E., 'Production of Virus-free Grapevines in NZ', *NZ Journal of Agricultural Research*, 13 Nov 1970, pp.991-1000.

  'Effect of Grapevine Leafroll Virus on Vine Growth and Fruit Yield and Quality', *NZ Journal of Agricultural Research*, 13 Aug 1970, pp.689-98.

Parle, J.N. and Di Menna, M.E., 'Source of Yeasts in NZ Wines', *NZ Journal of Agricultural Research* 9, Feb 1966, pp.98-105.

Parle, J.N. and Dodanis, D., 'Control of Botrytis Cinerea in grapes', *NZ Journal of Experimental Agriculture*, 1 Mar 1973, pp.81-3.

Peacocke, G.L., Notes on Waeranga and Ruakura State Farms, Christchurch 1973, pamphlet.

Quinn, J., 'Te Kauwhata Station Seeks Virus Free Grape Vines', *NZ Journal of Agriculture*, Vol. 113, 1966, pp.50-51.

Reeves, M.J., 'The Incidence of Red Wine from Hybrid Grapes in NZ Red Wines', *Food Technology in NZ*, 13, No. 6, pp.3-7, Jun 1978.

Robertson, G., 'A Case of Wine', *NZ Listener* 99, No. 2185, 5 Dec 1981, pp.48-57.

Robertson, J.M., 'The Chemical Composition of Some NZ Dry White Wines', *Food Technology in NZ* 10, No. 3, Mar 1975, pp.8-13.

Rodda, T.E., 'Recollections of an early pioneer of the Department of Agriculture', Auckland Historical Society Miscellaneous Manuscripts, Auckland Institute and Museum, MS 808 76/28-31.

Rush, G.M., 'NZ White Table Wines 1971 and 1977', *Food Technology in NZ*, Jul 1979, p.3.

Scott, D., *Fire on the Clay*, 1979. See pp.164-71, and 190-93 on pioneer wine maker Paul Groshek.

Scott, R., 'An NZ Export', (of wine in the 1870s and 1880s), *NZ Listener* 66, No. 1632, 8 Feb 1971, p.49.

'New Zealand's Wine Industry Matures', *Better Business*, Jun 1966.

'Shake-up for Wine Industry', *National Business Review*, 16 Apr 1984, p.1.

Shaw's Wine and Spirit Trade Directory, pub. annually.

Simon, A., 'New Zealand' in *Wines of the World* (ed. Simon), 1967, pp.637-44.

'New Zealand Holiday', in *Wine and Food*, No. 124, Winter 1964, pp.38-46.

Simpson, A., 'Monopolies and Wineries', *Affairs*, Nov 1971.

'Since the Days of Noah', *Te Ao Hou* Vol. 6, 1958, pp.38-40 (winemaking in a Maori community).

Soler, J., 'Kupu tohutohu mo te mahi whakato tapahanga waina Karepe' (Directions for propagating vines from cuttings), 2pp. 1896, Alexander Turnbull Library.

'Standard Export Wine Proposed', *National Business Review*, 23 Jan 1984, p.1.

'Superclone – send us a sign', *Southern Horticulture*, Autumn 1984, p.47.

Suttor, G., 'Culture of the Grapevine and the Orange in Australia and New Zealand', 1843.

Thompson, F.B., 'Use of Hormone Weedkillers near Vineyards', *NZ Journal of Agriculture* 113, No. 6, Dec 1966, pp.81-3.

Thorpy, F., 'The Winemakers', *New Zealand Heritage*, Vol. 7, part 91, p.2542, 1973.

'The Wine Industry: Heady Success and a possible Hangover', National Business Review Marketplace. No. 4, 1974, pp.8-18.

'Time for New Zealand Wine to Come of Age', *Food Technology in New Zealand*, Apr 1984, p.15.

Trickett, P., 'Vintage Years', *NZ Listener*, 25 Nov 1978, p.24.

Trlin, A.D., 'The Yugoslavs', in Thomson, R.W. and A.D. Trlin (eds), *Immigrants in New Zealand*, 1970.

'Yugoslav Settlement in New Zealand 1890-1961', *New Zealand Geographer*, Vol. 24, No. 1, Apr 1968.

Vaughan, J., 'NZ Still White Wine. A Consumer Survey', Auckland University Management Studies Department, 1978, unpublished paper.

'The Vivian Guide to NZ Wine Buying', Wellington, Vivian Wines, 1972, pamphlet.

'Villa Maria's Packaging Update: Wooing the Wine Market', *Designscape* No. 128, Sept 1980, p.19.

'Viticulture – suitable areas and basic requirements for commercial production', Ruakura Farm Conference Proceedings, 30, 1978.

Wallace, B., 'Wine Industry Moves to Cull the Hooch from the Hock', *National Business Review*, 4 Apr 1972, p.3.

Wilson, B., Interplanting Vines to Beat Phylloxera, *NZ Farmer* 104, No. 11, 9 Jun 1983, pp.14-15.

'Wine', *Encyclopaedia of New Zealand*, 1966.

'Wine – A Consumer Survey of Christchurch Households', Dept of Agricultural Economics and Marketing, Lincoln College, Research Report No. 79, 1977.

'Wine and Research', *NZ Manufacturer* 13, No. 9, Jul 1961, pp.64-7.

'Wine Bars', *Thursday*, 5 Sept 1974, pp.52-4.

'The Wine Fuss', *Food Technology in NZ*, Apr 1980, p.31.

'Wine Glass Tasting', *Designscape* No. 105, pp.20-4, Aug. 1978.

'Wine Industry for Otago first mooted 1903', *Otago Daily Times*, 14 Apr 1967, p.9.

'The Wine Industry is all a Flutter', *Consumer* 179, 1980, pp.323-329.

'Wine Industry of NZ', *Modern Manufacturing* 3, No. 6, Feb 1952, pp.45-53.

'Wine Intervention Not On – PM', *Horticulture*, Jan 1984, p.1.

'The Wine People', *The Sunday Herald*, 5 Aug 1973, special feature.

'The Wine Styles of New Zealand', *Wine and Spirit Buying Guide*, (Australia) Oct 1979, pp.59-62.

'Wine Surplus: Raise Your Glass to Freer Distribution', *National Business Review*, 20 Feb 1984, p.35.

'Winemakers Seek Better Deal', *New Zealand Manufacturer*, 15 Jul, 1952.

'Winemaking in New Zealand', *New Zealand Mail*, 5 Dec 1890, p.20. See also 16 Oct 1880, 19 a-b; 21 Oct 1882, 17 d-e; 16 Jan 1885, 22d; 5 Dec 1890, 209; 5 Dec 1895, 5 b-c; 7 May 1896, 18e; 14 May 1896 7 d-e.

'Winemaking in Auckland', *Southern Cross*, 14 Dec 1875, p.3.

'91 Wines Analysed for Water and Sugar, *Consumer* No. 179, Dec 1980, pp.323-29.

'Wining the British', *Exporter*, April 1984, p.6.

Woodfin, J.C., 'The Development of Viticulture', *NZ Journal of Agriculture*, 20 Aug 1938.

'Grapevines for NZ Conditions, *NZ Journal of Agriculture*, Vol. 36, 1928, pp.106-10.

'Grapevines for NZ Conditions', *NZ Journal of Agriculture*, Vol. 39, 1929, pp.262-66.

Wright, J.M. and Parle, J.N., 'Brettanomyces in the NZ Wine Industry', *NZ Journal of Agricultural Research* 17, May 1974, pp.273-78.

Yardin, Rev. Father, 'On Vine Growing in Hawkes Bay', in Transactions and Proceedings of the NZ Institute, Vol. 23, 1890, pp.528-31.

'The Year of the Grape Glut', *Management*, Jan 1984, p.23.

Magazines and Newsletters

The New Zealand Wineglass has appeared from 1980 on, originally every 2 months, then monthly.

The Wine Report, a monthly.

Wine Review was published 1964-1978, quarterly.

Wine Columns

Many newspapers and magazines carry regular wine columns and wine features. The following are among those that have recently included material of significance:

Hospitality	The Christchurch Star
Insight	Signature
National Business Review	The New Zealand Woman's Weekly
The New Zealand Herald	Auckland Metro
The Auckland Star	The Evening Post

Entries in bold type indicate vineyards. Entries in italics indicate grape varieties.

Page numbers in bold refer to main entries while page numbers in italics refer to pictures.

Index

Abel & Co. 84
Abel, Malcolm 84
Acidity 67
Aging 69,193
Agricultural and Horticultural Society 13
Albany Surprise 21, 22, 28, **46**
Albertz, Wendolin 13
American Diamond 81
Anderson, S.F. 21, 34
   diary *15*
Arataki 18, 19
Aspen Ridge 126, *126*
Averill brothers 101, 115
Babich 96-7, *96, 97, 98-9*
Babich, Joseph *96*
   Josip *20*, 96
   Peter 96
Back-blending 69
Baco No. 1 81
Baco 22A 26, 28, **40,** *40*, 80, 86
   Babich 40
   Collard 40
Balic 100, *100*
Balic, Diana *100*
   Joseph 100
Barrington, A.J. 12
Baruzzi, John 116
Becker, Dr Helmut 30
Beetham, William 14, 17
Bennett, Michael 163
Berg, Prof. A.R. 179
Bird, Robbie and Don 152
Bird, Robert 20
Blight 21
Botrytis 52, 53, 191
Bottling 69
Boyes, Peter 81
Bragato, Romeo *15,* 15-18, 21, 56, 78, 148
Brajkovich, Mate *25,* 30, 92, *92*
Breidecker, Heinrich 14
Brodie, Walter 29
Brookfields 150
Brown, Morton 132
Buck, John 163, 166
Busby, James *12,* 13
Butler, Rosemary 141
Cabernet Sauvignon 28, **46,** *46, 53,* 85
   acreage 39
   Babich 46, 97
   McWilliams 46, 156
   Nobilo 46, 90
   wood maturation 71
Carbonation 72
Chambers, Bernard 14, 163
Champagne 72-3, 188
Chan, Ah 134
Chan, Gilbert 134
   Ken 134, *135*
   Stanley 134
Chardonnay **40,** *40*
   acreage 39
   Cooks 40, 129
   Delegat's 40, 107
   McWilliam's 40, 154
Chasselas **41,** *41*
   acreage 39
Chateau Yelas 118
Chenin Blanc, **41,** *41*
   acreage 39
   Corbans 41, 104
Clarification of wine 68

Climate **34-6**
Clonal Section 58
Collard Bros 101-2, *101, 102*
Collard, J.W. 101
Competitions **192**
Continental 80, *80*
Cooks 28, 30, *55,* **127-30,** *127, 128*
Coopers Creek 85, *85*
Corban, A.A. 18, 28, 29, 56, 103
   Alex 103, *105*
   Alwyn 162
   Wadier *18,* 103
Corbans, *10, 82,* **103-5,** *103, 104, 105,* 147, 176
Crushing 64, *65*
Cyprian, Brother 158
Dalmatian immigrants 16, 18, 80, 94
Darwin, Charles 12
Delegat, Jim 107
   Nikola 106
Delegat's 106-7, *106, 107*
de Redcliffe 131 *131*
du Fresne, Viggo 168, *168,* 170
d'Urville, Dumont 12
Eastern Vineyards *29*
Ellis, Richard 150
Erceg, Ivan 112
   Mijo 112
   Paul 120
Eskdale *149,* **151**
Esk Valley 152
Evans, Len 101
Fermentation **67-71**
   Bottle fermentation 73
   Bulk fermentation 72
   Cold fermentation 68
   of red wine 70-1, *70*
   of white wine 67-8, *68*
   Stop fermentation 69
Finn, Tim and Judy 172
Fino Valley 108, *108*
Fistonich, George 26, 122, 166
Flavoured wine 29
Frankovich brothers 16
Fredatovich, Peter *25,* 109
Freeze concentration 69
Frey, Mel 114
Frost 36, *36*
Galvin, Keith 116
Gamay Beaujolais 47, *47*
   Abel 47, 84
   acreage 39
   Korepo 47, 170
   McWilliam's 47, 156
   Victory 47, 173
Gass, Craig 170
Gewürztraminer **41,** *41*
   acreage 39
   Matawhero 41, 140
Glassware *195*
Glenburn 86
Glenvale 152, *152, 153*
Green, Tina, *154*
   Tony 154
Grey Riesling, **42,** *42*
   Cooks 42, 129
   Matua Valley 42, 88
Grgic, Mara 96
Grk 87
Groshek, Paul 22-3
Hancock, John 106, 132
Hanlon, L. 78

Harvesting, 55, *55*
Heginbotham, Peter 167
Hendry, Andrew 85
Herekino 16
Hewlett, F.E. 21
Hitchcock, Kerry 129
Hladilo, Rado and Patricia 111
Hogan, Allen and Joyce 176, *177*
Hubscher, Peter 143
Hunter, Ernie 178
Hunter's 178
Hybrids 21, **38,** 188
Industries Development Commission 30
Irwin, Denis 140, *140*
Isabella 17, 21, 24, 44
Ivicevich, Anthony 113
   Mick 113
   Tony 113
Ivicevich, Victor 110
Jelas, Andrew 86
   Michael 86
Jelich, Stipan 18, 118
Johnson, Hugh 9
Judd, Kevin 93
Juice clarification 66, *66*
   separation 65-6
Kastel 117
Knappstein, Bob *155,* 156
Korepo 170, *171*
Kosovich, Ante 16
Labelling **188**
Lagan, Des 192
Lampila, Father 158
Langstone, F., MP 22
Latitude 34
Levet, Charles 13, 17
Licensing Amendment Act 19
Lincoln 109, *109*
Lincoln College 182
Lindeman, B.W. 22
Liqueurs
   Balic 100
   Lombardi 154
   Mayfair 110
   Totara SYC 135
Lombardi 154
Lorenz, Almuth *178*
Lucas, David 127
MacLennan, Ross 166
Markovina *87, 87*
Markovina, Ivan 87
Marsden, Samuel 12
Mason, Rex, MP 21, *25*
Massey, W.F. (Prime Minister) 19
Matawhero 140-1
Matua Valley *55, 64,* **88-9,** *89*
Mayfair 110, *110*
Mazuran 111, *111*
Mazuran, George *24, 27,* 28, *111*
McDonald, Tom 20, 21, 115, *156*
McDonnell, Lt. T. 12
McKissock, Alister 126
McWilliam's 26, 70, 74, 148, **154-7,** *157*
Merlot **47,** *47,* 85
   Babich 47, 97
   Collard 47, 102
Méthode Champenoise 73
Micro-climates 36
Milina 80
Mission *62,* **158-61,** *159, 160*
Montana 30, 67, **142-5,** *143,* 176, **179-80,** *179, 181*

Morris, Michael 163
Morton Estate 132, *133*
Mother's Cellar *95*
Muaga Vineyards 24
Müller-Thurgau 28, *39,* **42-3,** *43,* 64, *157,*
177, 178
  acreage 39
  Babich 43, 97
  Collard 43, 101
  Delegat's, 106
  Montana 43, 143
  Robard and Butler 43
Muscat **42,** *42*
  acreage 39
Music's 80
Nash, Walter 24, *25*
National Wine Competition 192
Neill, Rod 173
Neudorf 172, *172, 173*
New Zealand Viticultural Association 19
New Zealand Wine Council 22
Nobilo 90-1, *90, 91*
Nobilo, Mark 90
      Nick 90
      Nikola 90
      Steve 90
Ngatarawa 162, *162*
Oidium 14, 21
Old Railway 114
Olmo, Dr Harold 37, 58
Orchiston, Warwick *165,* 166
Ormond 146, *147*
Osika, Brother *161*
Pacific 112, *112*
Palomino **44,** *44*
  acreage 39
  Mazuran 44, 111
  Montana 44
Pannill, George 21, 44
Panorama 113
Pechar's 114
Pechar, Steve 114
Penfolds 26, 30, *68,* **115-7,** *116, 117,* 146,
176
Petrie, Hon. Henry W. 13
Phylloxera 16, 18, **59,** *59,*
Pierre 167
Pinòtage **47,** *47*
  acreage 39
  Montana 47, 144
  Nobilo 47, 90
Pinot Gris **44**
  Cooks 44, 130
  Mission 44
Pinot Meunier **48**
  Cooks 48, 130
Pinot Noir **48,** *48, 175*
  acreage 39
  Babich 48, 97
  Nobilo 48, 91
  St Helena 48, 182
Pleasant Valley *54,* **118,** *118*
Polglase, Mark 122
Pompallier, Bishop 13
Port 75
  Babich 97
  Balic 100
  Collard 102
  Matua Valley 89
  McWilliam's 156
  Pacific 112
  Penfolds 117
  Vidal 166
Powditch, William 12
Prohibition movement 14, 15, 19, *20*
Pruning 51, *52*
Puhara 158
Radaly, Joe 112
Rainfall 34, *35*
Randall, Mrs A.M. 15
Regionalism 78
Reichensteiner 58
Rhine Riesling **45,** *45, 183*
  acreage *39*
  Collard 45, 101
  Montana 45, 180

Ritchie, J.D. 19
Riverlea 104
Robard and Butler 104
Robertson, Peter and Ngaire 150
Robinson, Danny 143
Rootstock **59**
Rosé **72,** 102, 105
Royal Commission on Licensing 22, 24
St Helena 182-3, *183*
Salonius, Kim and Trish *151*
San Marino 92
Sauvignon Blanc **45,** *45*
  acreage 39
  Matua Valley 45, 89
  Montana 45
Schroder, Robert 84
Schuster, Danny 182
Seibel, Norbert 104
Seibels 48-9, *49*
  Abel 49
  Collard 49
  Seibel 5437 48
  Seibel 5455 48, 80, 86
Selak, Ivan 93
    Mate *25,* 93
Selaks 73, 93
Seifried, Agnes *175*
    Hermann 168, 175
Sémillon **45,** *45*
  Matua Valley 45
  Villa Maria 45, 123
Sherry **74**
  Babich 96
  Balic 100
  Corbans 29
  Glenburn 86
  Glenvale 152
  Lincoln 109
  Mazuran 111
  McWilliam's 156
  Pacific 112
  Penfolds 115, 117
  Soljans 118
  Totara SYC 135
Sherwood, Fred 21
Shiraz **49**
  Collard 49
  Matua Valley 49
Simes, John 179
Simon, André *27*
Smith, Dawson 14
Society of Mary, The 158
Soils **36-7,** *36, 37,* 51, 176
Soler, Joseph 13, 17, 165
Soljan, Frank 119
     Rex 119
     Tony 119
Soljans 119, *119*
Southee, Danny 84
Sparkling wine **72,** *73,* 188
  Balic 100
  Penfolds 116
  Selaks 93
Spence, Ross and Bill 88
Steinmetz, Bartholomew 155
Sugar 53, **66,** 69, 72-5
Sulphur 65
Sunshine 34
Sweetening 69
Sylvaner **45**
  Weingut Seifried 45, 175
Talyancich, Vic 100
Te Kauwhata 17-18
  Research Station **56-7,** *57*
Te Mata 163, *164*
Te Whare Ra *9,* 176
Temperature 34
Tiffen, Henry 14, 17, 160
Tikitiki **138,** *138*
Tolaga Bay **139,** *139*
Torduch, Ivan 108
Totara SYC 134-5, *134*
Transport Nelson *169*
Tutu berries 12
Vella, John 21
Victory 173

Vidal 165-6
Vidal, Anthony 165
    Cecil 166
    Frank 166
    Leslie 166
Villa Maria 65, **122-3,** *123*
Vine disease 53, 176
  See also Blight, Oidium, Pylloxera,
  Botrytis,
      Virus diseases
Vineyard surveys 39
Vintages 190-1
Virus diseases **58,** *59*
Viticultural Association of New Zealand
21-4
Vitis labrusca 17, 21, **38,** *59,* 188
Vitis vinifera 12, 21, **38,** *59*
Vuletich, Mario 80
     Mate 80
     Milica *80*
Waihirere 143, 145
Wairau Plains 176
Water, in wine 67
Weaver, Randy 85, *85, 115,* 142
Weingut Seifried 174-5, *174*
Whatitiri 81, *81*
Wilkinson, Peter, MP 111
Windy Hill 120, *121*
Williams, J.N. 14
Wine Industry Development Plan 30
Wohnsiedler, Friedrich 20, 146
Wood maturation 71
Woodfin, Charles 21-56
Wright, Harry *122*
Yardin, Rev. Father 17
Yeast 67, 72, 73
Yelas, Moscow 118
Yukich, Frank *115,* 143
    Ivan 26, 142
    Mate 143